Literature and Language Teaching

A guide for teachers and trainers

Gillian Lazar

CAMBRIDGE
UNIVERSITY PRESS

Published by the Press Syndicate of the University of Cambridge
The Pitt Building, Trumpington Street, Cambridge CB2 1RP
40 West 20th Street, New York, NY 10011–4211, USA
10 Stamford Road, Oakleigh, Victoria 3166, Australia

© Cambridge University Press 1993

First published 1993

Printed in Great Britain
by Bell and Bain Ltd, Glasgow

Library of Congress catalogue card number
Lazar, Gillian.
Literature and language teaching: a guide for teachers and
trainers / Gillian Lazar.
     p.   cm. – (Cambridge teacher training and development)
Includes bibliographical references.
ISBN 0-521-40480-0 (hc). – ISBN 0-521-40651-X (pb)
1. Literature – Study and teaching (Elementary) I. Title.
II. Series.
LB1575.L34 1992 92–8942
372.6'4044 – dc20 CIP

A catalogue record for this book is available from the British Library

ISBN 0 521 40480 0 hardback
ISBN 0 521 40651 X paperback

WD

Literature and Language Teaching

CAMBRIDGE TEACHER TRAINING AND DEVELOPMENT

General Editors: Ruth Gairns and Marion Williams

This series is designed for all those involved in language teacher training and development: teachers in training, trainers, directors of studies, advisers, teachers of in-service courses and seminars. Its aim is to provide a comprehensive, organised and authoritative resource for language teacher training and development.

Teach English – A training course for teachers
by Adrian Doff

Trainer's Handbook
Teacher's Workbook

Models and Metaphors in Language Teacher Training – Loop input and other strategies
by Tessa Woodward

Training Foreign Language Teachers – A reflective approach
by Michael J. Wallace

Literature and Language Teaching – A guide for teachers and trainers
by Gillian Lazar

Classroom Observation Tasks – A resource book for language teachers and trainers
by Ruth Wajnryb

Contents

Contents

9 Literature and self-access

Thanks

I would like to thank the students and teachers from all over the world who participated in the lessons and seminars, especially at International House in London, on which this book is based. I have learned a great deal from their ideas and responses.

My interest in using literature with the language learner started when I was an M.A. student at the London University Institute of Education, and I am grateful to Professor Henry Widdowson for encouraging this interest.

I owe a particular debt to Ruth Gairns for her thorough reading of the text, her helpful suggestions and her encouragement. Thanks also to Joanne Collie and Marion Williams for their useful comments on an earlier draft of parts of the text.

I am grateful, too, to Annemarie Young of Cambridge University Press for her patience and understanding, Maggie Aldhamland for her generosity and invaluable editorial advice and Elizabeth Serocold for her help.

Finally, many thanks to my family for their encouragement, especially my husband Michael Skapinker whose support and good humour has been unwavering.

Acknowledgements

The author and publishers are grateful to the authors, publishers and others who have given permission for the use of copyright material identified in the text. It has not been possible to identify the sources of all the material used and in such cases the publishers would welcome information from copyright owners.

Harvester Wheatsheaf for the extract on p. 2 from *A Reader's Guide to Contemporary Literary Theory* by Raman Selden; Basil Blackwell for the extract on p. 2 from *Literary Theory* by Terry Eagleton; the extract on p. 2 from *Literature and Language* by C. J. Brumfit and R. A. Carter (1986); the extract on p. 146 from *Hello and Goodbye* by Athol Fugard (1973); the extract on p. 151 from the introduction to *Boesman and Lane and Other Plays* by Athol Fugard (1974, 1978) and the extract on p. 97 from 'Lessons of the War: 1 Naming of Parts' by Henry Reed from *A Map of Verona* (published by Jonathan Cape in 1946) appearing in Henry Reed's *Collected Poems* edited by Jon Stallworthy (Oxford University Press, 1991) all by permission of Oxford University Press; Terence Whelan and *Ideal Home* for the extract on p. 5 from an article first published in *In Store* magazine; *The Spectator* for the extract on p. 5 from a restaurant review by Nigella Lawson; African Universities Press for the extract on p. 6 from 'Lagos Interlude' by Ralph C. Opara from *Reflections: Nigerian Prose and Verse* edited by Frances Ademola; Cambridge University Press for the extract on p. 22 from *Poem into Poem* by A. Maley and S. Moulding, the extract on p. 22 from *The Web of Words* by R. Carter and M. Long and for the extract on p. 81 from the *Cambridge Guide to Literature in English* edited by I. Ousby; Longman Group Ltd for the extract on p. 22 from *Reading Literature* by R. Gower and M. Pearson and for the extract on p. 113 from the *Longman Active Study Dictionary of English, New Edition*; Aitken and Stone for the annotated extract on p. 33 from *A House for Mr Biswas* by V. S. Naipaul; Naomi Lewis for the poem on p. 40 'Partly Because' by Ursula Laird from *Messages* edited by Naomi Lewis and published by Faber and Faber; the poem on p. 40 'A wish for my children' by Evangeline Paterson from *Lucifer at the Fair* published by Taxus Press at Stride Publications, 1991; the poem on p. 50 'Rodge Said' by Michael Rosen from *You tell Me* published by Puffin Kestrel reprinted with permission of the Peters Fraser & Dunlop Group; Rukhsana Ahmad for the extract on p. 49 from 'The Gatekeeper's Wife' by Rukhsana Ahmad in

Acknowledgements

The Inner Courtyard by Lakshmi Holstrom published by Virago; William Heinemann Ltd and HarperCollins Publishers, New York, for the extract on p. 63 from *Arrow of God* by Chinua Achebe; the Peters Fraser & Dunlop Group and the estate of Evelyn Waugh for the extract on p. 63 from *Brideshead Revisited* by Evelyn Waugh; the extract on p. 64 from *The Dragon's Village* by Yuan-tsung Chen, Copyright © 1980 by Yuan-tsung Chen, Reprinted by permission of Pantheon Books, a division of Random House Inc. Also by permission of The Women's Press; the extract on p. 259 is from *Dubliners* by James Joyce, published by Jonathan Cape; the estate of Elizabeth Bowen, Jonathan Cape and Random House, Inc. for the extract on p. 75 from 'Unwelcome Idea' from *The Collected Stories of Elizabeth Bowen*; Christopher Gillie for the extract on p. 80 and the adapted extract on p. 123 from the *Longman Companion to English Literature* by Christopher Gillie; the poem on p. 202 © MacGibbon & Kee, an imprint of HarperCollins Publishers Ltd 'maggie and milly and molly and may' by e e cummings from *The Complete Poems* 1913–1962. 'maggie and milly and molly and may' is reprinted from *Complete Poems* 1913–1962 by E. E. Cummings, by permission of Liveright Publishing Corporation. Copyright © 1923, 1925, 1931, 1935, 1938, 1939, 1940, 1944, 1945, 1946, 1947, 1948, 1949, 1950, 1951, 1952, 1953, 1954, 1955, 1956, 1957, 1958, 1959, 1960, 1961, 1962 by the Trustees of the E. E. Cummings Trust. Copyright © 1961, 1963, 1968 by Marion Morehouse Cummings; Evan Jones and Blake Friedmann Literary Agency Ltd for the poem on p. 98 'The Song of the Banana Man' which first appeared in *News for Babylon* edited by J. Berry, published by Chatto and Windus; Methuen, London, and St Martin's Press, Inc. New York, NY for the extract on p. 98 from *Nappy Edges* by Ntozake Shange. Copyright © 1972, 1974, 1975, 1976, 1977, 1978 by Ntozake Shange. From the book *Nappy Edges* and reprinted with permission from St Martin's Press Inc., New York, NY; Hale and Iremonger for the poem on p. 104 'The Gull's Flight' by Nigel Roberts (originally in *Steps for Astaire*); the estate of Robert Frost and Jonathan Cape for four lines on p. 105 from 'Stopping by Woods on a Snowy Evening' from *The Poetry of Robert Frost* edited by Edward Connery Lathem, published by Jonathan Cape; 'Stopping by Woods on a Snowy Evening' from *The Poetry of Robert Frost* edited by Edward Connery Lathem. Copyright 1923, © 1969 by Holt, Rinehart and Winston. Copyright 1951 by Robert Frost. Reprinted by permission of Henry Holt and Company, Inc. George Allen & Unwin, of HarperCollins Publishers, London, for the poem on p. 108 'A Small Dragon' by Brian Patten from *Notes to the Hurrying Man*; Faber and Faber Ltd for the poem on p. 112 'Days' by Philip Larkin from *The Whitsun Weddings*; Chatto and Windus for the poem on p. 114 'Old Mama Dot' from *Mama Dot* by Fred D'Aguiar; Penelope Mander for the poem on p. 117 and the annotated version of the poem on p. 119 'As it was' by John Mander in *Messages*, published by Faber and Faber; Methuen, London, for the adapted extract on p. 134 from *The Lower Depths* by Tunde Ikoli in *Black Plays* by Y. Brewster; Jonathan Cape for the extract on p. 139 from 'The Zoo Story' by Edward Albee in 'The Zoo Story and Other Plays'; reprinted by permission of The Putnam Publishing Group, from *The Zoo Story* by Edward Albee. Copyright © 1960 by Edward Albee. *The Zoo Story* is the sole property of the author and is fully protected by copyright. It may not be acted either by professionals or amateurs without written consent. Public readings, radio and television broadcasts likewise are forbidden. All inquiries concerning these rights should be addressed to the William Morris Agency, 1350 Avenue of the Americas, New York, NY 10019; Faber and Faber Ltd for the extract on p. 152 from *The Dumb Waiter* by Harold Pinter, Grove Weidenfeld for the extract from *The Dumb Waiter* by Harold Pinter published by Grove Press Inc.

Photographs on p. 122 South American Pictures, Tony and Marion Morrison and The Mansell Collection.

Introduction

Who is this book for?

- For any **language teacher** who wishes to explore the hows and whys of using literature in the language classroom. This includes:
  - teachers on pre-service and in-service training courses
  - teachers involved in the setting up and running of teacher development groups with their colleagues
  - teachers working on their own who want to improve their teaching skills.
- For those involved in the **training** and **development** of **language teachers**. This includes:
  - trainers working in teacher training institutions
  - directors of studies in private language schools
  - heads of departments in secondary schools
  - trainers working in-service on preparatory or refresher courses at different schools or institutions.

As a teacher or trainer you may have a background in literary studies, but be uncertain of how to use this when teaching a language. On the other hand, you may have sound practical experience in teaching or training, but be unfamiliar with literature. Whatever your past experience or interests, this book should help you to find practical ways of using literary texts in the language classroom.

What are the aims of this book?

In the last decade particularly, there has been an upsurge of interest in how literature can be used with the language learner. This book aims to help you develop a thoughtful and principled approach to using literature in the language classroom by asking you to think about some of the issues and debates which have arisen on this subject. At the same time, this book aims to provide you with the tools for developing your own classroom materials and for using these materials in a way that is relevant to your learners. You will find that quite a number of literary texts are featured. You may not want to use any of the texts themselves with your own students, but the tasks and activities organised around them should provide you with certain generalisable procedures and techniques which you can then apply or adapt to your own setting.

Literature is used most effectively with learners from intermediate level upwards. But this book also suggests a few ways of using literature with students at lower levels too (see Sections 6.6 and 7.7 for ideas on how to do this).

Literature itself has been greatly enriched by recent developments in the field of critical theory. Structuralism, deconstructionism, reader-response theory, feminist and Marxist criticism are just some of the branches of critical theory which have been challenging the ways in which we read and understand literature. In this book my overall aim is a practical one; it is to find ways of using literature which will help learners to achieve their main purpose for being in the classroom, that is, to improve their English. For most teachers this is the compelling goal when selecting and designing materials, and there is not really sufficient time to think about critical theory as well. I do hope, though, that one or two important insights from literary criticism which have important implications for teachers and their students will have seeped into certain sections of the book.

This book is intended very much as a starting point for teachers. If you find yourself wanting to explore a particular area in greater depth, then you might look at the 'Suggestions for Further Reading' at the end of each chapter. The lists included are not in any sense comprehensive. I have simply included some of the books and articles that I have found useful over the years, whether teaching or training.

How do I use this book?

The book consists largely of a series of tasks and activities for teachers to work through. These tasks are meant to actively involve the reader in 'learning by doing'. You could work through the tasks on your own, using the key at the back of the book to help you. Alternatively, you might like to work through them with a colleague or group of colleagues, discussing your ideas together. If you are responsible for the training and/or development of teachers, then you can make use of the tasks and activities in your training sessions. The Trainer's Notes at the back of the book suggest ways of using the tasks and activities with groups of teachers.

Each chapter of the book is designed to be relatively self-contained, although certain themes or ideas recur throughout the book. You can choose to read and study whichever you think will be most relevant to your teaching needs. Similarly, within each chapter, you may find that certain sections are more useful to you than others. From the title of each section you should be able to select those you feel are appropriate.

Introduction

You will notice two symbols which occur throughout the book: ⚷ denotes that there are answers for the activity in the key at the back of the book. There are quite a number of tasks and activities which do not have this symbol. This is usually because they are very open-ended and are intended to provoke discussion and reflection rather than to provide a single right answer.

The ☆ symbol next to an activity indicates that this particular task also develops English language skills. These activities might be of interest to you if you wish to use this book not only to improve your teaching skills, but also to improve your language skills and proficiency in English. By working through these activities your knowledge of English and how it is used will be extended. At the same time, you will be developing some methodological insights as to how the procedures and techniques in the task you have done can be applied to your own students.

You will notice that Chapter 8 consists largely of observation sheets designed to help you think about your lessons using literature, both before and after the lesson. You might find it useful to use some of these observation sheets as you work through the book and try out some of the ideas in your classroom. The observation tasks will help to focus your thinking on certain aspects of using literature in the language classroom.

1 Using literature in the language classroom: The issues

The emphasis in this chapter is mainly on exploring some of those underlying issues and concerns relevant to using literature with the language learner. It is not the aim of this chapter to focus on the development of materials for immediate use in the classroom, although many of the points raised in this chapter will have a bearing on what approaches and materials are finally selected. Rather, a number of thoughts and ideas are raised for reflection and discussion. Some of these thoughts and ideas should help in making more principled and coherent classroom decisions about why and how to use literature in language lessons. However, ideas generated in this chapter will not help to pinpoint the definitive, right or correct way to teach or use literature. This is because every teaching situation is different, every literary text is different and every theory explaining literature itself or how to use it in the classroom is different. The task for teachers is thus to draw on the range of insights available, and then to develop an approach appropriate and relevant to their students.

1.1 What is literature?

In this section we think about some of the possible ways of defining literature. This will enable us to focus on some of the implications of using literature with the language learner.

Task 1 ☆

A group of teachers from all over the world were each asked to write down a definition of literature. Read through their definitions and then write down your own definition of literature.

A. Literature is 'feelings' and 'thoughts' in black and white.
B. Literature is the use of language to evoke a personal response in the reader or listener.
C. Literature is a world of fantasy, horror, feelings, visions . . . put into words.
D. Literature means . . . to meet a lot of people, to know other different points of view, ideas, thoughts, minds . . . to know ourselves better.[1]

Task 2 ☆

Here are a number of other quotations which 'define' literature. As you read them, think about the following questions.

Using literature in the language classroom: The issues

a) Are there any similarities between the definitions given here and the ones above?
b) Which definition(s) do you reject? Why?
c) Which definition conforms most closely to your idea of what literature is? Why?

A. Literature could be said to be a sort of disciplined technique for arousing certain emotions. (Iris Murdoch, *The Listener*, 1978.)

B. Great literature is simply language charged with meaning to the utmost possible degree. (Ezra Pound, *How to Read*, Part II.)

C. The Formalists' technical focus led them to treat literature as a special use of language which achieves its distinctness by deviating from and distorting 'practical' language. Practical language is used for acts of communication, while literary language has no practical function at all and simply makes us *see* differently. (Selden, 1989, pp. 9–10.)

D. . . . one can think of literature less as some inherent quality or set of qualities displayed by certain kinds of writing all the way from *Beowulf* to Virginia Woolf, than as a number of ways in which people *relate themselves* to writing. It would not be easy to isolate, from all that has variously been called 'literature', some constant set of inherent features . . . Any bit of writing may be read 'non-pragmatically', if that is what reading a text as literature means, just as any writing may be read 'poetically'. If I pore over the railway timetable not to discover a train connection but to stimulate in myself general reflections on the speed and complexity of modern existence, then I might be said to be reading it as literature.[1] (Eagleton, 1983, p. 9.)

E. Literature is the question minus the answer. (Roland Barthes, *New York Times*, 1978.)

F. In the allocation of the label 'great literature' to a literary work we cannot be making a judgement which is objective or factual, however much we like to think that we are. A value judgement is constituted by the social and historical conditions which determine our particular ideology. The teachers and professors who have the power to decide which books make up an English Literature syllabus reflect in their choices, and in the knowledge of the literature which they purvey, a fundamental structure of beliefs and interests which reflect the particular culture or section of society into which they were born and in which they grew up. (Brumfit and Carter, 1986, p. 17.)

G. Literature, fiction, poetry, whatever, makes justice in the world. That's why it is almost always on the side of the underdog. (Grace Paley, *Ms*, 1974.)

Task 3 🗝

Each one of the quotations in Task 2 has certain implications for the approach we adopt to using literature in the language classroom. These implications are examined in the seven paragraphs below. Match each paragraph with the relevant quotation in Task 2.

1. One of our main aims in the classroom should be to teach our students to read literature using the appropriate literary strategies. This involves them not in reading for some practical purpose, for example to obtain information, but rather in analysing a text in terms of what it might mean symbolically or philosophically. Students may have already acquired this kind of literary competence in their own language, in which case we simply need to help them to transfer these skills. If not, we need to find ways of engendering the necessary competence.

2. Our main task in the classroom is to pinpoint how far literary language deviates from ordinary language. This obviously poses a problem for students – to what extent will they be confused or misled by studying deviant rather than normal language, and how far is this a useful activity for them?

3. Literary texts have a powerful function in raising moral and ethical concerns in the classroom. The tasks and activities we devise to exploit these texts should encourage our students to explore these concerns and connect them with the struggle for a better society.

4. The texts traditionally prescribed for classroom use may generally be accorded high status, but often seem remote from, and irrelevant to, the interests and concerns of our students. In fact, being made to read texts so alien to their own experience and background may only increase students' sense of frustration, inferiority and even power-lessness. We therefore need to select texts for classroom use which may not be part of the traditional literary canon, but which reflect the lives and interests of our students.

5. Our main aim when using literature with our students is to help them unravel the many meanings in a text. Students often need guidance when exploring these multiple levels of meaning in a literary text – we need to devise materials and tasks which help them to do this.

6. Literature provides wonderful source material for eliciting strong emotional responses from our students. Using literature in the class-room is a fruitful way of involving the learner as a whole person, and provides excellent opportunities for the learners to express their personal opinions, reactions and feelings.

7. We should not expect to reach any definitive interpretation of a literary text with our students. Rather we should use the text as the basis for generating discussion, controversy and critical thinking in the classroom.

Task 4

Think about a group of students you are teaching now, or have taught in the past. Perhaps you have used some literature with them already or perhaps you are planning to do so. Do any of the thoughts or ideas mentioned in the previous three activities seem relevant to your teaching of these students? If so, why? If not, why not? Are there any other implications arising from the various definitions of literature which you think should be considered with regard to these students?

Task 5

Figure 1.1 is a diagram which recaps and sums up some of the questions and thoughts raised about literature in Tasks 1 to 3. Look at it and then decide if there are any more ideas you want to add. Then think back to your original definition of literature in Task 1. Do you still agree with it or would you like to change it in some way? Why?

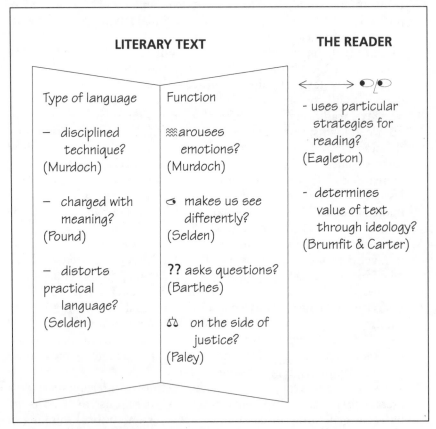

Figure 1.1 Defining literature: the issues

We have seen that defining literature is no easy task, and that there is considerable controversy among literary theorists and critics as to how this can be done. For the purposes of this book, we will take literature to mean those novels, short stories, plays and poems which are fictional and convey their message by paying considerable attention to language which is rich and multi-layered. In order for our definition of literature to be relevant to the classroom teacher, we will also go beyond the traditional literary canon to include contemporary works which recognise that the English language is no longer the preserve of a few nations, but is now used globally.

1.2 What is distinctive about the language of literature? ☆

One of the views of literature suggested in the previous section is that literature involves a special, or unusual, use of language. In this section we explore this idea further and consider any classroom implications arising from it.

Task 6

Here are a number of different texts. Read through each one and decide whether or not you think it is a literary text. If not, then think about where the text might have come from. Note down any language in the text which helped you to make your decision.

A. As this is a small Edwardian terraced house with limited natural light, Venetian blinds were chosen to cover the windows. They screen the street scene during the day and add to the impression of space given by the light walls and modern furniture. Curtains in deep coral would have looked heavy, but the sunshine that streams through the blinds keeps the overall effect light.

B. The windows were ajar and gleaming white against the fresh grass outside that seemed to grow a little way into the house. A breeze blew through the room, blew curtains in at one end and out the other like pale flags, twisting them up toward the frosted wedding-cake of the ceiling, and then rippled over the wine-coloured rug, making a shadow on it as the wind does at sea.

C. His breast of chicken with tarragon and girolles goes back to the classic French repertoire: the skin of the fowl crisped to gold, odoriferously swathed in a thick creamy sauce, golden also, piled with fleshy mushrooms fried in butter till they take on the gleam of varnished wood.

D. Just because we're deaf, it doesn't mean we've nothing between our ears.

E. Cousin Nwankechukukere came back with a wardrobe the size of the Eiffel tower and such impressive ideas indicative of her profound study of de Gaulle, the Common Market and slimming. She had become a woman. She even changed her name. There was no fanfare about this. I had expected the usual insertion in the papers: 'I, formerly known, called, addressed as . . . shall from today henceforward be known, called, addressed, etc.' and the bit about 'former documents remaining valid'. But no. Cousin Nwankechukukere just changed her name to 'Nwa'. To me there was a delicious crunchiness in 'Nwan-ke-chu-ku-ke-re', a crunchiness redolent of fried corn and groundnuts eaten with coconut. It was a pity to lose all that. Furthermore Nwankechukukere as a name should give the bearer a superiority complex. It is a name which literally means 'She-who-is-made-by-God.'

F. Three grey geese in a field grazing;
   Grey were the geese and green was the grazing.

G. She's been working on the project all week, but she's starting to run out of steam. She doesn't feel that her mind is operating any more.[2]

In Task 6 you may have found it quite difficult to identify which texts are literary and which ones are not. This is probably because there is no specialised literary language which can be isolated and analysed in the same way as the language of specific fields, such as law; or specific media, such as newspapers. It is also perfectly possible to imagine a literary context for many of the more obviously non-literary texts. For instance, example G. is an invented utterance, but it could easily be imagined as part of a dialogue in a play, novel or short story. Perhaps it is difficult deciding which texts are literary because one of the hallmarks of literature is that it feeds creatively on every possible style and register – it has become the one form of discourse in which any use of language is permissible. At the same time, many linguists have pointed out that there are a number of features of literary language which can be isolated. Many of these features occur in other forms of discourse as well, but in many literary texts they combine to form a highly unified and consistent effect, which strongly reinforces the message of the text (Brumfit and Carter, 1986, p. 8). Let us try to pinpoint some of these features.

Task 7 🗝

On the opposite page is a list of some linguistic features believed to be prevalent in literary texts. Read through the extracts in Task 6 again, and note down any examples of the linguistic features listed below. The first one has been done for you.

Linguistic feature	Example(s) in text
Metaphor	the frosted wedding-cake of the ceiling (B.) to run out of steam/her mind isn't working (G.)
Simile	
Assonance (repetition of vowel sounds)	
Alliteration (repetition of consonants)	
Repetition of word or phrase	
Unusual syntactic patterns (e.g. reversing the order of subject and verb)	
Double or multiple meaning of a word	
Poeticisms (poetic lexis)	
Mixing of styles/registers	

We have already said that literature does not constitute a particular type of language in itself, but that it may reveal a higher incidence of certain kinds of linguistic features which are tightly patterned in the text. The features listed in Task 7 are generally considered to be among those which tend to predominate in literary texts. On the other hand, we have also seen that they can be found in other forms of discourse as well, for example:
– metaphors and similes are used in everyday colloquial speech;
– assonance and alliteration can be found in children's rhymes and advertising jingles.

Task 8 🔑

Look again at the list of linguistic features we considered in Task 7. Next to each one write down any form of discourse, other than literature, in which you think you might find this feature.[3]

In this section we have explored the notion that literary language is relative rather than absolute, in that certain texts or parts of a text may exhibit more of those linguistic features associated with literature than others (Brumfit and Carter, 1986). Literary language is therefore not completely separate from other forms of language. This obviously has some implications for the use of literature in the language classroom. Think about your views on this as you complete the statements below.

Task 9 🔑

Read the statements below and complete them by choosing (a) or (b), according to your views on literary language and teaching.

1. Since literary language is not completely different or separate from other kinds of language
   a) there is no real point in using literature with language students.
   b) studying literary texts can help to improve students' overall knowledge of English.
2. By contrasting literary texts with other forms of discourse
   a) the superiority of literary language can be demonstrated.
   b) students can be sensitised to the wide range of styles in English and the different purposes for which they can be used.
3. Reading literary texts
   a) will help our students to understand and appreciate multiple levels of meaning, metaphors and phonological patterning in many other types of texts.
   b) is a limited skill which does not transfer easily to the reading of other types of texts.
4. In order to appreciate a literary text
   a) students will need some assistance in understanding and analysing the linguistic features which make up a text.
   b) imagination and intuition are all that are needed.

1.3 The reader and the text

In the previous section we concentrated on looking at the literary text and on the extent to which there are objective properties of literary language which clearly differentiate literature from other forms of discourse. In this section we transfer our attention to the reader of the text, which for the purposes of this book is usually the student of English. Below are two examples of ways in which the reader's experience has a bearing on the way a text will be interpreted.

Task 10 🗝

Read both examples and note down any implications for teachers using literature in the language classroom.

Example 1: From a university study

In 'Cultural Knowledge and Reading' by M. S. Steffensen and C. Joag-Dev (Alderson and Urquhart, 1984, p. 53) a study conducted at the University of Wisconsin is described. The study examined the way in which even highly proficient readers of English process texts when reading. Subjects from India and the United States were asked to recall two parallel texts describing Indian and American weddings. The information they recalled was then analysed for the amount recalled and the types of errors made, in order to ascertain whether cultural background made a difference.

From this analysis it was concluded that reading comprehension is a function of cultural background knowledge. If readers possess the schemata assumed by the writer, they easily understand what is said in the text and also make the necessary inferences about what is implicit, rather than stated. By schemata was meant the abstract cognitive structures which incorporate generalised knowledge about objects and events. For example, the schemata concerning a wedding might include knowledge about the roles of bride and groom and other family members, what clothing is traditionally worn, who is invited, where the wedding is held, what rituals form part of the ceremony and so on. Obviously, these schemata will differ cross-culturally.

Example 2: From two book reviews

The following are two different opinions of Mrs Ramsay, a character in *To the Lighthouse* by Virginia Woolf (published May 1927). The novel was reviewed in July 1927 by Conrad Aiken, an American novelist and poet (quoted in Majumdar and McLaurin). In his review Aiken admired Woolf's bold experimental technique, but he described her novels as having an 'odd and delicious air of parochialism, as of some small village-world, as bright and vivid and perfect in its tininess as a miniature: a small complete world which time has somehow missed'. He then went on to describe all Virginia Woolf's female characters, including Mrs Ramsay, as ' . . . the creatures of seclusion, the creatures of shelter; they are exquisite beings, so perfectly and elaborately adapted to their environment that they have taken on something of the roundness and perfection of works of art'.

In 1975 Barbara Bellow Watson, a feminist literary critic, said this of Mrs Ramsay: 'Because Mrs Ramsay in *To the Lighthouse* is a domestic, nurturing woman, her figure may not be immediately recognized as the powerful feminist statement it is.' (quoted in M. Evans, 1982, p. 405).

Task 11

What different views of Mrs Ramsay are being expressed by the two reviewers? Can you suggest any reasons for this? Do you think this has any implications for using literature with the language learner?

In both of the examples above, it was implied that the meaning of a text can never be fixed or frozen, but that different readers of a text make sense of it in their own way. As Selden (1989, p. 79) puts it, readers can be free to enter a text from any direction, but there is no correct route. Below are a few factors which may be important in influencing, or even determining, the interpretation that readers make of a literary text:[4]
- the historical period in which the reader is living;
- the class/social position of the reader;
- the reader's religious beliefs.

Task 12 🗝

a) What other factors could you add to this list?
b) Now decide which of the factors listed above, and the ones you may have added, might be the most important in influencing the interpretation that your own students might make of a literary text. Why?

Task 13 🗝

We have just suggested that the meaning of a literary text can never be fixed. But this view can be problematic for some teachers and students. Look at these possible objections to the suggestion that the meaning of a literary text can never be fixed. Think about your own response to the objections.

A. It is all very well to argue that the meaning of a literary text can never be fixed, but try telling that to my students! They insist that there is one way of understanding a text, and that I must know what it is. My refusal to provide this interpretation is seen as mean and wilful. I actually think my students have a point, since in their exams they are expected to come up with one particular interpretation and I doubt if variations on this would be acceptable.

Can you identify with the teacher's objections above? Can you think of any ways of overcoming the problems she describes?

B. If we accept that there is no fixed meaning to a literary text, are we then suggesting that *any* interpretation is valid? Surely the danger of this view is that we are then opening the way to accepting all and every interpretation of a text, however unlikely or implausible it may seem to us.

Do you think we should accept any interpretation of a text that our students offer us? Why? If we only find certain interpretations acceptable, what criteria do we use to decide what is acceptable or not?

In this section we have explored the notion that the meaning of a literary text can never be fixed, but is manufactured by the reader. Individual readers make sense of texts in very different ways, depending on the society they live in and their personal psychology.

Task 14 🔑

What implications do you think this might have for the kinds of tasks and activities we use to exploit literary texts with the language learner?

1.4 Literary competence and the language classroom

In Section 1.3 we considered the notion that the reader of a literary text is crucial in assigning meaning to the text. It was suggested that a great variety of factors might influence the meaning that a reader confers on a text, ranging from the individual psychology of readers to the social and political milieu in which they live. One factor which may be relevant to language teachers wishing to use literature in their lessons is the concept of 'literary competence'. This is something we will consider more fully in this section. But first read the two texts below and answer the questions which follow them.

TEXT A

> ...copters beating across the night sky. First a couple of security choppers, then the American Presidential helicopter, then two more military craft, then the presidential helicopter on its way back from depositing the President, and finally, more military overflights.

TEXT B
first . . .
a couple of security choppers,
then . . .
the American presidential helicopter
then . . .
two more military craft,
then . . .
the presidential helicopter (onitswayback
from DEPOSITING THE PRESIDENT),
and finally . . .
   more
      military
         overflights[5]

Task 15

a) In what contexts/where would you expect to find Text A and Text B?
b) Do you think there is any difference in meaning between the texts?

Task 16

Before reading the following text, think about these questions:
a) What is 'literary competence'?
b) How important is it for language teachers and students?

Most language teachers are familiar with Chomsky's notion of 'grammatical competence'. This is the idea that all speakers of any language possess an internalised grammar which allows them to produce and understand utterances which they may not have heard before, provided that these utterances conform to the grammatical rules of the language they are speaking. In the same way, some theorists, in particular Culler, have argued that effective readers of a literary text possess 'literary competence', in that they have an implicit understanding of, and familiarity with, certain conventions which allow them to take the words on the page of a play or other literary work and convert them into literary meanings. For example, when you were looking at the texts above – one a simple sentence taken at random from a newspaper and the other a rewriting of the same sentence as if it were a poem – the chances are that their form on the page cued you in to different ways of responding to them. Perhaps you treated the newspaper sentence in a rather objective way, simply using it to gain certain facts. On the other hand with the 'poem' sentence, you may have assigned certain meanings to it which had remained latent or unexplored in the newspaper text. For example, you might have read it as an ironic comment on the elaborate security surrounding a presidential visit. If so, you were implicitly drawing on certain conventions about how a poem is to be read and understood. And such conventions of interpretation apply equally well to other literary genres such as the novel, short stories and plays.

What exactly are these conventions which go towards making up a reader's literary competence? Defining them is no easy task. In very broad terms, it has been said that we are reading something as literature when we are interested in the 'general state of affairs' to which it refers rather than its pragmatic function in the real world (Brumfit and Carter, 1986 p. 16). Thus, when reading a newspaper article we expect it to be verifiable with reference to a world of facts, whereas when reading literary texts we are interested in what Brumfit has described as metaphorical or symbolic meanings which 'illuminate our self-awareness' (Brumfit, Carter and Walker, 1989, p. 27). More precisely, Jonathan Culler in *Structuralist Poetics* has attempted to pinpoint certain literary conventions which operate for particular genres, for example when reading a novel competent readers are able to follow the plot and recognise certain themes. (See 'Poetics of the Novel' in Culler, 1975, p. 189.) A skilled reader might also recognise how themes in the plot may be reflected by themes in the sub-plot, how particular characters come to embody certain values or attitudes, how the narration is shaped by a particular point of view, and so on. While it is extremely difficult to itemise all the skills that go towards making up 'literary competence', it is important for teachers to identify at least some of the more important skills which make up literary competence.

One reason for this is that too often when reading literature, students are expected, as if by osmosis, to acquire a kind of competence in reading literature. Teachers are able to recognise this competence when they see it (for example in an exam essay about a set book) but just what its components are remains mysterious to teachers and students alike. Far better for all would be an explicit and public statement of what skills and sub-skills students need to acquire as components of 'literary competence'. Depending on the nature of the course and the type of students involved these might include anything from recognising and appreciating a full range of genres (from sonnets to allegories) to simply following the plot of a short story. But by drawing up an explicit list of these skills, teachers would be able to plan their materials and courses with a clearer goal in mind and students would have clearer procedures and techniques for dealing with literary texts.

So just how important is it, for teachers using literature with the language learner, that students acquire 'literary competence'? This surely depends on the purpose for which the literature is being used. A useful distinction here is the one that has been made between the *study* of literature and the *use* of literature as a resource for language teaching (Maley, *ELT Documents*: 130, p. 10).

The study of literature makes literature itself the content or subject of a language course, while the use of literature as a resource draws on literature as one source among many different kinds of texts for promoting interesting language activities. Clearly, if it is the study of literature which is our aim then developing the 'literary competence' of our students is crucial. This, for example, might be the case for a group of learners at tertiary level. On the other hand, if we wish to use literature as a resource, then we may not aim to teach 'literary competence' but it is possible that our students will begin to acquire it through their exposure to literary texts. This might be the case if we are simply using literature as a resource on an occasional basis with our students, for example the use of a poem now and again with a class of adult learners. We should not expect such students to develop literary competence without deliberately developing and using tasks and activities which help them to do so.

Task 17

You are teaching a general English class. As part of their course, your learners are required to read and study a play on which they will be tested at the end of the year. Although your aim is to teach language, not literature, it is still important for your learners to begin to develop the necessary competence to understand and interpret a play. What specific literary skills do you think they need in order to be able to do this? Note down any skills connected with understanding and interpreting a play that you would like your learners to acquire over the year.

1.5 Why use literature in the language classroom?

In this chapter we have been considering some of the issues underlying the use of literature with the language learner. This leads inevitably to the question of why we should use literature in the language classroom.

Task 18

Below is a list of reasons for using literature with the language learner. Think about which reasons are the most important. List your reasons in order of importance.

Literature should be used with students because:
- it is very motivating
- it is authentic material
- it has general educational value

- it is found in many syllabuses
- it helps students to understand another culture
- it is a stimulus for language acquisition
- it develops students' interpretative abilities
- students enjoy it and it is fun
- it is highly valued and has a high status
- it expands students' language awareness
- it encourages students to talk about their opinions and feelings

Are there any other reasons for using literature that you want to add to this list?

Task 19

In the previous task you ranked reasons for using literature with the language learner in order of importance. The text which follows discusses some of these reasons in a little more depth. Read through the text, and then decide whether you would still rank the reasons for using literature in the way that you did.

Examining the reasons for using literature

MOTIVATING MATERIAL

In many countries around the world, literature is highly valued. For this reason, students of English may experience a real sense of achievement at tackling literary materials in the classroom. If students are familiar with literature in their own language, then studying some literature in English can provide an interesting and thought-provoking point of comparison. This may apply equally well if students come from a culture with a rich oral tradition, where the body of written literature is fairly restricted. Asking students to retell short stories from their own culture, for example, before getting them to read an authentic story in English on a similar theme, could be highly motivating.

Literature exposes students to complex themes and fresh, unexpected uses of language. A good novel or short story may be particularly gripping in that it involves students in the suspense of unravelling the plot. This involvement may be more absorbing for students than the pseudo-narratives frequently found in course books. A play may engage students in complicated adult dilemmas. A poem may elicit a powerful emotional response from students. If the materials are carefully chosen, students will feel that what they do in the classroom is relevant and meaningful to their own lives.

Using literature in the language classroom: The issues

Literature can provide students with access to the culture of the people whose language they are studying. But this is an area of some complexity. To begin with, the relationship between a culture and its literature is not at all simple, since few novels or poems could claim to be a purely factual documentation of their society. Some novels, short stories and plays may achieve the illusion of representing reality, but they are, in the end, works of fiction. It has been argued that poetry has possibly an even more indirect link with the 'real world' since it creates its meaning by an orientation towards language itself (Widdowson, 1984, p. 149).

Secondly, if we do assume that a literary text in some way 'reflects' its culture, then exactly what aspect of that culture is being mirrored and how reliably? There is a danger that students will fall into the fallacy of assuming that a novel, for example, represents the totality of a society, when in fact it is a highly atypical account of one particular milieu during a specific historical period. And if we are considering the issue of how far a literary work genuinely represents its culture, then we are inevitably drawn into the question of how culture is defined. Is our definition to be an anthropological one in which culture is defined loosely as the values, traditions and social practices of a particular group – which are then revealed in the literary text? Or do we define culture as the discernment and knowledge traditionally possessed by the well-educated, enlightened and cultivated native speaker which is passed on in 'good literature'? What then is the place of 'popular culture' which may in fact be of greater interest to many of our learners?

A further issue to consider is that English is now used globally as a first, second and foreign language.[6] How far the language can be separated from culture is a difficult and intriguing question. Literary texts in English reflect the rich and fascinating diversities of our world. They are written by authors living in many different countries and widely divergent cultures. By exposing our students to literature in English, it seems that we should be asking them to think about the range of cultures from which literature in English is produced. But frequently, the teaching of literature is identified with the imposition of particular imperialistic values. Chris Searle has described how in the Caribbean, students of British literature had the feeling that 'they had to pit the world and the people they knew around them against a barrage of hostile, alienated knowledge which bore no relation to the reality they saw around them' (Searle, 1984, p. 17). And writing of literature teaching in Kenyan schools, Ngugi wa Thiong'o describes how Kenyan school children are confronted 'with a distorted image of themselves and of their history as reflected in European imperialist literature' (Brumfit and Carter, 1986, p. 225).

It can be argued that reading literature in English does encourage students to become broadly aware of the social, political and historical events which form the background to a particular play or novel. At the same time, literature does seem to provide a way of contextualising how a member of a particular society might behave or react in a specific situation. A description of a farm in the outback, for example, in a short story by an Australian author, might familiarise students with the typical scenery and social structures to be expected in such a setting. More interestingly, it could provide them with insights into the possible relationships, emotions and attitudes of the inhabitants of the farm. In other words, using literature with our students may enable them to gain useful and often surprising perceptions about how the members of a society might describe or evaluate their experiences. But as this description is very likely to be only a partial one, we should encourage students to treat it critically. In fact, our response to the cultural aspect of literature should always be a critical one, so that the underlying cultural and ideological assumptions in the texts are not merely accepted and reinforced, but are questioned, evaluated and, if necessary, subverted.[7]

ENCOURAGING LANGUAGE ACQUISITION

In many countries around the world students have fairly limited access to spoken English, and written English often takes on primary importance for stimulating language acquisition. Literature may provide a particularly appropriate way of stimulating this acquisition, as it provides meaningful and memorable contexts for processing and interpreting new language. Obviously, at lower levels, students may be unable to cope on their own with an authentic novel or short story in English. Any extensive reading we encourage them to do outside the classroom would probably need to be of graded material, such as graded readers. But at higher levels, students may be so absorbed in the plot and characters of an authentic novel or short story, that they acquire a great deal of new language almost in passing. The reading of literature then becomes an important way of supplementing the inevitably restricted input of the classroom. And if recorded literary material is available, then students can acquire a great deal of new language by listening to it.

Within the classroom itself, the use of literary texts is often a particularly successful way of promoting activities where students need to share their feelings and opinions, such as discussions and groupwork. This is because literature is very rich in multiple levels of meaning. Focussing on a task which demands that students express their own personal responses to these multiple levels of meaning can only serve to accelerate the students' acquisition of language. Acquisition may also be accelerated because the overall context for processing the new language is so striking. Take, for example, a dramatised play reading with a group of intermediate learners. While reading an extract from the play on their own, they may find themselves unfamiliar with some of the vocabulary in the extract. But by listening to the extract read aloud by the teacher, or better still acted out on cassette, they may be able to hazard a useful guess as to the meaning of a new word; a guess facilitated by their understanding of the relationship between the speakers and the intonation they use to express this. Or, take a group of children who have only an elementary grasp of English. Asking them to read a simple poem aloud, possibly accompanied by gestures or mime, may be an effective way of helping them to internalise vocabulary, grammar patterns or even intonation.

EXPANDING STUDENTS' LANGUAGE AWARENESS

As we have seen in Section 1.2 one of the debates centred around literature teaching in the language classroom is whether literary language is somehow different from other forms of discourse in that it breaks the more usual rules of syntax, collocation and even cohesion. This seems to be particularly true of poetry.[8] Teachers often express concern that in using literature with our students, we are exposing them to 'wrong' uses of language. Let us consider these examples which seem to break, or at least bend, the usual rules and patterns we may be trying to teach:

A. A grief ago   (Dylan Thomas, *A Grief Ago.*)

B. . . . a fantastic farm where ashes grow like wheat into ridges and hills and grotesque gardens . . .   (F. Scott Fitzgerald, *The Great Gatsby*, Penguin, 1983, p. 29.)

C. Though wedded we have been
These twice ten tedious years . . .
(Cowper's *The Diverting History of John Gilpin* – quoted in Leech, 1988.)

In Example A the abstract noun *grief* replaces what is usually a noun denoting a time period, like *day* or *month*. In Example B *ashes* are described as growing – an unusual collocation, and one it is unlikely students will find in a dictionary. Example C is a poetic re-ordering of syntax, since usually the past participle *wedded* would follow *we have been*. The question for teachers is whether such original, but rather unconventional, uses of language are seriously going to confuse the learner.

It has been argued that by asking students to explore such sophisticated uses of language, we are also encouraging them to think about the norms of language use (Widdowson, 1975). In order to understand the stylistic effect of any of the examples above, students will need to be aware of how they differ from more common usage. In Example B, for instance, we might ask students to think of what usually grows; even perhaps to look up common collocations for it in the dictionary. The next stage is to consider what effect is conveyed by suggesting that the ashes are 'growing'. And in the context of a novel or short story this may even help students to interpret its underlying themes more easily. By focussing on the 'deviant' use of the verb here we are helping students not only to become aware of specific stylistic effects in this literary work, but also to consider how this effect is achieved by departing from a norm. At the same time, we are involving them in the process of discovering more generalisable features of language like collocation. In other words, using literature with students can help them to become more sensitive to some of the overall features of English.

DEVELOPING STUDENTS' INTERPRETATIVE ABILITIES

Any learning of a new language would seem to involve the learner in the forming of hypotheses and the drawing of inferences, whether these relate to when a particular idiom is used appropriately, how far a grammatical rule can be generalised or what is implied behind the literal meaning of what someone says in a conversation. It has been argued that literature is a particularly good source for developing students' abilities to infer meaning and to make interpretations (see Rossner's interview with Widdowson in *ELT Journal* 37/1). This is because literary texts are often rich in multiple levels of meaning, and demand that the reader/learner is actively involved in 'teasing out' the unstated implications and assumptions of the text. In a poem, for example, a word may take on a powerful figurative meaning beyond its fixed dictionary definition. Trying to ascertain this significance provides an excellent opportunity for students to discuss their own interpretations, based on the evidence in the text. Thus, by encouraging our students to grapple with the multiple ambiguities of the literary text, we are helping to develop their overall capacity to infer meaning. This very useful skill can then be transferred to other situations where students need to make an interpretation based on implicit or unstated evidence.

EDUCATING THE WHOLE PERSON

The linguistic benefits of using literature with the language learner have been mentioned. But literature may also have a wider educational function in the classroom in that it can help to stimulate the imagination of our students, to develop their critical abilities and to increase their emotional awareness. If we ask students to respond personally to the texts we give them, they will become increasingly confident about expressing their own ideas and emotions in English. They will feel empowered by their ability to grapple with the text and its language, and to relate it to the values and traditions of their own society.

B

Conclusion

In this chapter we have started to think about some of the underlying issues and concerns involved in using literature in the language classroom. You may find that you have more questions than answers relating to some of the areas we have touched on. If so, why not write down some of these questions, queries or points for discussion? You may find answers to them later on in the book or in some of the supplementary reading you might choose to do. Or you could discuss some of these ideas with your colleagues.

Endnotes

1. With thanks to the teachers who attended the summer courses in teaching literature at International House, London, in 1989 and 1990.
2. The texts are taken from:
   A. *In Store: The magazine of ideas for your home*, September 1985.
   B. F. Scott Fitzgerald, *The Great Gatsby*, p. 14 (Penguin, 1983).
   C. A restaurant review by Nigella Lawson in *The Spectator*, 4 August 1990.
   D. An advertisement for The Royal National Institute for the Deaf.
   E. Ralph C. Opara, 'Lagos Interlude', in Figueroa (1982).
   F. This is a nursery rhyme common in a number of anthologies.
   G. This is a piece of colloquial speech which I made up myself.
3. This activity is rather impressionistic, based as it is on the intuitions of the reader. With the advent of computer corpuses which make use of concordances, it would be possible to identify in a more systematic way whether or not certain types of discourse do indeed reveal a high incidence of particular linguistic features. For a useful book on this topic and its application to the classroom see Tribble and Jones (1990).
4. For a book which explores the different factors determining or influencing a reader's response to a literary text, see Suleiman and Crosman (eds.) (1980).
5. The idea of rewriting a newspaper text in the form of a poem comes from Culler (1975), Chapter 8. The sentence from the newspaper, which is then rewritten as a poem, was taken from *The Guardian*, 16 July 1991.
6. For a brief discussion of the socio-political implications of this fact see Crystal (1988), Chapter 1.
7. This concern with criticising and subverting the underlying ideological and cultural assumptions in literary texts is a hallmark of many recent examples of Marxist, feminist and deconstructionist critical theory. Some references for following up these theories are provided in the list of further references.
8. See 'The Deviant Language of Poetry' in Widdowson (1984).

Suggestions for further reading

Literary theory

Eagleton, T. (1983) *Literary Theory*.

Jefferson, A. and Robey, D. (1984) *Modern Literary Theory: A Comparative Introduction*.

Lodge, D. (ed.) (1990) *Twentieth Century Literary Criticism*.

Selden, R. (1989) *A Reader's Guide to Contemporary Literary Theory*.

The issues and debates behind using literature with the language learner

Brumfit, C. J. and Carter, R. A. (eds.) (1986) *Literature and Language Teaching*.

Brumfit, C. J. (ed.) (1983) 'Teaching Literature Overseas: Language-based Approaches' *ELT Documents 115*.

Brumfit, C., Carter, R. and Walker, R. (eds.) (1989) 'Literature and the Learner: Methodological Approaches' *ELT Documents 130*.

Carter, R. and Long, M. (1991) *Teaching Literature*.

Holden, S. (ed.) (1988) Literature and Language (1987 Sorrento Conference organised by the British Council).

Rossner, R. (1983) 'Talking Shop: H. G. Widdowson on literature and ELT' in *ELT Journal*, 37, 1.

2 Approaches to using literature with the language learner

The aim of this chapter is to examine the possible approaches which you could draw on when using literature with your students. Pinpointing possible approaches can help us to select and design materials for classroom use, as well as to assess the suitability of published materials. We begin by considering these approaches in very general terms; later sections will examine some of the issues and problems they raise in more general terms.

2.1 An overview

Below are three quotes taken from books which use literature in the language classroom. Although there is some overlap between the books in terms of overall aims and methodological assumptions, they do have slightly different ways of selecting, organising and exploiting their material. By examining these quotes more carefully, we may begin to gather together some clues about approaches we could adopt when using literature with our students. Read through the quotes and then think about the questions which follow.

A. If carefully selected, poems can open up themes which are common to us whatever our cultural background, and can thus act as a powerful stimulus to the students' own reflective thinking, which will lead to more mature and fruitful group discussion. **(Maley and Moulding (1985),** *Poem into Poem,* **p. 135.)**

B. *Reading Literature* provides students with an introduction to the reading of British and American literature. It concentrates on helping them actually read what are sometimes difficult texts, while at the same time giving them help with literary history, biography, differences in genre, technical literary terminology and literary criticism.

    (Gower and Pearson (1986), *Reading Literature*, p. 1.)

C. The aims and design of the book can be briefly summarised as follows: *The Web of Words* helps learners to understand and appreciate English literary texts. It does so by using a wide variety of learning techniques and exercises which often involve active group and pairwork in class. The book focuses particularly on language where this is relevant to appreciate the style, effects and techniques of writing. The main purpose is to help students to use response to language as a basis for reading and appreciating literary sources.

    (Carter and Long (1987), *The Web of Words*, p. 1.)

Task 1

a) What seems to be the overall aim of each book in using literature with the language learner?
b) How would you expect the material in each book to be selected and organised?
c) What types of tasks and activities would you expect to find in each book?

In Task 1 you began to think about some possible approaches to using literature with the language learner. Now follows a more detailed categorisation of three possible approaches to using literature. This categorisation is, to some extent, an idealised version of what is likely to be used on courses or in materials. In practice, many courses and materials make use of a range of approaches which are blended together in different ways. For the moment, however, we may find it useful to treat each approach as separate and distinct.

Task 2

Below are descriptions of three possible approaches, the methodological principles underlying each one and some notes about the selection and organisation of the material that they use. Read through them – are there any similarities between these approaches, and your thoughts on the quotes from published materials in Task 1?

1. A language-based approach

METHODOLOGICAL ASSUMPTIONS

Studying the language of the literary text will help to integrate the language and literature syllabuses more closely. Detailed analysis of the language of the literary text will help students to make meaningful interpretations or informed evaluations of it. At the same time, students will increase their general awareness and understanding of English. Students are encouraged to draw on their knowledge of familiar grammatical, lexical or discoursal categories to make aesthetic judgements of the text.

SELECTION AND ORGANISATION OF MATERIAL

Material is chosen for the way it illustrates certain stylistic features of the language but also for its literary merit.

2. Literature as content

METHODOLOGICAL ASSUMPTIONS

This is the most traditional approach, frequently used in tertiary education. Literature itself is the content of the course, which concentrates on areas such as the history and characteristics of literary movements; the social, political and historical background to a text; literary genres and rhetorical devices, etc. Students acquire English by focussing on course content, particularly through reading set texts and literary criticism relating to them. The mother tongue of the students may be used to discuss the texts, or students may be asked to translate texts from one language into the other.

SELECTION AND ORGANISATION OF MATERIAL

Texts are selected for their importance as part of a literary canon or tradition.

3. Literature for personal enrichment

METHODOLOGICAL ASSUMPTIONS

Literature is a useful tool for encouraging students to draw on their own personal experiences, feelings and opinions. It helps students to become more actively involved both intellectually and emotionally in learning English, and hence aids acquisition. Excellent stimulus for groupwork.

SELECTION AND ORGANISATION OF MATERIAL

Material is chosen on the basis of whether it is appropriate to students' interests and will stimulate a high level of personal involvement. Material is often organised thematically, and may be placed alongside non-literary materials which deal with a similar theme.

Task 3 🔑

Here is a list of the advantages and disadvantages of using each of the approaches mentioned above. They have all been jumbled together.
Decide which advantage and which disadvantage belong with each of the different approaches.

Advantages

1. Students are helped to develop a response to literature through examining the linguistic evidence in the text. Students are provided with analytic tools with which to reach their own interpretations. They are encouraged to draw on their knowledge of English, so this approach may provide useful exposure to, or revision of, grammar and vocabulary in interesting new contexts. It is a way of justifying the inclusion of literature in the language syllabus since it fulfils students' main aim – to improve their knowledge of the language.
2. Involves learner as whole person, and so is potentially highly motivating. Demystifies literature by placing it alongside non-literary texts.
3. Genuinely educational approach in that understanding of texts is enhanced by situating them within their literary and historical contexts. Students are exposed to a wide range of authentic materials.

Disadvantages

1. May demand a personal response from students without providing sufficient guidance in coping with the linguistic intricacies of the text. Some texts may be so remote from the students' own experience that they are unable to respond meaningfully to them. Alternatively, some groups of students may dislike having to discuss personal feelings or reactions.
2. If applied too rigidly, so that analysis of the text is undertaken in purely linguistic terms with little chance for personal interpretation, this approach could become very mechanical and demotivating. Also, it may not pay sufficient attention to the text's historical, social or political background which often provides students with the valuable cultural knowledge to interpret what they read.
3. This approach may be most appropriate to a fairly select group of 'literary-minded' students. Material may be very difficult linguistically, and therefore demotivating for the average student. The approach may rely too heavily on the teacher to paraphrase, clarify and explain, resulting in very little student participation. A large part of the lesson may be carried out in the students' mother tongue, with students dependent on ready-made interpretations from the teacher.

Are there any other advantages or disadvantages you would like to add to the lists above?

Using literature: When, with whom and how?

So far in this section we have thought about different approaches to using literature in the language classroom. We will now reflect on which approach or combination of approaches might be the most suitable for a particular group of learners.

Task 4

Look at the descriptions below of different groups of students and think about the following questions:
a) Do you think it is appropriate to use literature with this particular group of learners? Why?
b) If you do, what kinds of literature would be best – novels, short stories, plays or poetry?
c) Would any particular approach be the most appropriate?

1. A group of businessmen and women who have EFL lessons at their company premises for three hours a week after work. They are usually very tired.
2. A class of secondary school students who speak English as a second language. They are studying for an English exam at matriculation level which they hope will allow them to go to university.
3. A group of adult learners with few educational qualifications who are attending evening classes three hours a week to improve both their knowledge of English as a second language and their literacy in it.
4. A group of children who have EFL lessons for six hours a week at a private school. They are usually quite tired since they have already attended school in the morning.
5. A class of adult EFL learners from intermediate to advanced level who have been learning English on and off for ten years. They only have time to attend lessons for two hours a week and they feel quite discouraged when they don't seem to be making much progress.
6. A group of apprentices at a technical college who study English for two hours a week. English is spoken as a second language in their country, although technical instruction is in their first language. They will soon be leaving the college to look for work.
7. A woman living in Greece, who is at intermediate level and has two hours of private EFL lessons a week. She hopes to go to the United States as a tourist, and is very interested in American culture.
8. A group of beginners who are very highly educated and literate in their own language. They are on an intensive English course in Britain. They are studying for twenty-five hours a week and their course lasts three months. They need English for their jobs.

Task 5

Think about your own students. Would you use literature with them? If so, what approach do you think would be most suitable? Why? Would you use any particular genre with them? Why?

In the next four sections of this chapter we will discuss in more detail the possible approaches to using literature with the language learner which were delineated in Section 2.1. Since stylistics is a particular method-ology, though falling into the general category of language-based approaches, it is dealt with in its own section (2.3).

2.2 A language-based approach to using literature

Before we begin in this section to consider the idea of a language-based approach to using literature, you might like to jot down any ideas you have about what such an approach involves and then to compare your ideas with those which follow.

A language-based approach is quite a broad approach which covers a range of different goals and procedures. Generally speaking, proponents believe in a closer integration of language and literature in the classroom, since this will help the students in achieving their main aim – which is to improve their knowledge of, and proficiency in, English.

But proponents of this approach vary in their ultimate goals. Some focus not on studying or reading literature itself, but rather on how to use literature for language practice.[1] Literary texts are thus seen as a resource – one among many different types of texts – which provide stimulating language activities. The advantages of using literary texts for language activities are that they offer a wide range of styles and registers; they are open to multiple interpretations and hence provide excellent opportunities for classroom discussion; and they focus on genuinely interesting and motivating topics to explore in the classroom (Duff and Maley, 1990, p. 6).

At the other end of the spectrum, a language-based approach to using literature includes techniques and procedures which are concerned more directly with the study of the literary text itself. The aim here is to provide the students with the tools they need to interpret a text and to make competent critical judgements of it. Here the method of stylistics or stylistic analysis is frequently adopted. Stylistics involves the close study of the linguistic features of a text in order to arrive at an under-standing of how the meanings of the text are transmitted. (Stylistics, or stylistic analysis, will be dealt with more fully in Section 2.3.)

Finally, there are those who argue that students are not always ready to undertake stylistic analysis of a text, but that certain language-based study skills can act as important preliminary activities to studying literature (see Brumfit and Carter, 1986, p. 110). Many of these study skills will be familiar to language teachers since they are normal, every-day classroom procedures and activities. An example might be asking students to make predictions about what will happen next at key points in a short story (Brumfit and Carter, 1986, p. 111). This kind of procedure is likely to be familiar to students, and so provides an unintimidating way of bridging the gap between language study and the development of more literary-based skills.

We shall now look at some examples of language-based activities for exploiting literature with the language learner. We shall also examine two schemes of work which are based on this approach – although to two very different ends.

Task 6

Here are a number of fairly typical language-based activities which make use of a literary text in the classroom. While you read through them, decide what the main language aim of the teacher is in using this activity with his or her students.

ACTIVITY 1   (UPPER INTERMEDIATE UPWARDS)

Groups of students are each given different sections of a dialogue from a play, which they then have to rewrite in reported speech using a range of verbs (e.g. suggest, mumble, wonder, etc.). When they are finished, they give their reported versions to members of another group to trans-form into dialogues, which are then compared with the originals from the play. Finally, students are reminded about such points as tense changes, when moving from direct into reported speech.

ACTIVITY 2   (LATE INTERMEDIATE UPWARDS)

Students are given a piece of descriptive writing from a novel or short story from which all adverbs and adjectives are removed. They rewrite the text adding those they think will liven it up, and compare their version with the original. They may use dictionaries to help them.

ACTIVITY 3   (INTERMEDIATE UPWARDS)

After they have read it, students are given three different summaries of a short story. They have to decide which summary is the most accurate.

ACTIVITY 4   (INTERMEDIATE UPWARDS)

Students read a dialogue from a play or a novel and then improvise their own roleplay of what happens next.

ACTIVITY 5   (ELEMENTARY UPWARDS)

Students are given three very short and simple poems in English, but without their titles. They are also given a list of six titles – three genuine and three invented. After reading the poems, they have to decide which title is most appropriate for each poem.

ACTIVITY 6   (INTERMEDIATE UPWARDS)

Students are given an extract from a novel or short story in which all tenses are removed. They are provided with the actual verbs to fill in. After completing this task, they compare their text with the original.

ACTIVITY 7   (ADVANCED)

Students are given three different critical opinions of a play or novel they have read. They have to decide which they find the most convincing or accurate.

Task 7   ☛─0

After you have decided what the language aims of each activity are, think about these questions:
a) For which of the activities above do you think the teacher's aim could have been achieved equally well by using a non-literary text? What particular advantages might there be in using literary texts instead of non-literary texts to teach or revise a particular area of language?
b) Are there any activities above which you think would help students to improve their competence in reading a literary text?
c) Think about some of the activities or techniques that you commonly make use of in the classroom. For example, you may:
   – ask students to answer True/False questions about a reading comprehension
   – ask students to provide synonyms for any new items of vocabulary you teach
   – ask students to read a text aloud to practise their pronunciation, etc.
   Write down at least three techniques or activities that you use frequently in your teaching. Can you use any of these techniques and activities to exploit a literary text with your students? What would be your aim(s) in doing so?

Task 8 🗝️

Figures 2.1 and 2.2 are schemes of work, or timetables, for a week's work with two different classes. Look through them, and answer the questions below.
a) Which one is for intermediate learners at secondary level?
b) Which one is for advanced adult learners?
c) Which one uses literary texts to complement or reinforce the language aims of the syllabus?
d) Which one makes use of a prescribed text for extensive reading practice, but also to improve the students' language awareness?

Day 1	Day 2	Day 3
Students in groups prepare oral descriptions of three different urban landscapes. Groups then come together – all pictures on board. Other students identify pictures from their descriptions. ↓ Teacher elicits vocabulary, e.g. high-rise, smoke stacks, factories, etc. ↓ Students complete gap-fill to practise vocabulary.	Reading comprehension Descriptions of Coketown from Dickens' *Hard Times*. – vocabulary exercises – true/false questions – questions about style Students begin to prepare own descriptions (of their town) for homework.	Passive voice Teacher shows 'picture' of Coketown now – elicits passive sentences, e.g. 'old buildings have been demolished/ Town hall was redecorated last year', etc. ↓ Students compare two pictures of a town that has changed + make their own sentences. ↓ Students prepare and present radio commercial to visit the new Coketown.

Figure 2.1 Lesson plan A

Day 1	Day 2	Day 3
Listening comprehension Taped interview on radio 'Current fads and fashions in the U.S.' – comprehension questions – vocabulary exercise –discussion in groups: a) List some current fashions in clothing, food, etc. b) What do you think of them?	Phrasal verbs Students fill in gap-fill exercise using different phrasal verbs. (Text about youth fashions.) ↓ Homework: Read chapter VII of *The Great Gatsby* and note down 3 phrasal verbs in it. Review of past tenses and sequencing words, e.g. the minute that...	Sentence-completion and ordering activity to ensure students have understood chapter VII – use past tense + sequencing words. In groups, students prepare interviews with different witnesses to the crash described – who knows what + why→ role-play for class.

Figure 2.2 Lesson plan B

2.3　Stylistics in the classroom ☆

In the previous section, we concentrated on those activities and tasks which can be used with a literary text to promote interesting and motivating language practice. In this section, we focus on a method which can guide students towards a more sensitive understanding and appreciation of the literary text itself. Stylistics, which involves the close study of the literary text itself, has two main objectives: firstly, to enable students to make meaningful interpretations of the text itself; secondly, to expand students' knowledge and awareness of the language in general. Thus, although the aim of using stylistics is to help students to read and study literature more competently, it also provides them with excellent language practice.

Task 9

Before reading the text which follows, try to complete these four
sentences.
a) Practical criticism is ....
b) The problem with using practical criticism with students is that ....
c) Stylistics is ....
d) The advantages of using stylistics with students are ....

In the teaching of literature, traditional practical criticism has relied on the intuitions of the reader to form critical judgements. Students are presented with a text and expected to arrive spontaneously at an appreciation of its literary qualities, without any explicit guidance as to how this is to be done. The difficulty with this approach is that the language learners' intuitions about the language may be quite different from those of the native speaker, since their linguistic, cultural and literary backgrounds are likely to be different.

At the same time, such an approach seems to imply that understanding or appreciating literature is the result of a kind of mystic revelation, which is not available to everyone. Being expected to appreciate a text, therefore, without being given a clear strategy for doing so, might only make students feel bored, mystified or demotivated.

What is needed, instead, is a way of enabling students to reach an aesthetic appreciation of a text which connects its specific linguistic features with intuitions about its meanings. One way of doing this is by making use of stylistics – a method which 'uses the apparatus of linguistic description' (Leech and Short, 1981, p. 74) to analyse how meanings in a text are communicated. In his book, *Stylistics and the Teaching of Literature*, 1975, Widdowson has described such a method as a mediating discipline between linguistics and literary criticism (p. 4). Linguists are largely interested in the codes which transmit particular messages, but not really in the messages themselves. The literary critic, on the other hand, is concerned with the interpretation and evaluation of literary works. Stylistics provides a link between the two in that it uses linguistic analysis to understand how messages are conveyed.

For the language learner, stylistics has the advantage of illustrating how particular linguistic forms function to convey specific messages. It uses terminology and a set of procedures reasonably familiar to students (those of grammatical description) to reach and justify literary intuitions. In this way it not only helps students to use their existing knowledge of the language to understand and appreciate literary texts, it also deepens their knowledge of the language itself. Stylistic analysis can also provide a way of comparing different types of texts (whether literary or non-literary) in order to ascertain how they fulfil different social functions. For example, students may be asked to compare the description of a character in a novel with the information about someone given in a letter of reference or on a medical form (Widdowson, 1975, Chapter 6). The students will then be able to examine how these texts differ and the reason for this difference. The teaching of literature can thus be integrated more fully into the classroom, since literary texts can be studied alongside other kinds of texts.

Analysing a text for classroom use

In order to devise activities for our students which use stylistic analysis, we ourselves need a procedure or strategy for analysing the text. Here is one possible procedure which involves two main steps:

STEP 1

While looking at a particular text, note down any linguistic features which are particularly noticeable. These features may be noticeable because they recur with unexpected frequency in the text; because they deviate slightly from what might be considered more grammatically or lexically usual; or because, if these features were paraphrased or rewritten in a slightly different way, a very different effect would be created.

STEP 2

Develop a series of questions which alert students to these features, and encourage students to reach an interpretation or appreciation of the text bearing these features in mind.

We now apply this procedure to the opening paragraphs of V. S. Naipaul's novel *A House for Mr Biswas* (Penguin, 1969).

Task 10

In Figure 2.3 the opening paragraphs of the novel have been marked for any unusual or noticeable linguistic features. Decide if you would underline or add any others.

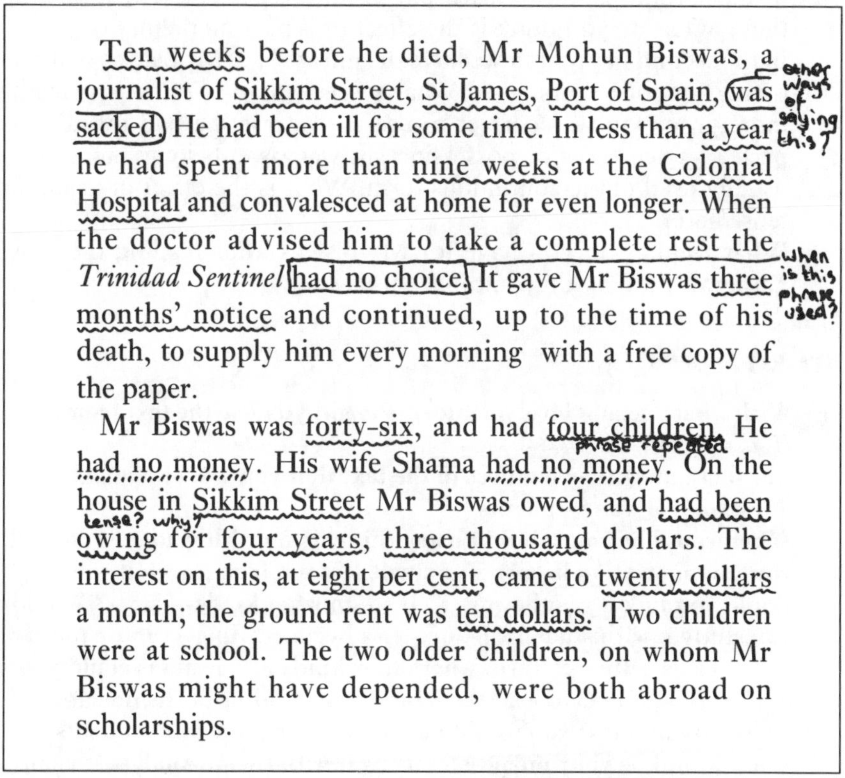
Ten weeks before he died, Mr Mohun Biswas, a journalist of Sikkim Street, St James, Port of Spain, was sacked. He had been ill for some time. In less than a year he had spent more than nine weeks at the Colonial Hospital and convalesced at home for even longer. When the doctor advised him to take a complete rest the *Trinidad Sentinel* had no choice. It gave Mr Biswas three months' notice and continued, up to the time of his death, to supply him every morning with a free copy of the paper.
Mr Biswas was forty-six, and had four children. He had no money. His wife Shama had no money. On the house in Sikkim Street Mr Biswas owed, and had been owing for four years, three thousand dollars. The interest on this, at eight per cent, came to twenty dollars a month; the ground rent was ten dollars. Two children were at school. The two older children, on whom Mr Biswas might have depended, were both abroad on scholarships.
other ways of saying this?
when is this phrase used?
phrase repeated
tense? why?

Figure 2.3 Extract annotated for noticeable linguistic features

Task 11

Here are some questions for students based on the text above. Go through the questions yourself and note your answers.

a) Write down all the examples you can find in the text of exact numbers, figures or other precise details describing Mr Biswas and his situation. What effect do you think is created by using all these details?

b) In the opening lines of the text we are told that Mr Biswas was sacked. The author could also have said:
'Mr Biswas was dismissed.'
'Mr Biswas lost his job.'

How would the use of these phrases in the passage have changed its meaning?

c) In what situation is it common to use the phrase 'I/We have no choice'? Do you think the newspaper had no choice in sacking Mr Biswas? What is the effect of using the phrase here?

d) In the second paragraph two phrases are repeated. Which ones are they? What do you think is the effect of repeating them?

e) In the second paragraph we have the phrase ' . . . Mr Biswas had been owing for four years . . . ' What tense is used here? It is probably more grammatically correct to use the phrase 'he had owed' (past perfect) since verbs of possession such as owe, belong, etc. are not usually used in the continuous form. What is the effect of using this tense here?

f) What feelings do you have for Mr Biswas after reading these two paragraphs? Why do you think this is so?

Task 12

a) With what age and level of students might you use the text from *A House for Mr Biswas*?

b) Are there any other features in the text that you would highlight in questions for your students?

c) What would be your aims in using this extract with students? Would you use the text on its own in a single lesson? If so, to what end? Could you link it to other texts? If so, to what kinds of texts? Would you study it with students before they begin reading *A House for Mr Biswas* as a setbook? If so, what other kinds of questions could you devise for students to lead them into their reading of the novel?

d) Think about a text you would like to use with your own students. What would be your purpose in using it with them? Analyse it using the two steps method described above and then decide what questions you would ask your students about it.

Task 13

Here are some statements about using stylistic analysis with your students. Decide whether you think each statement is **always true**, **sometimes true** or **never true**.[2]

a) Stylistic analysis can provide students with a basic procedure for appreciating or interpreting a text, but it cannot actually interpret the meaning of the text for them. This is because all interpretations of a text are necessarily incomplete and subjective, rather than complete and objective.

b) The use of grammatical terminology when doing stylistic analysis with students only serves to confuse and alienate them.

c) Stylistic analysis, if applied too rigidly, treats the text as a self-contained entity with little reference to the social, cultural or historical background in which it is grounded. By concentrating on the language of the text in isolation teachers may neglect to provide students with important background information which could be required to make sense of the text.

d) When doing stylistic analysis with their students teachers should avoid providing their own ready-made interpretation of the text. The aim of using stylistics is to engage students in the complex process of making sense of a text rather than of reaching a definitive view of that text's meaning.

e) Stylistic analysis is a rather mechanical approach to studying literature – it deadens the students' emotional response to what they are reading.

f) Stylistic analysis is a useful way of revising grammar and vocabulary with students, and increasing their overall language awareness.

2.4 Literature as content: How far to go?

One of the possible approaches to teaching literature, mentioned at the beginning of this chapter, is to make literature itself the content of the course. This kind of approach examines the history and characteristics of literary movements; the social, political and historical background to a text; the biography of the author and its relevance to his or her writings; the genre of the text, etc. Some language teachers would argue that this type of approach is really the province of the literature teacher rather than the language teacher, and is only successful when used with learners who have a specialist interest in the study of literature. Nevertheless, there are important elements in this approach which can be usefully applied to the teaching of literature in the language class. In this section we explore these elements further.

Task 14

Here is the beginning of a fairly long poem. Read it, and then write a very brief paragraph (not more than 50 words) describing what you think the poem is about.

Andrea del Sarto
(Called 'The Faultless Painter')

But do not let us quarrel any more,
No, my Lucrezia; bear with me for once:
Sit down and all shall happen as you wish.
You turn your face, but does it bring your heart?
5 I'll work then for your friend's friend, never fear,
Treat his own subject after his own way,
Fix his own time, accept too his own price,
And shut the money into this small hand
When next it takes mine. Will it? tenderly?
10 Oh, I'll content him, – but tomorrow, Love!
I often am much wearier than you think,
This evening more than usual, and it seems
As if – forgive now – should you let me sit
Here by the window with your hand in mine
15 And look a half-hour forth on Fiesole,
Both of one mind, as married people use,
Quietly, quietly the evening through,
I might get up tomorrow to my work
Cheerful and fresh as ever. Let us try.

Once you have finished Task 14, read the following information relating to the poem and then complete Task 15.

Background to 'Andrea del Sarto'

- The poem 'Andrea del Sarto' was written by Robert Browning (1812–1889) and first published in the second volume of *Men and Women* on 10 November 1855.
- Browning was a poet who successfully mastered a range of styles, and particularly delighted in the natural rhythms of everyday speech.
- Many of Browning's more famous poems, including 'Andrea del Sarto', are dramatic monologues. A dramatic monologue is a poem in which the poet invents a character, or more commonly, uses a character from history or legend. The poem is delivered as though by this person, sometimes but not always, to an imagined listener. The speaker in the poem is not identified with the poet, but is dramatised through what he or she says. In this way, the speaker is made to reveal himself or herself in an ironic way to the reader.
- Andrea del Sarto was a Renaissance painter and contemporary of Raphael and Michelangelo. He was born in Florence in 1486. In 1517 he married a beautiful widow, Lucrezia del Fede, who was often his model. Between 1518 and 1519 he went to France at the invitation of

Francis I. He died in 1531 at the time of the plague in Florence. He was known as the 'Faultless Painter' because of the perfection of his technique.

– Browning was generally familiar with the work of Andrea del Sarto, and probably based the information about the painter on Vasari's *Lives of the Artists*.

– Fiesole is a town in the hills just north-east of Florence.[3]

Task 15

Look again at the opening lines of *Andrea del Sarto* and the paragraph you wrote describing them. Has the background information you have just read altered your understanding or appreciation of the opening lines of the poem? In what way(s)? Which information did you find helpful to your understanding of the poem? Which information did you find irrelevant or distracting?[4]

Task 16

Below are some responses from teachers to the tasks you have just completed. Decide which one is closest to your own reaction. Would you want to add any more thoughts or feelings of your own?

A. I found that the background information provided really enhanced my understanding of the opening lines of the poem. It made the situation far more vivid, and gave me clues as to how to read the poem. Without knowing the context to which the poem relates it is difficult to understand what it is about.

B. I don't really see the point of providing background information. If a poem or piece of literature is good, then it should speak for itself and be universally understood.

C. The background information feels like a burden to me – as if I have the whole heavy weight of centuries of English literature bearing down on me. It makes me feel as if my own response to the poem will be totally inadequate compared to that of all the critics and professors who have written about the poem.

D. The background information made me feel I'd learned something new which I'd be able to apply to other poems by Browning – if I ever get round to reading them!

E. I find it a great relief to have a little help with reading the poem, rather than always having to fall back on my own interpretation.

F. Without background information, particularly of a cultural or historical kind, I think we fail to understand the way in which texts are often a unique expression of the historical or political period in which they are written.

Task 17

Think about a text that you might wish to use with your own students. With what background information might they need to be provided? What do you think their reaction is likely to be to this information?

The amount of background information about a text that you might wish to give a group of learners would clearly depend on a variety of factors, including the time available; to what extent the text refers to specific historical or mythological events or characters; the interest of the students in the literary characteristics of a text and so on. When designing materials, you will need to rely on your intuition about what information will enhance the students' understanding and enjoyment of the text. You will also need to decide how best to present this information – before or after the students have read the text, as a mini-lecture, as a reading or listening comprehension or as a research project in which students research the information themselves and present their findings to the class. Below is a list of a few of the areas that you might want to draw on when designing materials. Obviously, what kind of information you include will depend on what is relevant or appropriate to the text in question.

Background information which might be provided

– biographical information about the author
– historical or mythological events or characters to which a text refers
– philosophical, religious or political ideas debated or discussed in a text
– places, objects or other texts referred to in a text – either directly or indirectly
– genre of the text
– relationship of the text to the literary movements of its time
– historical, political or social background against which the text was written
– distinct features of the author's style.

Are there any other areas you would like to add to this list?

The titles of some books which provide information of the type listed above can be found in 'Suggestions for further reading' at the end of this chapter.

2.5 Literature for personal enrichment: Involving students

In Section 2.1 we said that literature is a useful tool for encouraging students to draw on their own experiences, feelings and opinions. In this section we explore ways of doing this more successfully when using a literary text.

Task 18 ☆

On the next page are two poems on a fairly similar theme. Before you read them, do the following activities

a) Think about someone who means a lot to you. Write down three wishes you have for them. Tell your partner about them.

b) Write down the three most important pieces of advice you think a parent could give a child. Discuss these in pairs or groups. Do you all agree?

c) Imagine you are a parent whose children are going away for a few weeks. Do you feel
   - relieved to have a bit of peace?
   - worried and anxious about their welfare?
   - guilty that you are not with them?
   - sad that you will miss them?
   - confident that they will be happy and secure without you?
   - any other feelings?

d) Think of a piece of advice that someone recently gave you or that you recently gave someone. Did you accept the advice that was given to you? Did the person act on your advice? Why?

Partly Because
Ursula Laird

Partly because of the mistakes I made
I felt obliged to say to my son
be kind to people
be a kind seller of seeds
5   or petrol pump attendant instead of an unkind lawyer
or an uncaring director of personnel.

I could only say it once
and he has gone away
chasing butterflies
10   but what he does to them
if they are caught
if they are in his power
I am never there to see.

(In Naomi Lewis (ed.) (1985) Messages, Faber and Faber, p. 227.)

A wish for my children
Evangeline Paterson

On this doorstep I stand
year after year
and watch you leaving

and think: May you not
5   skin your knees. May you
not catch your fingers
in car doors. May
your hearts not break.

May tide and weather
10 wait for your coming

and may you grow strong
to break
all webs of my weaving.

(In Veronica Zundel (ed.) (1991) Faith in her words, Lion Publishing, p. 133.)

Task 19 🗝

Think about the two poems above. With what level and age group of students would you use them? Then look back at Task 18. What is the purpose of these activities? Which one do you think would be the most effective warm-up activity to use with students before they read the two poems?

So far in this section we have looked at a few ways of cueing students into a text so that it seems more relevant to their own experience and they can respond personally to it. Below are four questions connected with this approach to using literature with the language learner.

Task 20

Think about your own answers or responses to the four questions below before reading the suggestions which follow. Then, while you read through the suggestions, put a tick next to any which you would like to try out with your own students in the future.

a) How can we select materials which encourage a strong personal response from students?
b) What if students are unwilling to give their personal responses or opinions in the classroom?
c) What are some ways to encourage students to respond personally to a text?
d) How can we help students to respond to texts which may seem very remote from their own experience?

How to make text more relevant to students' experience

HOW CAN WE SELECT MATERIALS WHICH ENCOURAGE PERSONAL RESPONSE?

It is best to select materials which are in line with the major interests of the students – a reasonable amount of time spent on a regular basis with a class usually allows a teacher to assess the students' interests. Alternatively, you could:

– Give students a list of certain literary texts with a brief summary of their content, and ask students to select the ones they would like to study.
– Provide students with a questionnaire designed to find out what kinds of material they read in their own language and what they would like to read in English (it may not be literature!).
– Give students a list of twenty to thirty topics and ask them to choose five that they find interesting – select literary texts connected with these topics or themes.
– Provide opportunities within the classroom for personalisation, by letting students work individually on those texts which interest them the most. (See Chapter 9 'Literature and self-access' for more ideas on how to do this.)

Approaches to using literature with the language learner

WHAT IF STUDENTS ARE UNWILLING TO RESPOND IN THE CLASSROOM?

There may be all sorts of reasons why students are unwilling to give their personal opinions or reactions in the classroom. Perhaps their traditional mode of education has stressed rote learning and a rather authoritarian role for the teacher. It may therefore not be part of the students' culture to discuss their own opinions and feelings in an educational context. Perhaps there are social factors in a class inhibiting students from expressing themselves. For example, students may be of different status or rank (e.g. a manager and one of the people working under her). Students may also be individually sensitive to particular issues raised in a text. Whatever the reasons, tasks and materials for exploiting literary texts should be designed with the likely behaviour of students in mind. With some classes it may be better to get students working in small groups, which may feel less threatening than talking to the class as a whole. And students may be more forthcoming if they actually choose with whom they would like to work in small groups. With some classes, students could be asked to reveal their own reactions to a text only when writing a short paragraph or essay for homework – to be read only by the teacher.

WHAT ARE SOME WAYS TO ENCOURAGE STUDENTS TO RESPOND?

It is probably a good idea to avoid asking very general questions about a text such as, 'Do you like it?' at least in the initial stages of studying it. Students often find questions of this nature too vague and intimidating. Instead make use of some of the following kinds of techniques.

- Ask students to free-associate/brainstorm around the central theme or title of a text before they read it. How do their own ideas compare with those in the text?
- Give students the bare outline of the situation in the text, for example, 'My first day at school'. Ask them to recount their own experiences of this situation before reading the text.
- Provide students with a questionnaire about some of the issues or situations raised in the text, and ask them to discuss their own views or responses to the questions before or after reading the text.
- Ask students to imagine that they themselves are certain characters in a text. What would they do in the situation of the characters in the text? They could even write a letter of advice from one character to another.
- Ask students to complete sentences which will lead them into the main themes or topics of the text. An example of this is shown in the chapter on poetry, in Section 6.6, where students at lower levels are asked to read a poem about old people and children. Before they read

the poem, they are asked to write two sentences of their own beginning:

Old people ....

Children ....

– Provide learners with a guided fantasy linked closely to the setting of the text. Students are told to close their eyes and imagine the noises, sights, sounds, feelings, etc. that they might experience in that setting.[5]

HOW TO HELP STUDENTS WHO MAY FEEL REMOTE FROM THE MATERIAL

Obviously it helps if texts are chosen on the basis of their relevance to students, but this is often not possible because of syllabus or other external requirements. Some of the procedures mentioned above may provide some point of entry for students. You should ask yourself whether there is anything in the text which has the core of a human situation which occurs cross-culturally. Can students be asked to compare their own experiences of this situation with the ones in the text? If not, can students be asked to imagine themselves in the situation described in the text – how would they react and behave? (See Section 4.3 for some ideas of different strategies for helping students to overcome cultural problems in literary texts.)

Finally, it may be vital to ensure that students have adequately understood the language of the text, and that you have provided the necessary historical, literary or cultural background for them to make sense of the text. In other words, a combination of the three approaches outlined in this chapter may be the best way of ensuring that students become enjoyably involved in using literature in the classroom.

Task 21

Think about a text that you would like to use with your students. How would you make it relevant to them, so that they feel motivated using it in the classroom?

2.6   The role of metalanguage ☆

In this chapter we have explored some possible approaches to using literature in the language classroom, and the implications of these different approaches. A further question which arises from such an exploration is how far we should make use of literary metalanguage or terminology with our students. In this section we review some of this terminology, and then think about how useful it might be in the classroom.

Below is a list of some of the terms which are often used when discussing literature.[6] In fact, some of them are terms for figures of speech which are equally common in everyday language. Each term is accompanied by a definition. Below the definitions are a list of examples. They match the definitions, but are in a different order.

Task 22 🔑

Match the terms with the examples of each one that follow.

Terms and definitions

METAPHOR: a comparison made between things which are unlike each other by describing one as if it were the other.

SIMILE: an explicit comparison made between two unlike things which is usually indicated by using the words *like* or *as*.

PERSONIFICATION: a kind of metaphor in which abstract or inanimate objects are described as if they were alive and animate.

PARADOX: a statement which appears to be contradictory or absurd, but may be true.

OXYMORON: a combination of neighbouring words which seem apparently contradictory or incongruous.

METONYMY: a figure of speech in which the name of a thing is substituted for another thing with which it is usually associated.

SYNECDOCHE: the whole of something is used to mean the part of it, or part of it is used to mean the whole.

APOSTROPHE: the direct addressing of an abstract quality, object or absent person.

ALLITERATION: the repetition of the initial consonant sounds in two or more consecutive words.

ASSONANCE: the repetition of identical or similar vowel sounds, usually in the middle of words.

Examples

A. '. . . with the smoking blueness of Pluto's gloom . . . ' (D. H. Lawrence, *Bavarian Gentians*.)

B. 'War is peace. Freedom is slavery. Ignorance is strength.' (George Orwell, *1984*.)

C. 'The pen is mightier than the sword.' (E. G. Bulwer-Lytton, *Richelieu*, II, 2, 1938.)

D. '. . . Mrs Spragg herself wore as complete an air of detachment as if she had been a wax figure in a shop-window.' (Edith Wharton, *The Custom of the Country*.)

E. 'O heavy lightness! serious vanity!' (W. Shakespeare, *Romeo and Juliet*.)

F. ' . . . His crypt the cloudy canopy . . . ' (Thomas Hardy, *The Darkling Thrush*.)

G. 'I have no relative but the universal mother Nature: I will seek her breast and ask repose.' (Charlotte Brontë, *Jane Eyre*.)

H. 'Milton! Thou shouldst be living at this hour.' (William Wordsworth, *London, 1802*.)

I. 'I should have been a pair of ragged claws
Scuttling across the floor of silent seas.'
(T. S. Eliot, *The Love Song of J. Alfred Prufrock*.)

J. 'Dorothea by this time had looked deep into the ungauged reservoir of Mr Casaubon's mind . . . ' (George Eliot, *Middlemarch*.)

Task 23 🗝

Would you use the activity you have just done with your own students? If so, to what end? If not, why not?

Task 24 🗝

Below are some arguments for using metalanguage or literary terminology with your students. Using this terminology means ensuring that students are familiar with it and encouraging them to apply metalinguistic terms to any texts that they are reading and studying. Can you think of any other arguments for using metalanguage? What about arguments against its inclusion in the language classroom?

1. Literary terminology provides students with the tools for identifying distinctive features in a literary text and so appreciating it more fully.
2. Students may expect to know the terminology, and will feel frustrated if they lack the means to acquire and use it, especially if they are expected to be familiar with it in exams, etc.
3. Students may be familiar with the terms in their own language, so providing the equivalents in English may be a simple and easy way of facilitating the transfer of literary knowledge from one language to the other.

Task 25 🗝

With what kinds of students do you think it would be most appropriate to use metalanguage? Think about student age, level and interests.

Endnotes

1. See the Introduction to Duff and Maley (1990). Also Alan Maley, 'Down from the Pedestal: Literature as Resource' in *ELT Documents 130*.
2. For further discussion on the limitations of using stylistics with students see Ronald Carter and Richard Walker, 'Literature and the Learner – Introduction', in *ELT Documents 130*. Also R. Gower, 'Can Stylistic Analysis Help the EFL Learner to Read Literature?' in *ELT Journal*, 40/2.
3. The information in this section was gleaned from M. Wynne-Davies, *Bloomsbury Guide to English Literature* and 'Notes' in *Browning: The Poems, Volume I*, edited by John Pettigrew and supplemented by Thomas J. Collins, Penguin 1981 pp. 643–644.
4. The procedure I have used in this section is adapted from an article by Roger Gower, 'Anyone for Beowulf? Literature as a Subject in ELT', SIGMA Issue No. 3, October 1990.
5. This idea was taken from Collie and Slater (1987), p. 18. A wealth of ideas for involving students personally in the reading and study of literary texts can be found in this book.
6. A fuller glossary of literary terms useful to teachers can be found in Hill (1986).

Suggestions for further reading

Collections of papers on different approaches to teaching literature

Brumfit, C. (ed.) (1983) 'Teaching Literature Overseas: Language-based Approaches', *ELT Documents, 115*.
Brumfit, C. J. and Carter, R. A. (eds.) (1986) *Literature and Language Teaching*.
Brumfit, C., Carter, R. and Walker, R. (eds.) (1989) 'Literature and the Learner: Methodological Approaches' *ELT Documents, No. 130*.
Holden, S. (ed.) (1988) 'Literature and Language'.

Stylistics and language-based approaches

Carter, R. (ed.) (1982) *Language and Literature: An Introductory Reader in Stylistics*.
Carter, R. and Burton, D. (eds.) (1982) *Literary Text and Language Study*.
Carter, R. and Long, M. (1991) *Teaching Literature*, Chapter 4.
Widdowson, H. G. (1974) 'Stylistics' in Corder, S. P. and Allen, J. P. B. *The Edinburgh Course in Applied Linguistics*, 3.
Widdowson, H. G. (1975) *Stylistics and the Teaching of Literature*.

Background information to literary texts

Gillie, C. (1972) *Longman Companion to English Literature.*
Swartridge, C. (1978) *British Fiction: A Student's A–Z.*
Wynne-Davies, Marion (ed.) (1989) *Bloomsbury Guide to English Literature.*

Texts with accompanying materials for classroom use

(These collections include texts from different literary genres – for materials based on specific genres see Chapters 5, 6 and 7.)
Carter, R. and Long, M. (1987) *The Web of Words.*
Gower, R. and Pearson, M. (1986) *Reading Literature.*
Gower, R. (1990) *Past into Present.*
Lott, B. (1986) *A Course in English Language and Literature.*
McRae, J. and Boardman, R. (1984) *Reading between the Lines.*
McRae, J. and Pantaleoni, L. (1990) *Chapter and Verse.*
Tomlinson, B. (1986) *Openings.*
Walker, R. (1983) *Language for Literature.*

3 Selecting and evaluating materials

In Chapter 2 we considered different approaches to using literature with the language learner, and in Section 2.1 we discussed whether it was appropriate to use literature with particular groups of learners. In this chapter we focus more specifically on how to select texts and materials which are suitable for use with your students. Of course, you may not have a choice of either texts or materials. Perhaps you are bound by a syllabus which sets out what literary texts you have to use with your students even though you can design the tasks to exploit these texts yourself. Or the syllabus may lay down both the texts and the exercises and tasks needed to exploit them. If you do have some choice in the selection of texts and materials, then Section 3.1 will help to pinpoint some criteria for selecting literary texts to use with your learners, while Section 3.2 suggests ways of evaluating published materials.

3.1 Selecting texts

In choosing a literary text for use with your students, you should think about three main areas. These are: the type of course you are teaching, the type of students who are doing the course and certain factors connected with the text itself. We begin by thinking about the first of these – the type of course you are teaching.

Task 1

Think about a group of students you have taught in the past, are teaching at the moment, or are going to teach in the future. Note down the information about them which is listed in the boxes opposite.

Type of course

Level of students:

Students' reasons for learning English:

Kind of English required on the course: (e.g. English for Academic Purposes, English for Business, General English, etc.)

How intensive is the course? (e.g. five hours a day for three months, four hours a week for a year, etc.)

Is there a syllabus?	Yes	No
1. Is it flexible?	Yes	No
2. Is literature included?	Yes	No

Can you include literary texts on this course? Why/Why not?

What kinds of texts will be most suitable? Extracts from novels? Poems? A full-length play? Why?

Task 2

Think again of the group of students you had in mind in Task 1 and fill in the following information:

Type of students

Age of students:

Interests/hobbies of students:

Cultural or ethnic background/nationality of students:

Students' previous experience of reading literary texts:

We are now going to connect the information you have just written down with criteria for selecting literary texts to use with your students. But first, read the two texts below.

TEXT A

> Rodge said,
> 'Teachers – they want it all ways –
> You're jumping up and down on a chair
> or something
> 5 and they grab hold of you and say,
> "Would you do that sort of thing in your own home?"

'So you say, "No."
And they say,
"Well don't do it here then."

10 'But if you say, "Yes, I do it at home."
they say,
"Well, we don't want that sort of thing
going on here
thank you very much."

15 'Teachers – they get you all ways,'
Rodge said.

(Michael Rosen (1979) in *You Tell Me: Poems by Roger McGough and Michael Rosen*, Penguin p. 17.)

TEXT B

Annette now sat down on the dried-out chair and looked through the
entries in all the ledgers whilst Hussain rummaged about in the store
weighing up and measuring out the grain for the birds and the fruit for
the monkeys. Madam preferred to check the weight of the fish and the
5 meat herself, so he would only weigh that when she'd finished reading
all the entries of food delivered into the stores that day. It took about
forty minutes to get all the food ready and then the two boys who also
assisted the head gardener to keep the drying lawns tidy would come to
help him feed the animals under the watchful eye of Memsahib.
10   He wondered about her sometimes. Who she was, where she came
from and what kind of love of animals this was that brought her out in
the afternoon sun when most other women of her class still drowsed in
darkened rooms. He knew that he had this job because of her in a way.
It was common knowledge that the previous superintendent had been
15 sacked because of her intervention. The gate-keeper had told him the
story many times . . . how she came to visit the zoo about two years
ago, saw that the animals looked thin and under-fed and decided to
complain. She wrote letters, made approaches and got them to change
the super. She was there with a letter from the governor himself the
20 day Hussain took charge saying she had permission from him to
'inspect' the food before it was given to the animals and that she
personally would make sure that the animals had a proper diet. To this
day she had not been late. Hussain got into a routine of being ready for
her, terrified of what might happen if she became angry again. The gate-
25 keeper, Maaja, thought her an interfering busybody. 'Poor Nawaz Sahib
who got turned out with his family of eight in such disgrace has still not
found a job, and was such a good man really!' he always ended with a
sigh. At this point in the conversation Hussain would lose interest in the
story and walk off remembering something important that needed doing.

(from Rukhsana Ahmad, 'The Gate-Keeper's Wife' in Lakshmi Holstrom (ed.) 1990
The Inner Courtyard, Virago Press, pp. 172–173.)

Task 3

Now that you have read Texts A and B, mark the letter A (for Text A) and B (for Text B) on the scales that follow, according to how far you think each text compares against the values of the scale. For example, if you think that Text A is too culturally far removed to be relevant or accessible to the group of learners you described, then you would mark A towards the end of the scale which says 'too remote from text to help comprehension'. But you might decide that Text B should go at the other end of the scale. Your scale would then look like Figure 3.1.

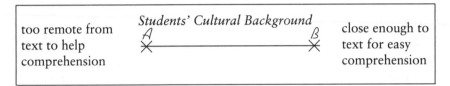

Figure 3.1

The relevance of the text

	Age of students	
too old to enjoy text	———————————	too young to enjoy text
too developed to find text challenging	*Intellectual maturity of students* ———————————	too immature to understand text
too developed to find text engaging	*Students' emotional understanding* ———————————	too immature to relate to text
too advanced to be challenged by the text	*Students' linguistic proficiency* ———————————	too elementary to cope with the text
too well–developed to be challenged by the text	*Students' literary background* ———————————	insufficient to cope with with the text

c

Selecting and evaluating materials

And now fill in the two scales below, which are slightly different from the ones you have just looked at.

far removed from themes/content of text	*Students' interests/hobbies* _____	close to themes/content of text
too remote from text to help comprehension	*Students' cultural background* _____	close enough to text for easy comprehension

After you have completed the scales above, finish these sentences:

I would/might try using Text .... with my students because ....
I'm not sure if I could use/I would not be able to use Text .... with my learners because ....
I think my students need a text that ....

In Task 3 you were asked to examine two texts fairly closely to decide whether or not they would be appropriate for use with your students. In fact, most teachers find that when selecting texts for their learners they generally proceed on an intuitive basis. With a good knowledge of, and rapport with, a group of learners this usually works well. But it is sometimes useful to focus more exactly on specific criteria for selection or rejection of texts, as we did using the scales above. Using the scales, for example, might have helped you to clarify that, although your learners are at quite an elementary level linguistically, their emotional and intellectual understanding is rather sophisticated. So you need to select texts which are linguistically relatively simple but which challenge them in other ways. In the section below we briefly discuss some of the more complicated criteria mentioned on the scales.

Criteria for selecting texts

It is probably fairly self-evident what is meant by criteria such as the age of students, their emotional and intellectual maturity and their interests and hobbies. The only difficulty when applying these categories to a whole class is that individual students within a group may vary considerably in their maturity and interests. Obviously, when selecting materials you will need to try to find texts that are suitable for the majority of students in the class. You may also find that developing the facility for self-access (see Chapter 9) is one way of personalising learning so that you can cater for the range of student development and interests within a group. We may find, however, that consideration of criteria involving the students' cultural background, linguistic proficiency and literary background is more complicated. The following is an attempt to examine these more complex criteria.

THE STUDENTS' CULTURAL BACKGROUND

When considering this factor, think about how far the students' cultural background and their social and political expectations will help or hinder their understanding of a text. It would be difficult, for example, for most readers to make sense of Jane Austen's novels without having some knowledge of the class system and the values of the society they describe. You will also need to consider how much background you will need to provide for your students to have at least a basic understanding of the text. (See Chapter 4 for some ways in which you can help students with the cultural problems in the text.)

On the other hand, it is also true that texts which may appear to be very remote in time and place from the world today may still have appeal for students in different countries around the world. This is either because they touch on themes (such as industrialisation or life in the city) which are relevant to the students, or they deal with human relationships and feelings (such as conflict between parents and children) which strike a chord in the students' own lives. In addition, many students may have a strong sense of curiosity about another culture and enjoy studying its literature because they believe it reveals key insights about that society.

THE STUDENTS' LINGUISTIC PROFICIENCY

This is an area of some complexity. It may well be that learners are classified as advanced and can communicate with ease in an English-speaking environment. Yet they might not be able to cope with the language of the text because it departs strikingly from the usual norms of language use; it includes a great many archaisms, rhetorical devices and metaphors; or it makes use of the dialect or register of a highly specialised field (such as law). You might need to ask yourself questions like these when deciding whether or not to use the text:

Are students sufficiently familiar with the usual norms of language use to recognise when these are subverted?

How much of the language in the text will students be able to infer?

Will students find it useful and enjoyable to study the text, or will they feel demotivated by the difficulties of the language?

Even if the language of the text is extremely difficult, will students be motivated by other factors to study the text (e.g. students often enjoy studying a difficult short story if there is a film based on it which they also enjoyed.

Finally, you may well ask yourself whether the text is too specialised in its language to be relevant to the type of language the students require to learn on the course.

THE STUDENTS' LITERARY BACKGROUND

There is an interesting relationship between the literary background of the students and their linguistic competence, since the two do not necessarily go together. Students may, for example, have studied literature in their own language. If it is a language (such as a Romance language) in which similar conventions to those in English operate for reading and interpreting literature, then they may already have a level of literary competence which will help them to make sense of a literary text even when their linguistic knowledge is rather limited. On the other hand, students who have little literary knowledge, but are linguistically proficient, may find themselves understanding each individual word on the page without being able to make sense of the literary meanings behind the texts. (This raises the issue of the students' literary competence – discussed more fully in Section 1.4.) When choosing texts to use with students, therefore, we should look not only at the grading of the language in the text, but at its specific literary qualities and whether our students can navigate their own way through these. A writer often cited in this regard is Ernest Hemingway – while his texts often appear to be linguistically simple, students may need guidance in making sense of their deeper literary meanings.

Task 4

In Tasks 1 and 2 we looked at the nature of a course you had identified and the type of students doing the course. There are other factors as well which can influence our choice of texts. Note down any factors you can think of. Then look at the following questionnaire. Are the points mentioned the same as the ones you have just noted down? What other criteria for selection would you include on the questionnaire?

Other factors to consider when selecting literary texts

AVAILABILITY OF TEXTS

1. What kinds of books and texts are available from which you can choose?
2. How easily can you make these texts available to your students?

LENGTH OF TEXT

1. Do you have enough time available to work on the text in class?
2. How much time do students have to work on the text at home?
3. Could you use only part of a text, or an abridged version of it? If so, how much background information will you need to give students to make the text intelligible?[1]

EXPLOITABILITY

1. What kinds of tasks and activities can you devise to exploit the text?
2. Are there resources available to help you exploit the text, for example a film of a particular novel the students are studying, recordings of a play or poem, library materials giving information about the life of an author, etc.?

FIT WITH SYLLABUS

1. How do the texts link with the rest of the syllabus? Thematically? In terms of vocabulary, grammar or discourse?
2. Can you devise tasks and activities for exploiting the text which link with the methodology you have used elsewhere in the syllabus? This often helps to put students at their ease. For example, if your students are used to using Multiple Choice or True/False questions when doing reading comprehension, then you could use similar tasks when exploiting a literary text.

A checklist of criteria for choosing literary texts

In this section we have thought about various criteria for selecting literary texts. The checklist below summarises these criteria. You can consult it as a quick reference when choosing texts, especially if you add any other criteria which you consider to be important.

Checklist for choosing literary texts

TYPE OF COURSE

Level of students
Students' reasons for learning English
Kind of English required
Length/intensity of course

TYPE OF STUDENTS

Age
Intellectual maturity
Emotional understanding
Interests/Hobbies
Cultural background
Linguistic proficiency
Literary background

OTHER TEXT-RELATED FACTORS

Availability of texts
Length of text
Exploitability
Fit with syllabus

3.2 Evaluating learning materials which make use of literary texts

In this section we think about evaluating materials which make use of literary texts. In the main, you will probably want to use the criteria we establish when choosing a book to use with your students, or when selecting a particular unit or section in a book. But you may also find yourself using some of the ideas in this section for thinking about materials produced by yourself or your colleagues.

It is not always easy to make this kind of assessment 'cold' without actually having used the material with the students, but it is possible to reach a few preliminary conclusions about the books and materials even if these are altered or modified after using them with a class. In this section, we suggest some criteria for assessing and evaluating books and materials.

First, let us think about what our needs, and those of other teachers are likely to be. The following are examples of the kinds of comments teachers might make about the type of published materials they feel they need to use with their students. Consider whether any of these comments reflect your own situation.

A.   My students are very academic and have to pass quite a stiff exam which deals with British literature through the ages. So I need a book which will take them chronologically through British literature and will provide lots of background information about history and literary trends. But since most books of this type seem to encourage students to learn by rote, I'd like to find a book which provides the necessary information but which actively involves the students in thinking for themselves as well.

B.   I just want a book that I can dip into now and again with my students – with a few nice poems or extracts that I can use to encourage discussion. My students need English for their work, but they enjoy a change of activity now and again, and they love a good discussion.

C.   I need a book that is going to help my students with their reading. This skill really needs improvement, and the students have promised they would be prepared to do some reading for homework. They are quite advanced, so I thought a collection of short stories might be suitable. Preferably with tasks or exercises they could do for homework and we could then discuss in class.

Task 5

Now think about your own situation and what kind of material you might like to use with your students. Write a short paragraph, or a few notes, describing the students and identifying the kind of material you would like to use.

Examples of evaluation sheets

We will now examine a number of evaluation sheets intended to help you decide whether a book, a piece of material from a book or a piece of material designed by you or a colleague is suitable for the students you have described in Task 5.[2]

The 'quickie' book evaluation sheet can be used if you only have time to look fairly rapidly through a book or number of books when trying to evaluate material.

'QUICKIE' BOOK EVALUATION			
Title of book			
Author(s)			
Publisher			
Level			
Overall aims/approach			
Types of text used			
Skill/language area which book will help to improve			
Strengths of material			
Weaknesses of material			
Suitable for my students? Yes/No (please give reasons)			

The detailed book evaluation sheet can be used if you have more time to assess a book in detail. Although you would certainly not expect the book to contain all the features mentioned on this questionnaire, the features do provide some overall guidelines as to what you might hope to find in a book using literature.

DETAILED BOOK EVALUATION

Title of book . . . .
Author(s)   . . . .
Publisher   . . . .

Aims and organisation

1. What are the overall aims of the book?
2. What approach to using literature seems to have been adopted? Is this approach suitable for your students?
3. How is the book organised? (thematically? according to linguistic difficulty? chronologically? etc.)
4. Are units/sections self-contained? Can you use some of the material, or do you need to work through it all?

Materials and activities

1. What kinds of text are used in the book? (poems? short stories? extracts from novels and plays? literary and non-literary texts?)
2. Are the texts sufficiently varied, interesting and relevant to students?
3. Are the tasks and activities sufficiently varied, interesting and relevant to students?
4. Are the students given sufficient linguistic guidance with the language of the texts (for example, vocabulary exercises, glossaries, etc.)?
5. Are students given adequate cultural, historical or literary backround information to make sense of the texts?
6. Are students encouraged to relate the materials to their own lives and experiences?
7. Is the material challenging enough for the students?
8. Could the material be adapted if necessary?

Instructions and layout

1. Are the instructions in the book clear and easy to follow?
2. Is the layout clear and attractive?
3. Are there visuals (pictures, photos, diagrams, etc.) to supplement the texts?

Accompanying resources

1. Is the teacher given sufficient guidance in how to use the book (either in the book itself or in a teacher's book)?
2. Is there recorded material available to accompany the book?
3. Could the book be used by students working on their own? (Is there a key, for example, to help them?)

Suitability for class/group

Would you use this book with your students? Please give reasons.

Selecting and evaluating materials

The following evaluation sheet can be used if you are evaluating a *piece* of published material fairly quickly, for example a section or unit of a book. If you have more time, you might want to expand your evaluation by giving more detailed reasons for ticking the columns as you did.

EVALUATING A PIECE OF MATERIAL

Title of book ....
Author(s) ....
Publisher ....
Page on which relevant material is found: ....

Please tick the relevant column.

	Excellent	Good	Adequate	Poor
1. Suitability of approach for your students.				
2. Suitability of level for your students.				
3. Relevance and interest of text/s chosen.				
4. Variety and appropriateness of tasks and activities.				
5. Staging and grading of tasks and activities.				
6. Opportunities for student participation and personalisation.				
7. Linguistic guidance (glossaries, exercises,etc.).				
8. Cultural/literary/ historical backround provided.				
9. Clarity of instructions.				
10. Layout and design.				

I would/would not use this material with my students because ....
....

Task 6

Now that you have looked through or used the forms in this section, you might like to make one of your own, listing all those criteria which you think are important in terms of the group of students that you yourself will be teaching. You can then use this form as a handy reference when you are assessing or evaluating any materials in the future.

Endnotes

1. The dangers of 'abridging' literary materials by making use of selected extracts from a text are discussed in Guy Cook's article, 'Texts, Extracts and Stylistic Texture' in Brumfit and Carter (eds.) (1986).
2. Some examples of books published which use literature with the language learner can be found in the Bibliography at the back of the book.

4 Reading literature cross-culturally

In Chapter 1 we touched very briefly on the problems of teaching literature across cultures. It was pointed out that readers invariably interpret texts in the light of their own world-view and cultural experience (Section 1.3). It was also mentioned that the relationship between a literary text and the culture in which it is produced is highly complex, since few texts are mere factual representations of their culture (Section 1.5).

In any teaching situation, there are obviously some literary texts which are likely to present fewer cultural problems for students than others. For example, a text in English by a writer of a similar cultural background to the group of students studying the text may be more culturally accessible than a text written by an author from a culture far removed from the students' own. On the other hand, a text from another culture which deals with themes relevant to the students' own society may prove to be both accessible and absorbing. In other words, the selection of suitable texts (as discussed in Chapter 3) can be quite complicated. And as there are many countries in the world where teachers have little say in the choice of texts, we may sometimes find ourselves using texts which are remote from our students' own experience. In addition, although students may find it easier to respond personally to a text from within their own culture, there is a strong argument for saying that exposing students to literature from other cultures is an enriching and exciting way of increasing their awareness of different values, beliefs, social structures and so on. Whatever the reasons, then, for using a text which students find culturally difficult, from the perspective of the teacher there are practical difficulties. In this chapter, we aim to identify what some of these problems might be so that we can suggest a few ways of overcoming them.

4.1 Being a student ☆

In this section we will experiment with putting ourselves in the position of our learners. We will be trying to step out of our own cultural skins so as to define more precisely the kinds of cultural problems our students may experience when reading literary texts. We will be doing this by reading three very different texts from around the world. One of the texts is in translation, one of them draws on a rich oral tradition and one of them is taken from a well-known British novel. Since all three texts are extracts, you may find you are slightly hampered in your understanding of them by not knowing what came before the extract in question. On the other hand, you should be able to focus quite clearly on the cultural difficulties in each text. This fits in with our aim in this section – to come up with a working list of those cultural aspects of texts which we find difficult, and which could prove problematic for our learners. Read through the following three texts, and then answer the questions which follow.

TEXT A

He beat his *ogene* GOME GOME GOME GOME . . . and immediately children's voices took up the news on all sides. *Onwa atuo! . . . onwa atuo! . . . onwa atuo! . . .* he put the stick back in the iron gong and leaned it on the wall.

5   The little children in Ezeulu's compound joined the rest in welcoming the moon. Obiageli's shrill voice stood out like a small *ogene* among drums and flutes. The Chief Priest could also make out the voice of his youngest son Nwafo. The women were in the open, talking.

'Moon,' said the senior wife, Matefi, 'may your face meeting mine
10   bring good fortune.'

'Where is it?' asked Ugoye, the younger wife. 'I don't see it. Or am I blind?'

'Don't you see beyond the top of the ukwa tree? Not there. Follow my finger.'

15   'Oho, I see it. Moon, may your face meeting mine bring good fortune. But how is it sitting? I don't like its posture.'

'Why?' asked Matefi.

'I think it sits awkwardly – like an evil moon.'

'No,' said Matefi. 'A bad moon does not leave anyone in doubt. Like
20   the one under which Okuata died. Its legs were up in the air.'

'Does the moon kill people?' asked Obiageli, tugging at her mother's cloth.

'What have I done to this child? Do you want to strip me naked?'

'I said does the moon kill people?'

25   'It kills little girls,' said Nwafo.

'I did not ask you, ant-hill nose.'

'You will soon cry, *Usa bulu Okpili.*'

'The moon kills little boys

The moon kills ant-hill nose

30   The moon kills little boys' . . . Obiageli turned everything into a song.

TEXT B

. . . Here, discordantly, in Eights Week, came a rabble of womankind, some hundreds strong, twittering and fluttering over the cobbles and up the steps, sightseeing and pleasure seeking, drinking claret cup, eating cucumber sandwiches; pushed in punts about the river, herded in
5   droves to the college barges; greeted in the *Isis* and in the Union by a

sudden display of peculiar, facetious, wholly distressing Gilbert-and-
Sullivan badinage, and by peculiar choral effects in the College chapels.
Echoes of the intruders penetrated every corner, and in my own college
was no echo, but an original fount of the grossest disturbance. We were
10   giving a ball. The front quad, where I lived, was floored and tented;
palms and azaleas were banked around the porter's lodge; worst of all,
the don who lived above me, a mouse of a man connected with the
Natural Sciences, had lent his rooms for a Ladies' Cloakroom, and a
printed notice proclaiming this outrage hung not six inches from my oak.
15   No one felt more strongly about it than my scout.
'Gentlemen who haven't got ladies are asked as far as possible to
take their meals out in the next few days,' he announced despondently.
'Will you be lunching in?'
'No, Lunt.'
20   'So as to give the servants a chance, they say. What a chance! I've
got to buy a *pin-cushion* for the Ladies' Cloakroom. What do they want
with dancing? I don't see the reason in it. There never was dancing
before in Eights Week. Commem. now is another matter being in the
vacation, but not in Eights Week, as if teas and the river wasn't enough.
25   If you ask me, sir, it's all on account of the war. It couldn't have
happened but for that.' For this was 1923 and for Lunt, as for thousands
of others, things could never be the same as they had been in 1914.

TEXT C

I hesitated to intrude on her sorrow, but I could not leave her in such a
state. I approached her slowly. She heard my footsteps and raised her
head.
'Please, don't go.' I put my hands over her shoulders. 'I want to talk
5   to you.'
'About what?' she asked dully.
'A lot. About you and about myself.'
We sat opposite each other on either side of the grave, motionless
and silent. She looked at me closely. I wondered if my face showed that
10   I, too, had cried out in the dark.
'Are you – are you the same as I?' She paused and waited for my
answer.
'You mean – was I given to a man by my family and he passed away
like — ' I looked down at the grave. 'It was not quite the same, but
15   something like that.'
Her interest was kindled.
'We sinners.' It was her soul speaking. Her face darkened and then
cleared, becoming younger and comelier. A struggle was going on
within her: her duty to mortify the flesh, as she had been taught was
20   the right thing to do, and the urgent, instinctive will to live and love.

'The man was my parents' friend,' I began. I was not inventing this
story. There had been a bachelor, a friend of the family. One day when
my aunt asked him why he did not get married, he dodged the question
by turning to me and saying that he was waiting for me to grow up and
25   be his bride. My uncle said that he would not object to having him as a
son-in-law. It was only half a joke.
'Did he give you any presents?'
'Yes, he gave me many presents, at the New Year, on my birthday — '
'Birthday?' she asked.
30   'The day I was born. It was a happy day for me, so he gave me nice
presents. You must have a birthday too.'

Task 1 🗝

a) In the texts you have read are there any cultural references that
   puzzle you, or which do not seem clear? Are there any sections of the
   text where you felt you understood individual words, but not their
   'meaning'? Jot down some notes or underline those sections of the
   text where you felt this was a problem.
b) How would you describe your responses when reading the texts?
   What kinds of feelings did you have while reading? Did these change
   according to the type of text?
c) Can you guess what society is being described in each text? Do you
   recognise where any of the texts are from?

4.2   A consideration of cultural aspects in texts

Here is a list of some cultural aspects to consider when using literary
texts with students. Examples to illustrate these aspects are taken from
the three texts that you have just read.

Task 2

Read through the list and tick any of those that you mentioned yourself
in Task 1(a). Would you like to add anything to the list?

1. Objects or products that exist in one society, but not in another (e.g.
   ogene in Text A, *cucumber sandwiches* in Text B).
2. Proverbs, idioms, formulaic expressions which embody cultural
   values (e.g. '*Moon, may your face meeting mine . . .*' in Text A).
3. Social structures, roles and relationships (e.g. number of wives in
   Text A, role of women in Texts B and C, hierarchies based on
   wealth or rank in Text B, relationships between parents and
   children in Texts A and C).

4. Customs/rituals/traditions/festivals (e.g. Eights Week in Text B or Welcoming the Moon in Text A)
5. Beliefs/values/superstitions (e.g. the meaning of the posture of the moon in Text A, mortifying the flesh in Text C)
6. Political, historic and economic background (e.g. England in the 1920s for Text B, The Chinese Revolution for Text C)
7. Institutions (e.g. the *compound* in Text A, the *Union* in Text B).
8. Taboos (e.g. discussion about the dead as in Text C)
9. Metaphorical/connotative meanings (e.g. the moon in Text A, Oxford in Text B)
10. Humour (e.g. Is calling someone 'ant-hill nose' as in Text A a genuine insult or merely humorous?)
11. Representativeness – to what slice of a culture or society does a text refer? Does it describe a particular class or subgroup? (e.g. how far does *Brideshead Revisited*, from which Text B is taken, represent life in England in the twenties?)
12. Genre – how far do different genres translate cross-culturally? Will students understand if a text is meant as a fable/representation of oral history in writing, etc.?
13. The status of the written language in different cultures and the resulting strategies for reading a text – will students believe they should accept the text as immutable and fixed? Will they expect to read a moral lesson from it? Will they feel comfortable questioning and analysing the text?[1]

We now have a working list of cultural aspects to consider in texts. We could refer to such a list when using literary texts with our students in order to anticipate some of the cultural problems students might experience when reading the text. Having done so, we might be in a position to decide how explicitly we should teach the culture in (or of) the text to our students. But the teaching of culture in the language classroom could prove controversial.[2] The two statements below high-light this controversy.

Task 3

Read the statements and decide which one is closest to your own views on this subject.

A. The aim of the language teacher is surely to teach language, not culture. Too much time would be taken up in classrooms if we had to constantly explain every cultural reference in texts. In any case, teaching the culture of a text usually means imposing a certain culture on our students. This seems absurd in an age in which English is an international language. The solution, therefore, is to select literary texts which are culturally universal or, at least culturally neutral, and which allow us to concentrate exclusively on language.

B. Our students' comprehension is frequently impeded not by linguistic features in a literary text, but by cultural ones. We owe it to them to help them to understand what these might be. Language can never be divorced from culture – by helping to explicate the cultural factors in a text, we are helping our students to understand more fully the language in which it is written.

4.3　Strategies for overcoming cultural problems

In the previous section we proposed a working list of those cultural aspects of texts which could impede student understanding. While preparing tasks and activities for use with a literary text you could refer to this list in order to identify the kinds of problems students might have when reading the text. The next step would be to help students overcome these problems and below is a list of suggested strategies to help them.

Task 4

Look again at the three texts in Section 4.1 and this time write down any strategies or activities you could use with students to help them cope with the cultural aspects of the text. Then compare your ideas against those which follow. Are any of your ideas similar to those suggested?

Personalising

Cue students in to the theme or topic of the text by making it relevant to their own experience, for example:

a) *A family gathering:* Think of a situation in which you and your family last spent time together. Where were you? Why were you together? Did you all get on together? Now read Text A. What occasion is being described? Who is there? Are they all getting on with each other?

b) Think of a situation in which someone you know has been sad. Why? Could you do anything to help them? Tell your partner about it. Then read Text C and write down who is sad and why.

Providing explanations/glosses

Provide brief cultural information in a note or gloss, for example:

a compound: an enclosure in an African village containing a collection of huts where a man lives with his wives and children (Text A).

Gilbert and Sullivan: a playwright and a composer (both British) who wrote a series of popular, satirical operettas including *The Pirates of Penzance* (1879) and *The Mikado* (1885) (Text B).

Asking students to infer cultural information

Provide questions designed to encourage students to infer cultural information from a text by making this information explicit, for example:
a) From the references to Lunt in the extract from *Brideshead Revisited* (Text B) do you think that a scout at Oxford university is:
   i)   a student who shares a room with another student who is senior to him or her?
   ii) a servant in an Oxford college?
   iii) a close friend of a student?
b) Do you think that an *ogene* (Text A) is:
   i)   a kind of leather drum used to summon people?
   ii) a musical instrument of some kind?
   iii) an iron gong which is beaten with a stick?

Making cultural comparisons

Get the students to brainstorm ideas about their own society and then compare them with those in the text, for example:
a) Think about a celebration or festival held by students in your country. Then fill in the first column of the following chart.

	Your country	Oxford
Name of festival/celebration		
Reason for holding it		
Where festival/celebration held		
Way in which it is celebrated		

Now read the extract from *Brideshead Revisited* (Text B) and complete the second column in the chart. What similarities or differences do you notice between the celebrations or traditions described in the two columns?

b) In your country are there any particular beliefs or superstitions relating to the moon? Write them down and then discuss them with your partner. Now read the extract from *Arrow of God* (Text A). What beliefs or superstitions about the moon do you notice in this text? Are they the same as, or different from, the ones you mentioned yourself?

Alternatively, you could ask students to take notes about any customs or beliefs described in a text before brainstorming 'parallel' customs or beliefs in their own society.

Making associations

Get students free-associating around a word or phrase that might have particular connotations or even figurative meanings for a native speaker of the language. How do these connotations compare from one country to another and from one individual to another? Do these words take on any particular symbolic meaning in the text? For example:

birthday   (Text C)
the moon   (Text A)
Oxford   (Text B)

Providing cultural background information as reading/ listening comprehension

Give the students a mini-comprehension, to listen to or to read, which provides more information about particular cultural aspects of the text. Then get them to apply this information to the text they have just read, for example:

a) a brief reading comprehension about the Chinese Revolution (for Text C, *The Dragon's Village*)

b) a brief listening comprehension about the dominant themes in the writings of Chinua Achebe (for Text A, *Arrow of God*)

Extension activities

These are activities for students to do after they have read the text, which ask them to think critically about, and become personally involved in, the cultural aspects of the text they have just read, for example:

a) *Roleplay/Simulation:* Imagine you are the students and dons (university teachers) at Oxford university in the days before most colleges admitted both male and female students. Colleges were usually for men only, although there were some colleges exclusively for women.

Decide who will take the role of a don and who the role of a student. Then discuss whether or not the colleges should become mixed, or whether the sexes should be kept separate. (Text B)

b) *Discussion:* What are the advantages and disadvantages of arranged marriages? (Text C)

c) *Project work:* If library facilities are available, ask students to write an essay or do a poster presentation on the changes in British society after the First World War. (Text B)

Task 5

Think about a literary text you want to use with your students, or have to use with them. Go through it slowly, underlining any cultural problems you think students might experience when studying it. Write down some ideas for tasks and activities which you can use with students to help them overcome these problems.

Endnotes

1. The differing attitudes of readers to written texts is discussed in an article by Karl-Heinz Osterloh, 'Intercultural differences and communicative approaches to foreign-language teaching in the Third World', in J. M. Valdes (ed.) (1986).

2. For an article which discusses how literature can actually be used to *teach* culture see Joyce Merill Valdes 'Culture in Literature' in J. M. Valdes (ed.) (1986).

Suggestions for further reading

Harrison, Brian (ed.) (1990) 'Culture and the Language Classroom', *ELT Documents 132* (particularly Harrison's own article 'Culture, Literature and the Language Classroom').

5 Materials design and lesson planning: Novels and short stories

In this chapter we explore some of the distinctive features of the short story and novel. Examining these features will enable us to develop ways of using short stories and novels with our students.

5.1 Writing your own story

We begin this chapter by inventing our own story based on the boxed paragraphs below. Before reading any further, cover all of the boxed paragraphs with a piece of paper. You are going to read these paragraphs, which are extracts from a short story, one at a time. At each stage of the reading ask yourself the following questions as a guide to making links between the separate paragraphs:

Who?

Why?

What?

How?

Begin by moving your sheet of paper to the end of the first box and reading the first paragraph. Then ask yourself the questions above, using your imagination to answer them. Move your sheet of paper down to the next paragraph, and ask yourself the same questions. Do this until you have read all the paragraphs and completed the activity.

> She sat at the window watching the evening invade the avenue. Her head was leaned against the window curtains, and in her nostrils was the odour of dusty cretonne. She was tired.

> She had consented to go away, to leave her home. Was that wise? She tried to weigh each side of the question.

> She was about to explore another life with Frank.

> The white of two letters in her lap grew indistinct. One was to Harry;
> the other was to her father.

Task 1

How do you think the story is going to end?

Task 2 ⚷

The story we have just been speculating about is called 'Eveline' and comes from *Dubliners* by James Joyce. Imagine that you were using this story with a class of students at upper intermediate level and that you decided to use the activity above with them. At what stage of the lesson would you use it, and what would be your aims in doing so? If you were to use a similar activity with another short story, what would you need to consider when selecting the paragraphs you want students to speculate about? Rather than giving students a worksheet with the paragraphs on them, in what other ways could you present the paragraphs?

It is unlikely that the story you conjured up in your imagination while reading the extracts would be identical to that of another teacher or student. On the other hand, you would have probably shaped it according to an implicit understanding or intuition of what elements make up a short story. In the next section, we try to pinpoint some of these distinctive elements of a short story, many of which can be found in novels as well. We do this for one important reason – by focussing on some of the unique characteristics of this genre we may also be able to anticipate some of the difficulties our students have when reading or studying a short story. And this will be of help when designing materials for exploiting the story successfully.

5.2 Distinctive features of a short story

The activities in Section 5.1 involved using your intuitive knowledge of the elements of a short story. In this section we go through some more activities in order to exploit this intuitive response and to pinpoint the unique elements of the short story.

Task 3

Imagine that you were asked to explain or define what a short story is, perhaps to a Martian. What would you say? Compare your answer with some of those given below by other teachers.

It's a work of fiction, so it involves the imagination.

A short story tells of one event in a very concentrated way.

It's about people who don't really exist.

It describes something at a moment of crisis.

It has a plot, and characters who are somehow connected with each other.[1]

Task 4 ☛

Most people would agree that a short story, as the name suggests, involves the telling of a story. But what exactly is a story? Which of the following would you describe as a story? Which ones seem to you to be more 'storyish' than others?
A. Little Miss Muffet sat on a tuffet.
B. Little Miss Muffet sat on a tuffet, eating her curds and whey.
C. Little Miss Muffet sat on a tuffet, eating her curds and whey. Along came a spider, and sat down beside her.
D. Little Miss Muffet sat on a tuffet, eating her curds and whey. Along came a spider, and sat down beside her, and ate its curds and whey.
E. Little Miss Muffet sat on a tuffet, eating her curds and whey. Along came a spider, and sat down beside her, and frightened Miss Muffet away.
F. Little Miss Muffet sat on a tuffet, eating her curds and whey. Little Jack Horner sat in a corner, eating his pudding and pie.

Task 5 ☛

a) Once you have decided which of the one(s) above are stories, can you suggest why this is the case? What characteristics does a story have which makes it different from a 'non-story'?
b) It has been mentioned that a typical story involves chronology, or a sequence of events, and causation – the fact that events are somehow connected with each other, and that one event may result from another.[2] Think about any short story or novel that you know well. Is the chronology of events clearly sequenced? Are the relationships of cause and effect clear to the reader? If not, then what kinds of problems might a foreign language student have when reading the story?

Task 6 ☛

Look at paragraphs A. to D. below. Which one do you think you are most likely to find in a short story or novel? Why do you think this is the case?

A. The train was about three-quarters of an hour from its destination and was travelling at a good sixty miles an hour when Mr Harraby-Ribston, a prosperous businessman, rose from his seat, lifted his suitcase down from the rack and threw it out of the window. The only other occupant of the carriage, a small, thin man, a Mr Crowther, had raised his eyes from his book when his travelling-companion stirred from his seat and had noticed the occurrence. Then the two men exchanged a sharp glance and immediately Mr Crowther continued his reading, while Mr Harraby-Ribston resumed his seat and sat for a while puffing a little and with a heightened colour as a result of his exertion.

B. Suddenly this business-looking man just stands up and chucks his suitcase out of the window just like that. And this other bloke in the train doesn't say anything – just carries on, you know, reading his book. Can you believe it?

C. A businessman on a train threw his suitcase out of the window. The only other passenger in his compartment carried on reading, and did not say anything.

D. A businessman, Mr J. Harraby-Ribston of Slough, recently threw a suitcase weighing about twenty pounds out of the window of a train. The only witness to the event was Mr P. Crowther of Swindon, the other occupant of the railway carriage. The train, which was due to arrive at Bristol Temple Meads within three-quarters of an hour, was travelling at approximately sixty miles an hour.

Task 7 ☛

It has just been suggested that much of the meaning of a short story is communicated by the kind of language used and the style of the delivery. What kinds of problems do you think students learning English are likely to have with the language and style of a short story or a novel?

Task 8 ☛

a) Look at the following paragraphs from two short stories. Try to decide who is telling the story in each one.
b) How important is it for students to understand who is narrating the story they are reading? Why?

TEXT A

I took the house of Brentwood on my return from India in 18—, for the temporary accommodation of my family, until I could find a permanent home for them. It had many advantages which made it peculiarly appropriate. It was within reach of Edinburgh, and my boy Roland,
5 whose education had been considerably neglected, could go in and out to school, which was thought to be better for him than leaving home altogether or staying there always with a tutor. The first of these expedients would have seemed preferable to me, the second commended itself to his mother.

(from Margaret Oliphant, 'The Open Door' in R. Dalby (ed.) (1988)
The Virago Book of Victorian Ghost Stories, p. 150.)

TEXT B

. . . Mrs Kearney has finished wedging her parcels between her hip and the side of the tram and is intending to look at her magazine when she stares hard ahead and shows interest in someone's back. She moves herself and everything three seats up, leans forward and gives a poke at
5 the back. 'Isn't that you?' she says.
    Miss Kevin jumps round so wholeheartedly that the brims of the two hats almost clash. 'Why, for goodness sake! . . . Are you on the tram?' She settled round in her seat with her elbow hooked over the back – it is bare and sharp, with a rubbed joint: she and Mrs Kearney are of an
10 age, and the age is about thirty-five. They both wear printed dresses that in this weather stick to their backs; they are enthusiastic, not close friends but as close as they are ever likely to be. They both have high, fresh, pink colouring: Mrs Kearney could do with a little less weight and Miss Kevin could do with a little more. (from Elizabeth Bowen, 'Unwelcome Idea'
in Janet Madden-Simpson (ed.) (1984) *Women's Part*, Arlen House, p. 155.)

5.3 Anticipating student problems when using a short story

In the previous section we examined three problems students might have when reading or studying a short story: understanding the plot; understanding the language in which the story is written; and understanding how the type of narrator who tells the story can shape or influence the way the story is told. Obviously, students may also have other kinds of problems when reading or studying a short story.

Task 9

Think about a group of students you are teaching or have taught. Have you ever used a short story with them? Did they have any difficulties with it? What were they? If you haven't used a short story with them, what kind of problems do you think they would be likely to have?

Figure 5.1 summarises some of the problems that a group of teachers believed their students to have when reading a short story.

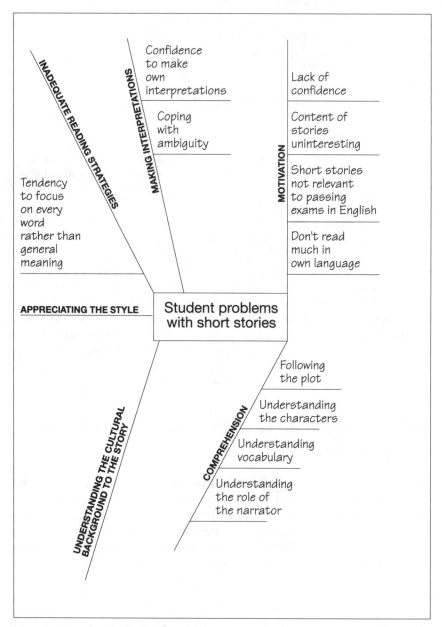

Figure 5.1 Anticipating student problems with short stories

Task 10

How many of these problems did you mention in Task 9? How many do you think are applicable to a class you have taught or are teaching at the moment? What others would you add to the diagram?

5.4 Planning a lesson for use with a short story ☆

In the next two sections, we go on to consider the kinds of activities and tasks you can draw on when designing materials to use with a short story. It is worth bearing in mind that many of these tasks and activities are designed to help students overcome the difficulties highlighted in Figure 5.1.

In Section 5.1 we built up a story based on some paragraphs from James Joyce's *Eveline*. The complete story can be found in the Appendix. Read it, and then look through the tasks and activities below which are designed to be used with the story with a group of learners at late intermediate level.

Task 11 ☛━◑

While you look at the activities and tasks, think about these two questions:
a) What is the aim of using each activity?
b) What would be a good order for using the activities in a lesson?

ACTIVITY 1

Divide into two groups. Group A look at Word List 1, Group B look at Word List 2. Discuss what the words on your list mean in the context of the story. You can use your dictionaries to help you. When you have finished, explain the meaning of the words to the students in the other group.

Word List 1	*Word List 2*
clacking (line 5)	squander (line 60)
palpitations (line 50)	squabble (line 56)
the air (line 111)	elated (line 81)
sacrifice (line 120)	to court (line 84)
impulse (line 124)	fervent (line 141)

ACTIVITY 2

In *Eveline*, Joyce describes one character who is experiencing a crisis or conflict in their family.

a) Think of a situation in which a family is experiencing a crisis or conflict. Perhaps it is something that has happened in your family. Or perhaps it is something that has happened in a family you know.

b) Imagine that you are one of the members of the family. Where are you? What kinds of sounds can you hear in the background? What kinds of noises and smells are you aware of? Are you looking at anything in particular?

c) What kinds of thoughts and feelings are you experiencing?

d) Now write two or three paragraphs based on your thoughts about (a) to (c). Try to make your description as 'vivid' as possible. When you have finished read your description to the other students. Get them to guess what situation is being described.

ACTIVITY 3

Think about the following situations, and discuss them with your partner. Give reasons for the advice you would give each person in that situation.

a) Tom is nineteen years old and lives with his invalid mother. They have no other relatives living nearby and Tom is responsible for looking after her. When he was at school he would come home every day and do all the housework as well as nursing her. Now he has been offered a place to study architecture at a university a three hour train trip from his home. What should he do?

b) Jessie has three young children to support since her husband was injured in a mine accident. She works at a local hospital as a cleaner. She has heard that it is possible to get a job for triple her annual salary if she goes to work and live in a neighbouring country. But she would not be allowed to take her family with her. What should she do?

c) Agnes, who is French, has recently fallen in love with an American called Jeff. He runs his own company in New York, while she runs her own business in Lyons. They would like to get married and be together, but neither one wants to give up their business. Each of them would prefer to live in their own country. What should they do?

d) Cynthia is a sixteen-year-old who quarrels all the time with her parents. She finds living with them depressing and difficult, and wants to move out. The only problem is that she has no job and no money, and her parents believe she should stay on at school until she has more qualifications. What should she do?

e) Peter is strongly opposed to the government of his country, and worries that his political activities could cause problems for his family. He sometimes thinks it would be better to leave and try to carry on his activities from abroad. What should he do?

ACTIVITY 4

a) Think about events in your own country at the beginning of the century. What was daily life like for most people?
b) Your teacher is going to tell you a little about life in Ireland at the same time. If necessary, take a few notes about what he or she says.

ACTIVITY 5

Now read the text again. This time take notes summarising the main point of each paragraph in the story. For example:
Paragraph 1: Setting the scene – Eveline at the window.
Paragraph 2: Eveline's childhood memories of the street and her neighbours.
Paragraph 3: ....

Then discuss these questions in pairs or groups:
a) Is there any logical sequence to Eveline's thoughts?
b) What kind of connections can you find between the different paragraphs? What effect does this have?

ACTIVITY 6

Read the story and answer these questions:
a) Who is Eveline?
b) What is her dilemma?
c) What do you think is her final decision?

ACTIVITY 7

a) In the story, Eveline is in the middle of an emotional crisis. In groups, note down the reasons she has for staying and the reasons she has for leaving, both conscious and possibly unconscious. For example:

Reason for leaving	*Reason for staying*
Frank– he is manly and attractive	Her father doesn't like sailors – can she trust Frank?

b) What decision does Eveline finally make?
c) In her position, would you have made the same decision? Why or why not?

ACTIVITY 8 🔑

Look at the last few paragraphs in the story. In pairs or groups discuss the questions below:
a) What is a *maze*? What is it usually used to describe? What is the effect of the phrase 'a maze of distress' in line 135?
b) Look at the sentence in line 139: 'Could she still draw back after all he had done for her?'
   Rewrite this sentence as if it was:
   i) direct speech
   ii) reported speech
c) The sentence in the story is an example of what is called 'free indirect speech'. Can you find any other examples of it in the text? What effect do you think they have?
d) Look at line 134: 'She answered nothing.'
   Is this usually grammatically correct?
   What effect does this have?
   What is a more usual way of saying this?
e) Look at the order of the sentences from lines 129 to 138. Do they seem to be organised in any particular way? What effect does this have?

ACTIVITY 9

Divide into two groups. Group A read Extract A and Group B read Extract B. Then answer these questions:

Group A
What are Joyce's main themes in *Dubliners*? How far do you see these reflected in *Eveline*?

Group B
What is 'stream of consciousness' technique? How far do you think Joyce uses it in *Eveline*?

Groups A and B
a) When you have finished discussing your extract tell the other group what you have discovered in your reading.
b) Can you think of any writers in your own language who may have used similar techniques to Joyce?

Extract A
Dubliners (1914)
A volume of short stories by James Joyce. Joyce later wrote: 'My intention was to write a chapter of the moral history of my country and I chose Dublin for the scene because that city seemed to me the centre of paralysis. I have tried to present it . . . under four of its aspects:
5 childhood, adolescence, maturity and public life. The stories are

arranged in this order.' He adds that he has used in them 'a style of scrupulous meanness', by which he is evidently referring to the bare realism of the stories, and the moral and spiritual poverty which they present. This poverty of spirit is no doubt what Joyce means by
10 speaking of the 'paralysis' of Dublin, the capital city of Ireland. The stories are based on Joyce's theory of the 'epiphanies', by which he meant that deep insights might be gained through incidents and circumstances which seem outwardly insignificant. Their effect is thus often through delicate implication, like the stories of Chekhov. Some of
15 them have sharp humour, however, notably 'Grace', and more have very sensitive poignance, especially the last and longest, 'The Dead', which is often regarded as a masterpiece.

(C. Gillie (1977) *Longman Companion to English Literature*, Longman, p. 489.)

Extract B

stream of consciousness A technique used by novelists to represent a character's thoughts and sense impressions without syntax or logical sequence. Four main types have been identified: soliloquy, omniscient narration of mental processes, and both direct and indirect interior
5 monologue.

The phrase 'stream of consciousness' was first used by William James in his *Principles of Psychology* (1890) to describe the random flux of conscious and sub-conscious thoughts and impressions in the mind. A parallel description can be found in Bergson's account (1889) of the
10 'élan vital', popularized in England by George Bernard Shaw. Literature can show many examples before both James and Bergson of the attempt to capture inner consciousness, notably Laurence Sterne's *Tristram Shandy* (1767). But stream of consciousness becomes important as a technique with the rise of modernism in the 20th
15 century. It can be seen in the works of Joyce (who claimed to have inherited it from Edouard Dujardin's *Les Lauriers Sont Coupés*, 1888), Dorothy Richardson, Virginia Woolf and, among Americans, William Faulkner . . .   (I. Ousby (ed.) (1988) *Cambridge Guide to Literature*, CUP, p. 956.)

ACTIVITY 10

a) At what age is it common for people in your country to leave home?
b) What are their reasons for doing so?
c) How do you think most people feel when they leave home? How did you feel when you left home?

ACTIVITY 11

Here are some statements which describe the main characters in the story. Read the statements and check the meanings of any words you don't know in your dictionary. Then decide whether you agree or disagree with the statement. Give some examples from the text to support your opinion.

a) Frank is a warm-hearted, kind and extrovert person with a zest for life.
b) Eveline is a timid, passive person with very little sense of adventure.
c) Eveline's father is a selfish bully, who behaves in an authoritarian way to his children.
d) Eveline is a sensitive, conscientious person with a strong sense of responsibility.
e) Frank is an easygoing, superficial person who is unable to form close ties with anyone.
f) Eveline's father is an affectionate, humorous man worn down by poverty and drink.

Task 12 🗝

Assessment of the lesson plan for *Eveline*
After you have considered the aim of each activity in the lesson plan and a logical order for them, think about these more detailed questions:

a) One of the main difficulties learners complain about when using a story is understanding the vocabulary. In the lesson plan for *Eveline* students were asked to look up the meaning of certain words in the story (Activity 1). If you were designing an exercise of this type, which of the following criteria would you bear in mind, and why?
  – The words included should be crucial for the students' understanding of the gist of the story.
  – The words included should be impossible for students to guess from the context.
  – The words included would be those you are certain the students did not know.
  – The words included would be useful for students in writing exam essays.
  – The words included would be those you think students should be able to use actively.
  What other factors would you need to think about when designing materials to help students with the vocabulary in a short story?
b) In at least two activities in the lesson plan, students were asked to respond personally to the themes of the story, or think about their own feelings and experiences. Which ones? Why do you think this is important?
c) In Activity 4, students are given a brief lecture on events in Ireland at the time that the story is set. Do you think that this lecture is necessary for their understanding of the story? Why/Why not? If you were to give them the lecture, what information would you want to

include in it? Is there any other cultural information that you think students should be given in order to understand the story?

d) Activities 5, 6 and 7 are all designed to practise some kind of reading skill with students. Which skills are being practised? In what order? Do you think it is necessary to provide students with all three activities when doing the story with them?

e) Which activity do you think would be suitable for a class with strong literary interests? What could be the result of using it with a class who do not have a strong interest in literature?

f) Are there any activities in the lesson plan that you would not use? Why? Can you suggest any activities that you might wish to add to the plan?

5.5 Further tasks and activities for use with a short story

In the previous section we looked at some activities and tasks for exploiting a short story. In this section we look at some other ways of doing this and classify them into three groups: pre-reading, while-reading and post-reading activities. Before reading through the activities listed below, you are invited to recall your own experience of activities for exploiting a text by completing Task 13.

Task 13

Before you read the list of suggested activities, write down your own ideas for tasks and activities to use with a short story. The following headings will help you to organise your ideas.

Pre-reading activities

1. Helping students with cultural background
2. Stimulating student interest in the story
3. Pre-teaching vocabulary

While-reading activities

1. Helping students to understand the plot
2. Helping students to understand the characters
3. Helping students with difficult vocabulary
4. Helping students with style and language

D

Post-reading activities

1. Helping students to make interpretations of the text
2. Understanding narrative point of view
3. Follow-up writing activities
4. Follow-up fluency practice

Task 14

As you read about the tasks and activities below, think about these questions:

a) Are many of the activities similar to the ones you mentioned in Task 13? Do you think any might work particularly well with your own students?

b) Think back to the kinds of student problems mentioned in Section 5.3. Which ones do you think could be successfully overcome by using the kinds of tasks and activities suggested on the list?

List of suggested tasks and activities

PRE-READING ACTIVITIES

1. *Helping students with cultural background*
   a) Reading or listening comprehension about the author's life or the historical and cultural background to the story.
   b) If library facilities are available, students do a mini-project on the social or historical background to the story (e.g. life in Ireland at the turn of the century for *Eveline*). Projects presented as a talk, essay or poster.
   c) Predictions about the genre of the short story (e.g. What would students expect of a story entitled *Murder in a Country House*?).
   d) Discussion about events in students' own country during the period of the story. How do they compare and contrast with the historical or cultural background in the story?

2. *Creating student interest in the story*
   a) Students make very general predictions about the story, using pictures or the dustjacket on the cover of the book from which it is taken.
   b) Group discussion about what the title of the story suggests.
   c) Prediction about the story based on reading the first paragraph only.
   d) Prediction about the story based on three or four words or on phrases which the teacher selects from the story.
   e) General discussion questions about some of the themes which occur in the story.

3. *Pre-teaching vocabulary*
   a) Students brainstorm a lexical set which is important in the story, for example legal vocabulary in a story about crime.
   b) Matching important words in the story with their dictionary definitions.

WHILE-READING ACTIVITIES

1. *Helping students to understand the plot*
   a) Providing students with two or three overall questions to check they have understood the gist of the story.
   b) Students write a brief summary of the plot in 50 words. They then write another summary in 100 words and see what they have added.
   c) Students provide 'titles' for each paragraph.
   d) Students are given a series of 'jumbled' sentences which summarise the plot. They have to re-order them.
   e) Sentence completion activities (i.e. students are given the beginning of a sentence about the story which they then complete). This is a way of helping them to understand 'cause-effect' relationships within the story.
   f) Students are given three slightly different summaries. They have to decide which is the best one.

2. *Helping students to understand the characters*
   a) Students choose from a list of adjectives which ones are most appropriate for describing a particular character.
   b) Students rank the characters in the story according to certain traits; for example which character is the most or least active, passive, aggressive, gentle, decisive, etc.
   c) Students write 'references' for different characters as if they were applying for a particular job.

3. *Helping students with difficult vocabulary*
   a) Give the text to one student or group of students in advance. Let them look up any difficult words in a dictionary and prepare a glossary for the others.
   b) Provide multiple choice questions to encourage the guessing of meaning from context.
   c) Provide definitions for certain words in the text – students match word to definition.

4. *Helping students with language and style*
   a) Close textual analysis of a section of the text.
   b) Using a section of the text to focus on a particular grammatical problem that students may have; for example blanking out all

verb forms in a section of the text and asking students to supply the correct tenses. The 'student version' is then compared with the original, and their stylistic differences discussed.

POST-READING ACTIVITIES

1. *Interpretation of the main themes of the story*
   a) Providing students with different critical interpretations of the story which they then discuss.
   b) Providing general questions to 'debate', focussing on any contentious points in the story.
   c) Asking students to note down any lexical areas which might take on a symbolic meaning in the story (e.g. darkness might be a kind of metaphor for death in a particular story). Students then speculate about possible symbolic associations for these sets.

2. *Helping students to understand narrative point of view*
   a) Students write diary entries or a letter describing the events of the story, as if they were one of the characters in the story.
   b) If the story is told by a first person narrator, then students write a brief character description of the narrator based on the evidence in the text.

3. *Writing activities*
   a) Writing a few paragraphs using certain stylistic features of the story.
   b) Writing a review of the story.

4. *Discussion*
   a) Reading and discussion of critical literary writings about the author of the story or his or her works in general.
   b) Roleplay or acting out of a scene from the story.
   c) Critical discussion or debate about the world-view of values which seem to be depicted in the text.

5.6 Designing your own materials for use with a short story

When you start working on the design of your own materials, you need, first, to try to pinpoint any problems you think your students may have when reading and studying the story. Your tasks and activities should then be designed to help students through these difficulties. Figures 5.2 and 5.3 are examples of lesson plans designed by two groups of teachers in a seminar.[3] The story they are based on is by Graham Greene and is entitled *The Case for the Defence* (from *Collected Stories*).

Preactivities

List of crimes   - which punishments fit?
Vocabulary of crime   - trial, witness, etc.

Creating anticipation

either   • some words from text – predict plot

or   • stop in the middle of story just before
                          we see other twin – what now?

During reading

1 Help students with difficult first paragraph: write it all on
   board - students come up and eliminate all the unnecessary
   words until they get to the nitty gritty
2 Timed reading in class up to a certain point - we would not
   give them the last section

$\boxed{\text{predict in groups}}$ ⟶ predictions correct?

Follow-up activities in class

1 Students write comprehension questions for each other
2 Grammar – play alibi to practise past tenses
3 Court role plays

Written homework

- Mrs Salmon's next few weeks
- Her letter to a member of her family

Figure 5.2 'The Case for the Defence' – Lesson Plan A

1   BRAINSTORM for LEGAL VOCABULARY

2   Short DISCUSSION: CAPITAL PUNISHMENT

3   Read FIRST SENTENCE: predict

   | Who's talking? |

4   Read to "but the hanging"
    Overhead projector — students sequence events leading to murder

5   Read to "a face one forgets"
    Teacher tells class — accused was acquitted
    Group discussion — Why?

6   Read to "an extraordinary end"
    Students predict end
    Read to end

7   FOLLOW UP ACTIVITIES
    a) Writing a newspaper article based on the story
    b) Conducting interviews with characters, eg Mrs Salmon

Figure 5.3 'The Case for the Defence' – Lesson Plan B

Task 15

Using a short story of your own choosing, and suitable for a class you are teaching, design a lesson plan incorporating some of the ideas and activities that have been mentioned in this chapter.

5.7 Using novels in the language classroom

In the previous sections we identified some of the characteristic features of the short story and novel. We focussed on some of the typical problems students experience when reading a short story and suggested some techniques and activities to help them overcome these problems. In this section we think about using a novel with the language learner. In fact, a great many of the ideas discussed in Sections 5.1 to 5.6 are as relevant to the novel as to the short story, but in this section we aim to pinpoint any problems specific to using a novel in the language classroom.

What are the differences between the novel and the short story?

We have already said that novels and short stories share a great many features in common. Like the short story, the traditional novel involves a chronological sequence of events, linked by relations of cause and effect. The description of events in a novel is shaped by a narrator, and the language of the novel is used in a highly self-conscious way to convey particular effects. Nevertheless, there are a few generic features which we are more likely to find in a novel than in a short story, although we cannot say rigidly that these features are exclusive to the novel rather than the short story. As in all literary texts there may be considerable overlap between the characteristics of one genre and another.

Task 16 ☛○

Look at the following list of features. Write N next to those you think are more *likely* to be found in the novel and S next to those that are more *likely* to be found in the short story:
– focusses on a moment of crisis
– narrative told from different perspectives
– mood and tone fairly unified throughout the text
– large cast of characters
– numerous flashbacks to past events
– highly complicated plot
– very economic, suggestive use of language
Can you think of any other differences between the novel and the short story?

We have seen that in a novel there is likely to be a larger cast of characters than in a short story, the plot may be more complicated and methods of narration can sometimes be more complex. (For example, in a novel like John Fowles' *The Collector* the same events are related by two different narrators who are themselves the main characters in the novel. On the whole, short stories tend to rely on a single narrative voice.)

If the novel you were intending to use with your students demonstrated any of these features, then you would need to account for them in the tasks and activities you devised to use with the novel. For example, if the plot of the novel is very complicated then you may need to do quite a few activities with students which help them to follow the sequence of events (such as writing summaries, providing sentence-completion exercises, reordering jumbled sentences, etc. – see Section 5.5 for activities which help students to understand plot). Similarly, if the same events are described by two different narrators in the novel you will use, you could devise a jigsaw reading activity in which groups of students read the two different descriptions and then compare notes. In fact, many of the tasks and activities listed in Section 5.5 could be used to guide your students in their reading of the novel. However, while these activities can help students with the more specifically literary problems of reading the novel, a number of practical problems remain. Among those which teachers commonly mention are:

1. Coping with the length of many novels.
2. Helping students to cope with the volume of unfamiliar vocabulary in the novel.
3. How to adapt activities which work well for short stories (like those listed in Section 5.5) to use with a novel rather than a short story.

Before reading the text that follows think of some ideas for helping to overcome these three problems. Then compare your ideas with those in the text.

COPING WITH THE LENGTH OF THE NOVEL

Obviously the amount of time you spend in class reading the novel depends on your syllabus. Generally speaking, it is best to choose a novel that is fairly short. You might get students to do most of the reading of the novel at home – for example, a chapter every fortnight if the novel is to be used over a year. Class time could then be spent on activities (such as those described in Section 5.5) which help the students explore the text further. If time is short, or the novel is very long, you could think about dividing the class into groups. Over a period of a few weeks, each group could then be responsible for reading a different chapter and summarising the contents for the whole class, either verbally or in writing. Selected chapters could be read by the whole class. Students usually take great pains to produce good summaries if they know that their classmates' understanding of the novel depends on them.

HELPING STUDENTS TO COPE WITH THE VOLUME OF UNFAMILIAR VOCABULARY

Clearly the amount of unfamiliar vocabulary in a novel should be a prime factor in determining whether or not the novel is selected for classroom use. Students should be able to extend their vocabulary while reading without feeling the need to look up the meaning of every second word on the page. It is best to choose a text where students will not feel overwhelmed by unfamiliar language. Two strategies can be useful in helping students with any vocabulary they don't know. The first is to encourage students to read for gist rather than detail. This can be done by setting homework tasks which demand an overall comprehension of the chapter, for example, summary writing. You might even accustom inexperienced readers to this way of reading by asking them to read a chapter for homework, underlining only those unfamiliar words which they feel are crucial to their basic comprehension of the chapter. Which words they chose and the reasons for choosing them could then be discussed in class.

A second strategy for helping students with vocabulary is to give students some kind of glossary to use while reading. This could provide the meaning of important words in the text, either in English or in the mother tongue. You could provide this yourself, or you could make groups of students responsible for compiling a glossary for different chapters. These glossaries could then be distributed among the whole class before the chapter is read.

ADAPTING ACTIVITIES TO USE WITH THE NOVEL

You would be unlikely to use the activities listed in Section 5.5 with a novel in the concentrated way that they can be used with a short story (as in Section 5.4). Since a novel will probably be used in class over a period of a few weeks or months, you could select two or three activities from Section 5.5 to use each week in class. Which activities you chose to use with each chapter of the novel would depend on the difficulties students might be having with a particular chapter and/or your syllabus for that week. For example, if students are having difficulties with a chapter because of its complex presentation of different characters then you might wish to provide activities which help students with this (as in *Helping students to understand the characters* in the 'While-reading activities'). If, on the other hand, a section of the chapter that students are reading is very rich in its use of tenses, and you happen to be revising tenses in class that week, you could use that section for a close stylistic analysis to review the way in which different tenses can be used.

Task 17

Are there any other problems that you or your students might have when reading or studying a novel? What could you do to overcome these problems?

Task 18

Think of a novel that you would like to use with your students. Plan:
- what pre-reading activities you would use to stimulate student interest in the text;
- how much of the novel would be read at home and how much in class;
- how you would help students with any difficult vocabulary;
- what tasks and activities you could use in class to exploit the first two chapters of the novel with students (use the suggestions in Section 5.5 to help you).

Endnotes

1. With thanks to the teachers attending the summer courses in using literature at International House, London, in 1989 and 1990.
2. For a detailed discussion of these elements see Rimmon-Kenan (1983) Chapter 2.
3. With thanks to the teachers who attended the seminar on *Using Literature in the EFL Classroom* at the Teachers' Centre, International House, London in October 1989.

Suggestions for further reading

On narrative/linguistic theory

Fowler, R. (1977) *Linguistics and the Novel.*
Rimmon-Kenan, S. (1983) *Narrative Fiction: Contemporary Poetics.*

Practical classroom ideas

Collie, J. and Slater, S. (1987) *Literature in the Language Classroom.*
Greenwood, J. (1988) *Class Readers.*
Lazar, G. (1990) *Using novels in the language-learning classroom*, ELT Journal, **44**, 3.

Anthologies of short stories with accompanying classroom materials

Adkins, A. and Shackleton, M. (eds.) (1980) *Recollections.*

Pierce, T. and Cochrane, E. (eds.) (1979) *Twentieth Century English Short Stories.*

Pervan-Plavec, M. (1990) *Reading for Study and Pleasure.*

Rossner, R. (1988) *The Whole Story.*

For a list of possible novels and short stories to use in the classroom see J. Collie and S. Slater (1987) *Literature in the Language Classroom,* p. 260.

6 Materials design and lesson planning: Poetry

This chapter discusses the place of poetry in the language classroom. It begins by focussing on those aspects of poetry which are linguistically distinctive and then asks teachers to examine their own beliefs about the relevance of poetry in the language classroom. Activities for use with students at both lower and upper levels of language competence are presented for discussion. Finally, teachers have an opportunity to plan learning material for use with their own students.

6.1 Putting a poem back together again ☆

In this section, we think about some of the distinctive features of poetry as well as ways of using poetry in the language classroom. We begin by looking at a type of activity which could be used with students. It involves the reordering of the lines of a poem.

Task 1

a) Think about the word *sea*. Write down any associations the word has for you.
b) Here is a poem with twelve lines. All the lines have been jumbled up so they are not in the correct order. Try to reorder them so that they make a complete poem. The title of the poem is 'maggie and milly and molly and may'.

and molly was chased by a horrible thing
so sweetly she couldn't remember her troubles,and
went down to the beach(to play one day)
may came home with a smooth round stone
which raced sideways while blowing bubbles:and
it's always ourselves we find in the sea
maggie and milly and molly and may
and maggie discovered a shell that sang
milly befriended a stranded star
For whatever we lose(like a you or a me)
as small as a world and as large as alone.
whose rays five languid fingers were;

Task 2 🔑

Now compare your version with the original poem which is given in the key. Is your version the same as, or different from, the original? If it is different, in what way? Which one do you prefer and why? Think about the reasons why you ordered the poem in the way that you did.

Making decisions about the correct order of the lines in the poem above involves far more than comprehension of meaning. It involves drawing on your knowledge and experience of the way poetry is structured. For example, if your ordering was the same or similar to the original you may have begun with the verse:

'maggie and milly and molly and may
went down to the beach (to play one day)'

because it seemed a fairly typical way of beginning a story – by identifying the characters and the setting. On the other hand, you may have felt confused initially about making these lines the beginning of the poem because they do not start with a capital letter – an example of cummings' stretching the rules of punctuation. Or you may have put lines 9 and 10 together because of the two rhyming words at the end of each line – *stone* and *alone*.

Thinking about how we put the poem back together again is a way of focussing on how the overall discourse of the poem is structured and webbed together. Many of the discoursal features you may have mentioned in identifying your reasons for the order you chose will also be common to other forms of discourse, for example a collocational link like 'sang so sweetly' might equally be used in a conversation or a newspaper article. Others will be more specific to poetry.

Task 3 🔑

Look back at your reasons for ordering the poem as you did and identify those links and connections more likely to be found in poetry.

Task 4

What kind of reaction do you have to cummings' original poem? Do you like it? If so, why? If not, why not?

Task 5 🔑

Could you use the activities above with your own students, even if the actual poem you chose was a different one? If so, to what end? What might you need to do before giving them the poem to reorder? Can you think of any poems or lyrics from songs with which you could use this technique?

6.2 What is distinctive about poetry? ☆

Two significant points emerge from using the activity in Section 6.1. Firstly, it is clear that many of the techniques we commonly use in the classroom (in this case, jumbling up a text and asking students to reorganise it) can equally be used when teaching poetry. Secondly, poetry does have some fairly distinctive features which differentiate it from other forms of discourse. It is useful to identify these features because by doing so we might be able to help our students grapple with certain problems they may encounter when reading poetry. It will also enable us to decide how poetry can be of value to the language learner.

Task 6 ☛⊶0

Look at the examples below which are taken from different poems. Decide in what way the language in the extract differs from more usual or standard English. In some cases, part of the text has been underlined to help you.

EXAMPLE A

Delicate mother Kangaroo
Sitting up there <u>rabbit-wise</u>, but huge <u>plumb-weighted</u>,
And lifting her beautiful slender face, oh! so much more
   gently and finely lined than a rabbit's, or than a hare's,
5 Lifting her face to nibble at a round peppermint drop,
   which she loves, sensitive mother Kangaroo.

                (from D. H. Lawrence, 'Kangaroo' in A. Freer and J. Andrew (eds.) (1970)
                 The Cambridge Book of English Verse 1900–1939, CUP.)

EXAMPLE B

'Twas <u>brillig</u>, and the <u>slithy</u> toves
Did <u>gyre</u> and <u>gimble</u> in the <u>wabe</u> . . .
All <u>mimsy</u> were the <u>borogroves</u>,
And the <u>mome raths outgrabe</u>

            (from Lewis Carroll, 'Jabberwocky' in C. Ricks (ed.) (1987)
        The New Oxford Book of Victorian Verse, Oxford University Press, p. 190.)

EXAMPLE C

Silent is the house: all are laid asleep
One alone looks out o'er the snow-wreaths deep,
Watching every cloud, dreading every breeze
That whirls the 'wildering drift, and bends the groaning trees.

(from Emily Brontë, 'The Visionary' in P. Dickinson and S. Shannon (eds.)
(1967) *Poet's Choice*, Evans Brothers, p. 254.)

EXAMPLE D

Today we have naming of parts. Yesterday,
We had daily cleaning. And to-morrow morning,
we shall have what to do after firing. But today,
To-day we have naming of parts. Japonica
5 Glistens like coral in all of the neighbouring gardens,
    And today we have naming of parts.

(from Henry Reed, 'Lessons of the War: 1. Naming of Parts' in J. Rowe (ed.) (1971)
Modern Poetry: A Selection by John Rowe, Oxford University Press, p. 24.)

EXAMPLE E

Busy old fool, unruly Sun,
Why dost thou thus,
Through windows, and through curtains call on us?
Must to thy motions lovers' seasons run?
5 Saucy pedantic wretch, go chide
Late school-boys and sour 'prentices,
Go tell court-huntsmen that the King will ride,
Call country ants to harvest offices;
Love, all alike, no season knows, nor clime,
10 Nor hours, days, months, which are the rags of time.

(from John Donne, 'The Sun Rising' in A. J. Smith (ed.) (1971)
John Donne: The Complete English Poems, Allen Lane, p. 80.)

EXAMPLE F

Beneath the vast
Cathedral of sky
With the sun for steeple
Evangeling with laughter
5 Go the shining ones
The little people

(from Roger Mais, 'Children Coming from School' in John J. Figueroa (ed.) (1982) *An Anthology of
African and Caribbean Writing in English*, Heinemann/The Open University, p. 279.)

Materials design and lesson planning: Poetry

EXAMPLE G

> "I leave m' yard early-mawnin' time
> An' set m' foot to de mountain climb,
> I ben' m' back to de hot-sun toil,
> An' m' cutlass rings on de stony soil,
> 5 Ploughin' an' weedin', diggin' an' plantin'
> Till Massa Sun drop back o' John Crow mountain,
> Den home again in cool evenin' time,
> Perhaps whistlin' dis likkle rhyme,
>
> "Praise God an' m' big right han'
> 10 I will live an' die a banana man.

(from Evan Jones, 'The Song of the Banana Man'
in J. Berry (ed.) (1984) *News for Babylon*, Chatto and Windus, p. 92.)

EXAMPLE H

> he made the journey
>   to deliver her   to freedom
>   the carpenter   tendin   to his   own
>   movin   north

(from Ntozake Shange 'frank albert and viola benzena owens' in (1987) *Nappy Edges*, Methuen, p. 64.)

EXAMPLE I

> <u>My heart is like</u> a singing bird
> <u>Whose</u> nest is in a water'd <u>shoot</u>;
> <u>My heart is like</u> an apple-tree
> <u>Whose</u> boughs are bent with thick-set fruit;
> 5 <u>My heart is like</u> a rainbow shell
> That paddles in a halcyon <u>sea</u>;
> <u>My heart</u> is gladder than all these,
> Because my love is come to <u>me</u>.

(from Christina Rossetti, 'A birthday' in V. Zundel (ed.) (1991)
Faith in her words, Lion Publishing, p. 100.)

In Task 6 we looked at some of the ways that poetry may differ linguistically from more usual or standard forms of English. We saw that poetry reorganises syntax, invents its own vocabulary, freely mixes registers and creates its own punctuation. Poetry draws creatively on a full range of archaisms and dialects, and generates vivid new metaphors. It patterns sounds and orders rhythms. Of course, as we said in Section 2.2, none of these effects are exclusive to poetry. Advertisements, nursery rhymes, jokes, riddles, political slogans, hymns and songs may also use such linguistic devices. But it is probably true to say that poetry employs a higher concentration of such devices or effects than other forms of discourse. For this reason, poetry has been described as deviating from the norms of language (Leech, 1988, p. 5). This clearly has some important implications for the use of poetry in the language classroom.

Task 7

What do you think are some of the implications of the poetic use of language for using poetry in the language classroom?

6.3 Why use poetry with the language learner?

Task 8

Look at the following remarks, all made by language teachers. Do you agree with them? If so, why? If not, then why not?

If poetry's deviant language, what's the point of using it with language learners? They want to know what's right, not what's wrong!

I've got a very demanding syllabus to get through, so there's no real time for playing around with poetry in my lessons.

My students don't read poetry in their own language, so how can they possibly read it in English?

It's alright to use poetry with students who intend to study literature further when they leave school. But reading poetry is too specialised an activity for most students, isn't it?

I've tried using a poem with students, but they found it difficult to understand, and just wanted me to give them the 'right' interpretation of what it meant.

I sometimes wonder if I've really understood the meaning of a poem myself – it's a bit daunting then to explain it to a group of students.

Can you add any other reasons for not using poetry with your students?

Task 9

Now read the text below. As you read, note down any points which you think provide counterarguments to the remarks made above.

Poetry has been characterised as deviating from the norms of language (Widdowson, 1984, p. 146). It has been argued that poetry frequently breaks the 'rules' of language, but by so doing it communicates with us in a fresh, original way. For the language teacher, this poses two questions. Firstly, in order to make sense of what is a new, original use of language the student needs some familiarity with the norms or rules from which this use deviates. Teachers may feel that the knowledge of norms or 'correct' language is not yet sufficiently well-established by students for them to appreciate when the norms are being stretched. Secondly, teachers might worry that exposing students to more creative uses of language could, in fact, legitimise the use of deviant or 'incorrect' language in the classroom.

An important point to bear in mind is that language may not be quite as rigidly governed by rules as we think. If you listen to two native speakers of English having a relaxed casual conversation there may be many examples of slips of the tongue which are actually 'incorrect' uses of grammar and vocabulary, and yet communication between the speakers remains unimpeded. On the other hand, most teachers would agree that it is pedagogically useful and necessary to provide students with idealised language rules. When using poetry in the classroom, we could therefore exploit the more 'deviant' or unusual use of language we find in it as a basis for expanding the student's language awareness and interpretative abilities. For example, if a poem contains unusual syntax then students could be asked to pinpoint in what way it is unusual and to contrast this with more commonly accepted uses. In so doing, they would be reaching some kind of conclusion about the stylistic effect conveyed by the language, and hence the meaning of the poem. Or if a poem is rich in words coined by the poet, students could be asked to guess which words in the poem are neologisms, to check by using a dictionary if this is indeed the case, and to then comment on the way in which these coinages contribute to the overall meaning of the poem. Naturally, the usual principles of grading material appropriately to the level of the students would still apply. It would only be fair to expect students to identify 'deviant' or less common uses if they already had a reasonable grasp of the grammar and vocabulary from which these uses depart. Provided the teacher is clear about what constitutes the more poetic uses of language, then activities of the type mentioned may serve as a useful way of reinforcing the students' knowledge of the norms of language use, and the manner in which they can be adapted to achieve different communicative purposes.

Making the language of a poem the basis of classroom study is also a way of integrating poetry into the syllabus. Using poetry is not then seen simply as an activity done for its own sake, but as a way of improving language knowledge. The occasional use of a poem linked linguistically to a lexical or grammatical area being taught in a particular lesson is often an enjoyable way of reinforcing or revising that area. Similarly, if we can identify certain linguistic features in a poem which mesh with areas specified in the syllabus, then the poem could be used as the basis for a lesson which increases student awareness of those features. For example, a poem which mixes formal and informal registers could be used as the starting point for a lesson sensitising students to different uses of register.

Making the language of the poem the basis for classroom study is a helpful first step towards enabling students to make confident interpretations of a poem. Since many students read little poetry in their own language, reading poetry in another may seem a daunting prospect. Without an even elementary understanding of the language of the poem it becomes impossible. Teachers obviously need to ensure that they choose poems suitably graded to the level of the students and that the students are given as much help as possible in understanding the language of the poem. At the same time, it is often the case that students do, in fact, understand the literal meaning of each element in the poem without being able to engage in an interpretation of its deeper meaning. Students may lack confidence in doing so; they may lack appropriate strategies for making interpretations; or the notion of playing with different interpretations may quite simply be culturally alien to them. As teachers, we can devise activities which gently lead students towards making interpretations of their own, rather than demanding that students produce their own interpretations from the start. We can also encourage students to make use of certain interpretative strategies while reading, for example speculating about the symbolic meaning of certain key words in the text rather than dwelling solely on their literal meaning.[1] Finally, placing the language of the poem at the centre of classroom activities should never degenerate into a sterile linguistic exercise. This can only be avoided if the students' own interests and experience are drawn on fully at all stages of the lesson, and if we accept that the interpretation of a poem varies from reader to reader.

Think back to the remarks you read for Task 8. Have any of your views on them altered?

6.4   Exploiting unusual language features

In the previous two sections, we looked at some of the more unusual or 'deviant' features of poetry, and what implications this might have in the classroom. In this section we look at how these features might influence the design of tasks and activities to be used with a poem.

Task 10

Look at the following poem. With what level of students do you think it could be used? Underline any parts of it which you think are linguistically unusual in any way.

Autobahnmotorwayautoroute
Around the gleaming map of Europe
A gigantic wedding ring
Slowly revolves through Londonoslowestberlin
Athensromemadridparis and home again,
5 Slowly revolving.

That's no ring,
It's the Great European Limousine,
The Famous Goldenwhite Circular Car

Slowly revolving

10 All the cars in Europe have been welded together
Into a mortal unity,
A roundaboutgrandtourroundabout
Trafficjamroundaboutagain,
All the cars melted together,
15 Citroenjaguarbugattivolkswagenporschedaf.

Each passenger, lugging his
Colourpiano, frozenmagazines, high-fidog,
Clambers over the seat in front of him
Towards what looks like the front of the car.
20 They are dragging behind them
Worksofart, lampshades made of human money,
Instant children and exploding clocks.

But the car's a circle
No front no back
25 No driver no steering wheel no windscreen no brakes no

(Adrian Mitchell, 'Autobahnmotorwayautoroute' in S. Heaney and T. Hughes (ed.) (1982)
The Rattle Bag, Faber and Faber, p. 52.)

Here are two possible activities and tasks to use with students when exploiting the poem in the classroom.

Task 11 ☛━◦

As you look through these activities, decide which of the unusual language features in the poem each activity is designed to exploit. Are they the same as the ones you mentioned in Task 10?

ACTIVITY 1

Before the students read it, dictate the first verse of the poem as if it were punctuated normally, with commas between the names of the cities. Tell the students to punctuate it as they think appropriate. When they have finished let them compare their punctuation with the text of the poem.

What effect is created by the layout and punctuation used in the first verse of the poem? Can the students find other examples in the poem where separate words are placed right next to each other? What effect is created by doing this?

ACTIVITY 2

Match the adjectives with the nouns in the box below to make some new words. The first one has been done for you.

| coffee | illustrations | magazines | food | milk |
| pictures | soup | chicken | photos | television |

FROZEN ← *food*   INSTANT ←   COLOUR ←

Now look at the penultimate verse of the poem. Can you find any examples of words formed from the combination of an adjective and a noun? Do you think you would find these combinations in a dictionary? What effect does the poet create by using these combinations?

Task 12

In Tasks 10 and 11 we implicitly draw on a possible procedure for providing students with an entry point into a poem. Here are two paragraphs summarising and discussing this procedure. With which one do you agree? Why?

A. When designing materials to use with a poem, teachers should firstly analyse what is unusual or distinctive about the language in the poem. The materials or tasks for students should be devised around these unusual features, since this will increase both their understanding of the poem and their knowledge of the language in general.

B. Focussing on the unusual linguistic features of a poem can only be part of our procedure for using a poem with our students. We might begin by analysing what is linguistically unusual about a poem and then devise activities which exploit these features. But this procedure can never be complete in itself. Students may also need help in understanding the historical or cultural background to the poem, in inferring the attitude of the poet to his or her theme, in responding to the figurative meanings in the poem. The theme of the poem should somehow be made relevant to the students' personal experience as they can draw on this when grappling with its underlying meaning.

6.5   Helping students with figurative meanings ☆

In the previous sections we considered how poetry sometimes departs from linguistic norms, the difficulty that this can cause for students, and the implications for designing materials. Another difficulty students often have with poetry is understanding the multiple ambiguities of metaphorical language – and many poems are rich in metaphors or other figurative uses of language. In this section we think about ways of helping our students to decipher (and enjoy!) many of the figurative uses of language we find in poems.

Task 13 ☛─◑

a) Here is a definition of the word *metaphor*. Can you complete it by filling in the two missing words:
   A metaphor is a .... (i) made between two essentially ....
   (ii) things by identifying one with the other.
b) In each of the following examples there is at least one metaphor. Read carefully through the examples and then answer the questions about them which follow.

A.   She sweeps with many-coloured brooms,
   And leaves the shreds behind;
   Oh, housewife in the evening west,
   Come back, and dust the pond!

(from Emily Dickinson, 'Evening' in V. Zundel (ed.) (1991) p. 29.)

B.   I think the idea is to bring Meg in as a new broom – you know, to revitalise the department and get everything going again.

C.   The gull's flight
   is low
           flat
       & hard
       they go
   to sea
           to the edge
   where the day's fire
       is lit
       they go
   as shiftworkers
       to the dawn.

(Nigel Roberts, 'The Gull's Flight' in L. A. Murray (ed.) (1986)
The New Oxford Book of Australian Verse, Oxford University Press, p. 305.)

D. It was really an awful situation. There I was – no job and nowhere to live. And then I was stupid enough to leave my bag on a train – with all my money in it! And somebody must have taken it, because it never turned up at Lost Property or the police. So there it was – from the frying pan into the fire!

E. These woods are lovely, dark and deep,
But I have promises to keep,
And miles to go before I sleep,
And miles to go before I sleep.

(from Robert Frost, 'Stopping by woods on a snowy evening'
in Heaney and Hughes (1982) p. 407.)

F. Although the financial situation of the firm has improved, they're still not out of the woods yet.

Task 14 🗝

a) We have said that a metaphor involves a comparison between two things which are different or unlike each other. In each of the examples above what two different or dissimilar things are being compared?
b) Which of the metaphorical uses above would you expect to find in a dictionary? Why? Does this have any implications for the way we use poetry with our students?
c) What kinds of problems do you think students might have in identifying the meaning of the metaphors used in the examples above?

The problem with metaphors

In Task 13, we defined a metaphor as a connection or comparison made between things which are usually considered to be unlike each other. Students might find it difficult to understand and interpret a metaphor in a poem for a number of reasons.

To begin with, it may not be very clear to students that a metaphor is being used, or rather that a metaphorical reading of a poem is required. We can quite happily read Frost's poem (Example E) as a simple account of a journey – but because it is a poem, we start to ask ourselves what the journey and the woods represent symbolically. If students are used to learning English in a way that parcels up meaning tidily, they may feel uncomfortable when asked to speculate on the possible metaphorical meanings for the woods in the poem.

Secondly, students may find it difficult to unravel the connections between apparently dissimilar objects or concepts. Take, for example, the metaphor used in the poem 'The Gull's Flight' (Example C). In this poem the sun is described as the 'day's fire' lit at the edge of the sea. To be able to understand this metaphor, students need to infer that one object (the sun) is being implicitly compared to another (the day's fire), so that the fire 'stands for' the sun. They do this by inferring what characteristics or qualities they have in common, for example brightness, warmth, etc. Then they need to be able to infer what effect is created by describing one in terms of the other. In other words, understanding metaphors involves engaging in a series of linguistic inferences. Students might find this problematic, particularly if two very disparate objects or concepts are somehow conjoined in the metaphor, or if it is not very clear what is being compared to what. In the first verse of Emily Dickinson's *Evening*, for example, the sunset and the evening are never named directly in the poem, but are described figuratively in terms of a housewife sweeping the sky with coloured brooms.

Another problem that can arise is that readers interpret metaphors by drawing on their own individual associations. To some extent these associations will be determined by the customs and conventions of their society. A red rose in British society, for example, generally signifies love, romance, passion. But we may find that students from other societies have different cultural associations when interpreting this metaphor. We need to strike a balance between allowing the integrity of the students' own interpretations, while simultaneously pointing to the likely symbolic meaning for members of that community to which a writer might belong.[2]

Helping students with metaphorical meaning

In this section we examine some practical ideas for helping students to unravel the often complicated metaphorical or figurative meanings in poems. Below are two activities we can do with students. Both of them involve techniques which can be used with fairly complicated poems and with students at higher levels. Here we apply them to two poems which could be used with students at intermediate level.

ACTIVITY 1

a) Divide students into two groups. Ask one group to look at the following lines from a poem, from which two words have been removed. Ask students to predict what words could go in the blanks. They can use dictionaries for any words that they do not know. (The lines are from 'Little Fish' by D. H. Lawrence in Heaney and Hughes 1982, p. 247.)

The .... enjoy themselves
in the sea.
Quick little splinters of life,
their little lives are fun to them
in the sea.

Ask the other group to look at the same lines from the poem but with
different words removed, and to do the same as the other group.

The tiny fish enjoy themselves
in the sea.
Quick .... of life,
their little lives are fun to them
in the sea.

b) Put students into pairs so that each pair consists of a student from
each group. Ask students to discuss how they filled in the blanks and
why. In the original poem what are the little fish being compared to?
What is the effect of this comparison? Obviously, the word 'splinter'
might be difficult for students at this level, so encourage the students
to use dictionaries to establish its meaning.

ACTIVITY 2

a) Divide students into two groups and ask them to write down any
associations they have for the following cluster of words:
forest   green   dragon
(There might be a cultural problem here – either because the students'
connotations for the word *dragon* are different from those held by
most native English speakers, or because students may not know
what a dragon is. If this is the case, then you might need to explain
the meaning of the word, allow the students to use their own
imaginations in suggesting associations and possibly explain some of
the associations likely to be held by native speakers.)
b) Ask students to read the following poem and underline any of the
words mentioned in a). Are there any other words in the poem which
seem connected with this cluster? What symbolic or metaphorical
meaning do all these words seem to have in the poem?

A Small Dragon
I've found a small dragon in the woodshed.
Think it must have come from deep inside a forest
because it's damp and green and leaves
are still reflecting in its eyes.

5   I fed it on many things, tried grass,
     the roots of stars, hazel-nut and dandelion,
     but it stared up at me as if to say, I need
     foods you can't provide.

     It made a nest among the coal,
10   not unlike a bird's but larger,
     it is out of place here
     and is quite silent.

     If you believed in it I would come
     hurrying to your house to let you share my wonder,
15 But I want instead to see
     if you yourself will pass this way.

(Brian Patten, 'A small dragon' in M. Harrison and C. Stuart-Clark (ed.) (1977)
The New Dragon Book of Verse, Oxford University Press, p. 190.)

Task 15 🔑

Below are four statements summarising the procedures used to help
students to come to grips with the metaphorical/figurative meanings in
the two poems used in Activities 1 and 2. They have been jumbled up.
Reorganise them so that they provide you with a summary of the
procedure used in Activity 1 and another summary of the procedure
used in Activity 2.

a) Students read the poem and underline any words connected with the
    lexical grouping or cluster they discussed before reading the poem.
    Are there any other words in the poem which seem connected with
    this grouping? What metaphorical or symbolic meaning do these
    words seem to take on in the poem? (In some poems, you may find
    a few different clusters or groupings which often function
    contrastively.)

b) Divide students into two groups. One group will be given the first
    verse of the poem from which most figurative uses of language are
    removed, the other the same verse from which most literal ones have
    been taken out.[3]

c) In some poems a grouping or cluster of words are linked together
    associatively and come to take on a metaphorical or figurative mean-
    ing in the poem. Before they read the poem ask students to write
    down any associations they have for this grouping. Does this cluster
    take on any particular symbolic meaning in the poem?

d) Students from the one group then discuss with students from the
    other how they completed the cloze exercise. What do they think of
    the original version of the poem? What two things are being
    compared? What is the effect of this comparison?

6.6   Using poetry with lower levels

In the previous sections, we have thought mainly about some of the more distinctive features of poetry, and the problems they could present for our learners. In the rest of this chapter we turn our attention to some of the practical tasks and activities we can use to exploit poems in the classroom. In this section we look at some ways in which poetry can be used with students at elementary and low-intermediate level.

Task 16

Here are a number of statements about using poetry with students at lower levels. Next to each one write either True or False.

- It's impossible to find poems in language simple enough for students at lower levels to understand.
- Lower level students may understand the individual meaning of each word in a poem but completely miss its deeper meaning.
- We can use activities similar to those we use with other kinds of texts to exploit a poem with students at lower levels.
- Students at lower levels may enjoy and understand the deeper meaning of a poem without actually having sufficient oral skills to discuss it.
- Poems do not have to be used as an end in themselves, but can be used as a way of extending students' knowledge of the language.
- It's too intimidating for both students and teachers to use poetry at lower levels.
- Poetry works particularly well with students who are very literate or well-educated in their own language, even if their proficiency in English is limited.

Examples of activities for lower levels

Below are four poems with activities and tasks to accompany them for use with students at lower levels.

EXAMPLE A: CHILDREN

1. In pairs, complete the following sentences:
   Children always ....
   Children never ....
   Old people always ....
   Old people never ....
   Then read your sentences aloud to the other students in the class.

2. You are going to read a poem called 'Children'. With a partner complete the poem using the words in the box below.

heads	ones	morning	is	only
old	ears	sleep	are	eyes

Children
Children .... at night.
Children never wake up
When .... comes.
.... the old ones wake up.
Old Trouble .... always awake.

Children can't see over their ....
Children can't hear beyond their ....
Children can't know outside of their ....

The old ones see.
The .... ones hear.
The old .... know.
The old ones .... old.

(part of Laura Riding, 'Forgotten Childhood' in Heaney and Hughes (1982), p. 163.)

3. Compare your finished poem with those of the other students in your class. Are they the same or different?

4. Look at these pairs of words:
WAKE – SLEEP   EYES – SEE
Can you see how the words in the pairs are connected? Now here is a list of some other words. Arrange them in pairs in the two columns below. The first ones have been done for you.

heavy	short	carry	nose	arrive	thin	write	arms
fat	day	light	tall	sad	night	mouth	legs
smell	hands	eat	leave	happy	think	brain	walk

wake – sleep   **eyes – see**
heavy – light   nose – smell

5. For homework, write a short poem entitled *Teenagers*.[4]

EXAMPLE B: WHAT'S IT FOR?

1. Match the following pictures with the words below.

| dishwasher | hammer | microwave | word-processor |
| windscreen wipers | lawn mower | washing machine | saw |

2. Now match the pictures and words with these definitions:
   - they're for cleaning the front and back windows of a car when it rains
   - it's for washing clothes
   - it's a type of oven used for cooking food quicker than usual
   - it's a machine used to cut grass
   - it's for knocking nails in a wall
   - it's used to clean dirty plates
   - it's a computer used for typing
   - it's for cutting wood or metal

3. Think of a useful object we use at home or at work. Write a definition of it, beginning . . .

It's for ....

or

It's used for ....

or

It's used to ....

Get the other students in your class to guess what object you're describing.

4. Read this poem.

> *Days*
> What are days for?
> Days are where we live.
> They come, they wake us
> Time and time over.
> 5 They are to be happy in:
> Where can we live but days?
> Ah, solving that question
> Brings the priest and the doctor
> In their long coats
> 10 Running over the fields.

(Philip Larkin, 'Days' in Heaney and Hughes (1982) p. 121.)

Write your own definition:
Days are for ....
Read it aloud to your class.

EXAMPLE C: HE TREATS THEM TO ICE-CREAM

Note to teachers: When doing this activity instruct students to cover everything below the line with a sheet of paper. They only move down below the next solid line when they have completed the exercise at hand. Alternatively, you can write it up, section by section, on the blackboard or on an overhead projector transparency.

---

1. You are going to read a poem called 'He Treats them to Ice-cream' by Anna Swirszczynskia (in C. Rumens (ed.) (1985) *Making for the Open*, Chatto and Windus, p. 51). What does the verb 'to treat' mean here? Write down what you think the poem is about. Talk about your ideas to your partner.

2. Now read the first verse of the poem. After you have read it, write down what you think happens next. Read this aloud to your class.

> Every Sunday they went for a walk together.
> He, she
> And the three children.

3. Now read the next verse of the poem:

> One night
> when she tried to stop him going
> to his other woman,
> he pulled out a flick-knife
> from under the mattress.

Were you right about what happened next in the poem? Now write a last verse for this poem, and read it aloud to the class.

4. Here is the last verse of the poem.

> They still go for a walk
> every Sunday,
> he, she and the three children.
> He treats them to ice-cream and they all laugh.
> She too.

Does it have the kind of ending you expected? What do you think of the ending?

5. Look at the title of the poem again: 'He Treats them to Ice-cream'. Then look at these definitions for the word *to treat*.

> **treat**¹ /triːt/ *v* [T] **1** to act or behave towards someone in a particular way: *She treats us like children.* **2** to handle something in a particular way: *This glass must be treated with care* | *He treated the idea as a joke.* **3** to try to cure an illness by medical means: *a new drug to*
> 5 *treat this disease* **4** to buy or give someone something special: *I'm going to treat myself to a holiday in Spain.* **5** to put a special substance on something to protect it or give it a special quality: *The wood has been treated to make it waterproof.* – **treatable** *adj.*
>
> (*Longman Active Study Dictionary of English*, New Edition, Longman 1991, pp. 712–13.)

How many different meanings does it have? Do you think any of these other meanings are connected with the poem?

EXAMPLE D: SOLOMON GRUNDY

1. Look at this old English nursery rhyme:

    Solomon Grundy
    <u>Born</u> on a Monday
    <u>Christened</u> on Tuesday
    <u>Married</u> on Wednesday
    <u>Took ill</u> on Thursday
    Worse on Friday
    <u>Died</u> on Saturday
    <u>Buried</u> on Sunday
    This is the end
    of Solomon Grundy.

    Do you know what all the underlined words mean? Use your dictionary to help you.

2. What is a slave? Do you think the life of a slave would be the same as the life of Solomon Grundy? Now read this poem about Old Mama Dot, a slave.

    Born on a sunday
    In the kingdom of Asante

    Sold on a monday
    Into slavery

    5   Ran away on tuesday
    Cause she born free

    Lost a foot on wednesday
    When they catch she

    Worked all thursday
    10 Till her head grey

    Dropped on friday
    Where they burn she

    Freed on saturday
    In a new century

    (Frederick D'Aguiar, 'Old Mama Dot' in J. Berry (ed.) (1984)
    News for Babylon, Chatto and Windus, p. 26.)

3. Here are some sentences about the life of Old Mama Dot. Put them in the right order.
    She became a free woman.
    She worked hard until she felt very old.
    She tried to run away from her master.
    She died from working so hard.

She was born in Africa.
They punished her by cutting off her foot.
She was sold as a slave.

4. In the poem, the poet uses the special English which Mama Dot, the slave, would use. Can you see any examples of it in the poem? What could we say instead in standard English?

5. Now write a short poem about the life of a typical person from your country.

Task 17 🔑

Here is a list of some of the types of activities used with the four poems. Some of the activities have been used with one poem only, some of them with more than one. Next to each activity, write down at least one poem with which this activity is used.

sentence completion
matching words to definitions
predictive writing
ordering sentences in the correct sequence
writing your own poem
gap-fill/cloze
matching words to pictures
checking word meaning in a dictionary
organising words according to lexical relationships

Task 18 🔑

Here are some brief descriptions of the aims behind using each of the four poems. Decide which poem and accompanying activities belong with which description.

a) The aim of this series of activities is to revise some vocabulary, and to introduce a new function by providing three ways of expressing it. The use of a poem at the end of the lesson is intended as a fairly light-hearted and enjoyable way of reinforcing this function.

b) The aim of this sequence of activities is to promote oral practice and practice in imaginative writing by involving students in a simple, but powerful narrative poem. The poem usually excites strong reactions, and many students find it interesting and helpful to write an alternative ending to it. A secondary aim is to show how one word can have a number of different meanings, particularly in a poem.

c) These activities encourage students to focus on some basic grammatical rules, particularly those relating to the use of the present simple tense. They also aim to provide revision in some basic vocabulary in the form of a problem-solving exercise.

E

d) These tasks teach some basic vocabulary, encourage students to decode a simple poem, and sensitise students to the notion that non-standard forms exist in English. Both the nursery rhyme and the poem can then be used to provide models for students' own imaginative writing.

Task 19

Think back to the statements made in Task 16 at the very beginning of this section. Since working your way through the poems used with students at lower levels have your views on these statements changed at all? Can you think of any poems that you would like to use yourself with students at lower levels? How would you exploit them?

6.7   Using poetry to develop oral skills ☆

In Sections 6.4 and 6.5 we looked at some of the difficulties that students commonly have with poems – coping with unusual language and decoding figurative language. We have assumed that students should be alerted to the use of striking metaphors, unusual syntax or inventive games with punctuation. But this approach tends to stress what the eye sees when a poem is read, and ignores the rich patterns of sound that contribute to the special qualities of most poems. In this section, we consider a few ways of using a poem so that these sound patterns can be fully enjoyed and appreciated by students.

Below is a worksheet which incorporates a series of activities designed to help students understand and respond personally to a poem before they prepare a choral reading of it.

Activities for developing understanding of 'As It was'

1. In groups discuss what you might do in the following situations:
   - You are walking along when you see a very large, drunken man beating a dog with a stick.
   - You are in a large department store and you see a woman with a small baby secretly putting some baby clothes in her bag without paying for them.
   - You know your neighbours are away for the weekend and late on Saturday evening you hear strange noises coming from their house.
2. Look at these two sentences:
   It did not seem important at the time.
   We walked away: it was not our concern.

In pairs or groups, decide in what situations you might use sentences like these. Can you think of any other similar sentences you might use in that situation?

3. Read the poem below. In the poem, the poet uses the sentence, 'We walked away: it was not our concern.' To what situation does this sentence seem to refer?

> As It was
> It did not seem important at the time:
> We gave them pity when they wanted gold,
> We could not help it: we were never told.
>
> We'd lost our glasses, so we could not see:
> 5 We went home early from the Pantomime –
> It did not seem important at the time.
>
> We walked away: it was not our concern.
> No doubt there was some fruit upon the Tree:
> We'd lost our glasses, so we could not see.
>
> 10 We could not help it: we were never told.
> We heard a shot: the guards looked very stern.
> We walked away: it was not our concern.
>
> We could not help it: we were never told.
> No doubt there were some rumours of a crime,
> 15 We'd lost our glasses, so we could not see.
> We walked away: it was not our concern.
> The streets were dark and it was very cold.
> It did not seem important at the time.

(John Mander, 'As It was' in Lewis (1985), p. 231.)

4. With a partner, talk about what you think is meant by the following lines from the poem:

'We went home early from the Pantomime.' (line 5)
'No doubt there was some fruit upon the Tree.' (line 8)
'We'd lost our glasses, so we could not see.' (lines 4, 9, 15)

Discuss your ideas with your teacher, and the other students in the class.

5. Some of the lines in the poem are repeated. Which ones? What effect is created by repeating these lines?

6. How do you think the speaker in the poem feels about the events which are referred to in the poem? Tick some of the adjectives below:

| satisfied | nostalgic | horrified | depressed | guilty | remorseful |
| angry | calm | tormented | ashamed | objective | self-justifying |

Task 20 🗝

Below is a list of aims which motivated the use of the activities above. Next to each aim write the activity or activities which best fulfils it. The first has been done for you.

- to understand the emotional tone of the poem (6.)
- to understand the overall gist of the poem
- to understand some of the figurative or metaphorical meanings in the poem
- to stimulate student interest and to encourage personal involvement in the underlying themes of the poem
- to analyse how the stylistic device of repetition of key phrases contributes to the overall effect of the poem
- to understand the tone of the poem.

Choral reading of 'As It was'

After ensuring that students have a reasonable understanding of the poem, and are aware of how its stylistic features contribute to its meaning, we are now able to turn our attention to how it can be used for choral reading. A choral reading is a kind of performance in which the poem is read aloud by a group of students. The reading can also make limited use of movements, gesture, facial expressions and the changing qualities of the voice (variations in speed of delivery, loudness or softness, stress, etc.).

Task 21

Think about how you might make use of 'As It was' for choral reading. The checklist below will provide you with some points to consider.

CHECKLIST FOR PREPARING CHORAL READINGS

When preparing a poem for choral reading, it would be useful to ask yourself questions like the ones below.
1. Are there any specific points of pronunciation you would like to practise with students before doing the reading? Stress? Intonation? Sounds?
2. How will students be divided for the reading? In groups? Or will the whole class work together?
3. How much freedom will the class have to devise its own reading? Can students work it out for themselves? Or will you provide them with instructions detailing who is to say what?
4. When devising the reading or getting students to do it for themselves are there any particular qualities in the poem you think should be

emphasised when it is read aloud? For example, if lines are repeated should the same speaker always deliver them? Which sections of the poem should be said by individual students, and which by a pair or group? Do you need to appoint a 'conductor' to get students to join in at the appropriate times?

5. Does the classroom need to be reorganised to do the reading? What do you do if space is very limited and furniture not easily moved?

6. How will rehearsals be fitted into classroom time? Will you do preparation and practice all in one session? Or will you rehearse for a shortish time over a series of lessons and then get students to do an end-of-term performance for other classes?

Here are the notes of one teacher who used 'As It was' for choral reading. While you read them decide how far the techniques used or comments made could apply to the students you teach.

TEACHING NOTES

Level: Mid-Intermediate

Description of class: Mixed nationality – adult students from Middle East, Africa and Europe, 15 altogether.

Procedure: To begin with, I gave students in pairs four sentences to practise reading aloud. Here they are:

■ ■
We could not help it: we were never told.

■ ■
We could not help it: we were never told.

■ ■
We walked away: it was not our concern.

■ ■
We walked away: it was not our concern.

The squares on the words show which words students had to stress or emphasise. I asked them to think about how the meaning of the sentences changed according to where they put the stress. I went around the class unobtrusively monitoring and correcting punctuation. It is quite a useful way of practising stress as students are really sensitised to how stressing different words conveys different meanings. They enjoyed it!

Students then divided into groups of five and I handed out copies of 'As It was' marked for choral reading [Figure 6.1]. I explained the point of a choral reading and said we'd rehearse it for half an hour and then perform it for each other. I assigned different letters of the alphabet to students, and explained that where a line was marked A, A should read, and so on. I told them this was a guide; they should feel free to vary it if they wanted or even to ignore it and work out their own reading. I also suggested that when they were practising, they should think about who was going to stand where, to decide whether they would move about, what gestures they would use, etc.

Evaluation: Reading went off quite well. Students from some countries said there was a strong oral tradition at home, and they enjoyed having a go at it in English. Some students said that next time they would bring some instruments, like drums, whistles and percussion instruments from their own countries into class with them to beat out rhythms to the poem! They thought saying it aloud was great practice for pronunciation. I think children or teenage learners would particularly like this activity.

As It was

It did not seem important at the time:	*A step forward – matter-of-fact*
We gave them pity when they wanted gold,	*B shake head*
We could not help it: we were never told.	*C, D shrug*
We'd lost our glasses, so we could not see:	*E shade your eyes to look*
We went home early from the Pantomime –	*B walk jauntily*
It did not seem important at the time.	*A step forward*
We walked away: it was not our concern.	*C, D, E softly*
No doubt there was some fruit upon the Tree:	*B gesture up to tree*
We'd lost our glasses, so we could not see.	*E shade eyes*
We could not help it: we were never told.	*C, D point at themselves*
We heard a shot: the guards looked very stern.	*A all turn suddenly to the right*
We walked away: it was not our concern.	*C, D, E softly*
We could not help it: we were never told.	*C, D*
No doubt there were some rumours of a crime,	*B kneel down*
We'd lost our glasses, so we could not see.	*E whining voice*
We walked away: it was not our concern.	*C, D, E crossly*
The streets were dark and it was very cold.	*B, C, D, E turn to right and talk quickly*
It did not seem important at the time.	*A quietly after long pause*

Figure 6.1 'As It was' marked for choral reading

Task 22

Can you think of any poems you would like to use for a choral reading? Plan how you would use them with your students.

6.8 Using a poem with students at higher levels ☆

In this section, we look at a famous poem by William Blake and consider what kinds of difficulties students at advanced levels may have with a poem written nearly two centuries ago. We also move beyond treating the poem largely as a linguistic artefact, and think about what kinds of background information students could find useful when reading the poem.

Task 23

Read Blake's poem 'London'. Imagine you wanted to use it with students at an advanced level. What kind of problems do you think they might have with it?

> *London*
> I wander thro' each charter'd street,
> Near where the charter'd Thames does flow,
> And mark in every face I meet
> Marks of weakness, marks of woe.
>
> 5 In every cry of every Man,
> In every Infant's cry of fear,
> In every voice, in every ban,
> The mind-forg'd manacles I hear.
>
> How the Chimney-sweeper's cry
> 10 Every blackening Church appals;
> And the hapless Soldier's sigh
> Runs in blood down Palace walls.
>
> But most, thro' midnight streets I hear
> How the youthful Harlot's curse
> 15 Blasts the new-born Infant's tear,
> And blights with plagues the Marriage hearse.

Task 24

Here is a list of a few difficulties that advanced students might have when reading 'London'. Which ones are the same as the ones you have already noted down? What other difficulties could you add to the list?

Difficulties for advanced students reading 'London'

- Understanding individual words in the poem (e.g. charter'd, ban, blight, etc. – particularly difficult since the historical meaning of the words may have changed over the last two centuries).
- Understanding the metaphorical/symbolic meaning behind phrases or lines in the poem (e.g. 'And blights with plagues the Marriage hearse').
- Understanding the historical context which forms the background to the text.
- Understanding the poet's attitude to what he sees around him.
- Responding personally to the themes of the poem.
- Feeling threatened or intimidated by the apparent level of difficulty of the poem.

Can you think of any ways you could help students to overcome these problems?

Activities for use with 'London'

The following are possible activities and tasks which could be used with a group of advanced students studying Blake's poem 'London'. You are unlikely to ever want to use all of these activities at the same time, but you could choose some. After you have worked your way through them, we will think about how the activities could help to overcome some of the problems students might have when reading Blake's poem.

PRE-READING ACTIVITIES

1. Look at these two pictures. How are they different? What do they have in common? What do you think life is like for the inhabitants in both these places?

2. 🛎 In groups, think of all the reasons why people might leave their villages in the country to go and live in a big city. Your teacher will give you a large poster on which to write your ideas. When you have done so, you will get a chance to compare your poster with those of other groups.

3. Here are a number of words and phrases. Decide for yourself which three best fit your views on city life, and which ones best fit your opinion about life in the country. Write these words under the two headings below. Explain your choices to your partner.

| opportunities   poverty   isolation   freedom |
| wealth   community   violence   excitement   tranquillity |
| sense of belonging   security   boredom   oppression |
| lack of morality   dirt   anonymity |

City life	*Country life*

4. Here is a text which describes some of the historical changes in England between 1750 and 1850. Use your dictionary to look up any of the words you don't understand. Then answer the questions which follow.

> The biggest social change in English history is the transfer, between 1750 and 1850, of large masses of the population from the countryside to the towns; the basic social classes were transformed from small farmers and rural craftsmen into an urban
> 5 proletariat and a lower middle class of industrial employers. The movement was hastened by two forces: (i) the agricultural revolution carried out by the landowners drove the peasants off the land, and (ii) they were drawn to the towns by the demand for labour in the factories and mills, operated by machines driven by
> 10 steam-power. It affected the north of England and parts of the Midlands far more than the south, and this, too, was a big transformation; hitherto it had been the south that had been advanced and relatively populous while the north had remained relatively empty, backward and conservative, but now the north
> 15 was pushing against the conservatism of the south.
>   The new industrial towns were places of great distress for the workers. The poor were indeed having the worst period of suffering since serfdom had been practically extinguished in the 14th century. The prosperous peasant farmer, the yeoman, who

20   had won battles for the Plantagenet kings in the Hundred Years'
War, had long been considered the solid base of English society,
but by the 19th century he had largely disappeared. If he had not
sunk to the level of a labourer on the land of a bigger farmer or
become a factory-worker and little better than a serf, he had turned

25   into an industrial employer. The employers themselves often
struggled very hard to get their heads above the level of
wretchedness, and they commonly achieved it by a narrow range
of human virtues – thrift, industriousness, sobriety – and were apt
to conclude that these were the only estimable virtues, because

30   they were the only ones that had proved useful to themselves.

(adapted from C. Gillie (1972) *Longman Companion to English Literature*, Longman, p. 29.)

a) What major change was there in the English class system between 1750 and 1850?

b) What two forces accelerated the urbanisation of English society?

c) What kinds of jobs do you think industrial employers performed? How did they manage to get ahead?

d) 'The new industrial towns were places of great distress for workers.' What kind of conditions do you think people worked in? If they were unable to find work in factories, how else do you think people supported themselves? What kind of conditions do you think people lived in? What did the cities look like?

5. You are going to read a poem called 'London' by William Blake who lived from 1757 to 1827. Blake has been described in the following ways:

– a political radical of his time who supported the French revolution

– a man who fought against the greedy materialism of his age

– a mystic visionary who opposed the narrow dogma of traditional Christianity

– a prophet who warned of the dangers of reducing man to a cog in an industrial revolution

– a romantic poet who believed passionately in the importance of the imagination

– a man of humble origins who used the strong simple language of popular culture in his writings.

In the light of what you know about Blake's character and the important changes taking place in English society at the time he was writing, what do you think the poem 'London' is going to be about?

6. Now read the poem 'London'. Does it surprise you in any way, or is it as you expected?

7. ☛⊖ Here are a number of words from the poem. Some possible definitions or explanations of their meaning are provided – all of these could be found in the dictionary. Decide which definition fits best with the word as it is used in the poem. If you think both or all definitions apply, give reasons why you think this:

charter'd (lines 1 and 2)
1) established by a written document from the ruler or parliament which creates a borough, university or company
2) established by a written document from the ruler or parliament which grants certain privileges or rights

marks (line 4)
1) a device, seal or label indicating ownership
2) a boundary, frontier or limit
3) a sign

ban (line 7)
1) a formal prohibition
2) a curse with power to harm

appal (line 10)
1) to grow pale
2) to lose heart and become dismayed

blast (line 15)
1) to blow violently
2) to blow on a trumpet
3) to blow up by explosion

blight (line 16)
1) to affect plants with a disease that destroys them suddenly
2) to wither hopes or prospects

8. In groups or pairs discuss what you think is meant by the following lines or phrases:
    1) the mind-forg'd manacles (line 8)
    2) Marks of weakness, marks of woe (line 4)
    3) the Marriage hearse (line 16)

9. In the poem there are a number of different words connected with certain ideas or images. While you read the poem again, note down all the words or phrases connected with:
restrictions/limitations
sound/noise
disease/destruction
What overall effect is achieved by using these images in the poem?

10. In the poem two institutions are mentioned – the Church and the Palace. What do you think these represent? What is the relationship between the Church and the Chimney-sweeper as expressed in lines 9 and 10? What is the relationship between the Palace and the soldier as expressed in lines 11–12?

11. Look at the last verse of the poem. What is unusual about the phrase 'Marriage hearse'? In what way does the 'Harlot's curse' damage the infant and the institution of marriage?

12. In the poem there are a number of repetitions – of words and phrases. Note down what these are and what effect you think they have.

13. Here are a number of critical comments made about Blake's poem. Which one do you find the most convincing?

Blake's 'London' is a revolutionary document which ferociously attacks the corruption of urban life.

In 'London' Blake seems to be writing in the tradition of the popular ballad, but his apocalyptic vision of life in the city goes beyond a mere protest against social injustice.

In 'London' we see a city which is truly a vision of hell – of life after The Fall.

Despite the fury of the attack on the institutions of the time, Blake's 'London' always retains its tone of compassion for suffering.

In 'London' Blake's angry denunciation of social institutions never loses sight of the way an individual is enslaved by his or her own fear and brutality.

Now write a short paragraph summarising your own feelings and opinions about the poem.

Task 25 ⚷

a) Look again at the list of difficulties that advanced students might have with the poem (Task 24). Next to each difficulty write down any of the tasks or activities for use with 'London' which could help to overcome these problems. Can you think of any other activities which could help student understanding when reading the poem?

b) Which activities would you, yourself, use with a group of students? Why? Which activities might you leave out? Why?

c) How necessary is it to provide students with the kind of background information given in Activities 4 and 5?

d) Why is it necessary to provide students with alternative definitions of the words in the poem (Activity 7)?

e) Is it always necessary to provide students with different critical views as in Activity 13? Why?

126

f) What kinds of activities could you use as follow-up or post-reading activities for this poem?

Task 26

Figure 6.2 is a diagram summarising the possible stages of a lesson using 'London'. Think of a poem you would like to use with your students and use the diagram to help you plan a lesson based around that poem.

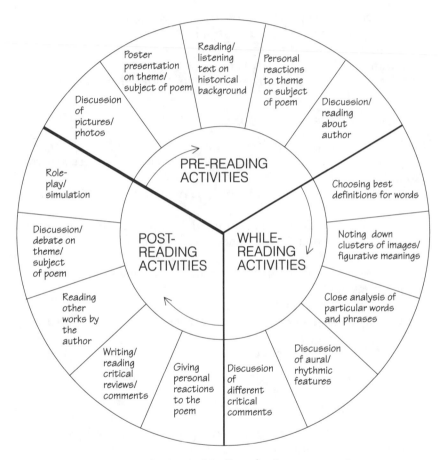

Figure 6.2 Stages in a lesson using 'London'

6.9 Anticipating student problems

In this chapter we have already looked at a number of tasks and activities for exploiting poems with students. When planning a lesson using a poem it is always useful to try to anticipate some of the

127

difficulties students may face when reading or studying a poem, since by
doing so you can design materials which help the students through some
of the difficulties. Below is a checklist of some possible questions you
might ask yourself when trying to predict these problems.

**Before you read the checklist, think about the areas such a checklist
should cover.**

1.   The background to the poem

To make sense of the poem do the students need to know about:
– any cultural or historical information?
– the collection from which the poem is taken?
– the author's life or other works?
– what genre the poem is or to what literary movement it belongs?

2.   The language of the poem

Do you need to help the students with:
– any unusual language in the poem which stretches the norms or rules
  of language use?
– any unfamiliar words, phrases, grammatical constructions or
  syntactic features?
– any important discoursal or formal features of the poem (e.g.
  rhyming, repetition of certain lines or conformity to set genres such as
  the sonnet, etc.)?
– any ambiguities in meaning (e.g. multiple meanings for a particular
  word, puns, etc.)?
– any figurative or symbolic meanings?
– any figures of speech or rhetorical devices in the poem (e.g.
  apostrophe)?
– any aural or musical qualities in the poem (e.g. alliteration, assonance,
  etc.)?

3.   Motivating and involving students

– How can the theme or topic of the poem be made relevant to the
  student's own experience?
– How does the use of a poem in class mesh with the requirements of
  the syllabus and the students' perceptions of their own needs? Can the
  poem be exploited in such a way that both of these demands are met?
– What activities will most suit the learning styles of the students? Being
  asked to discuss the poem in a very open-ended way? Being given only
  two set interpretations of the poem from which to choose? Being
  asked to read a lot of background to the literary period? Being asked
  to recite the poem aloud?

Task 27

Think about a poem you would like to use with your own students. Use the questions above to help you begin to plan your lesson. A checklist of ideas for tasks and activities to use can be found in the next section.

6.10   Further tasks and activities

In this chapter, we have looked at a variety of ways of exploiting poems in the classroom. Here is a list of these and some others which might be useful for designing materials.

Pre-reading activities

STIMULATING STUDENT INTEREST IN THE TEXT

1. Students predict the theme of the poem from its title or a few key words or phrases in the poem.
2. Students or groups of students are given different lines from the poem and asked to suggest the subject or theme of the poem. Does this change when they hear the other lines read aloud to the class?
3. Students discuss or describe pictures or photographs relevant to the theme of the poem.
4. Students are asked what they would do, and how they would respond, if they were in a situation similar to the one in the poem.

PROVIDING THE NECESSARY HISTORICAL OR CULTURAL BACKGROUND

1. Students read or listen to a text which describes the historical or cultural background to the poem.
2. Students read or listen to a text about the author's life which may deepen their understanding of the themes of the poem.
3. Students discuss what are appropriate behaviours or feelings in their culture or society in a particular situation. Then they compare this with the emotions in the poem – are these individual to the writer or indicative of cultural norms?
4. More literary-minded students could be given information about the genre of the poem or the literary movement to which the author belongs before reading it.

HELPING STUDENTS WITH THE LANGUAGE OF THE POEM

1. If there is unusual or deviant language in the poem, students could be asked to work on activities exploring more normative uses of language. For example, if certain verbs in a poem collate with unusual nouns students could be asked to predict what the usual collocates for the verbs are before comparing this with the language of the poem.
2. To guide students towards an understanding of more metaphorical or symbolic meanings in the poem, students could be asked to free-associate round some of those words in the poem which carry powerful symbolic connotations.
3. The teacher preteaches any important words, phrases or grammatical constructions that appear in the poem.

While-reading activities

1. Students are given a jumbled version of the poem (either lines or verses) and asked to put it together again. Jumbling up verses works particularly well for poems with a strong narrative, for example ballads.
2. Certain words are removed from the poem, and students have to fill in the gaps – either by themselves or using a list of words provided.
3. Students read only one verse at a time and then try to predict what's coming next – this works well with narrative poems.
4. Students underline all the words connected with a particular lexical set and then speculate on their metaphorical or symbolic meaning.
5. Students decide which definitions of a particular word in the dictionary is the one that best fits the meaning of the word in the poem.
6. Students answer comprehension questions about the meaning of certain words or phrases in the poem.

Post-reading activities

HELPING STUDENTS TOWARDS AN INTERPRETATION OF THE POEM

1. Students are given a series of statements about the possible under-lying meanings of the poem, and they decide which ones are true or false.
2. Students are given two or three brief interpretations of a poem (possibly from critics) and they decide which one they think is the most plausible or appropriate.
3. If a poem is written in rather archaic language, students are asked to

compare this to two versions of it in modern English – which version best captures the meaning and tone of the poem?
4. Very advanced students can be asked to compare a poem with two different translations of it in their own language. Which translation is the most satisfactory?
5. Students imagine they are filming the poem. They have to decide what visual image they would provide for each line or verse of the poem as it is recited.
6. Students practise reading the poem aloud and decide what mime or gestures would accompany a choral reading.

FURTHER FOLLOW-UP ACTIVITIES

1. Students rewrite the poem as a different form of discourse. This works particularly well with ballads or narrative poems – students either rewrite the story as if it were a newspaper article or the script for a soap opera.
2. Students read and discuss other poems by the same author, or other poems on the same theme.
3. Students write their own poem, using the original as a model.
4. Students do some language work based around any unusual language in the poem, for example, punctuating a poem with unconventional punctuation; creating words using suffixes and affixes the poet may have used in an unusual way and then checking them in the dictionary; 'correcting' unusual syntax; etc.
5. Discussion or roleplay based on the theme or subject of the poem.
6. Students discuss the values and world-view which are either implicitly or explicitly expressed in the poem. Do they agree with them?

Endnotes

1. For a fuller discussion of what conventions or strategies students need in order to understand poetry see Keith Jones, 'On the goals of a reading programme for students of English as a foreign literature' in Brumfit (1983).
2. Many of the ideas for this section first appeared in an article by the author: Lazar, 'Metaphorically Speaking' in SIGMA, Issue No. 1, October 1989. SIGMA is the newsletter of the IATEFL Literature Special Interest Group.
3. A procedure for analysing metaphors on which this exercise is based can be found in Leech (1988) *A Linguistic Guide to English Poetry*, pp. 153–156.
4. The ideas for using this poem and the poems in Sections 6.1 and 6.4 were originally published in an article by the author: Lazar (1989).

Suggestions for further reading

On poetic discourse

Leech, G. (1988) *A Linguistic Guide to English Poetry.*
Widdowson, H. G. (1984) 'The deviant language of poetry' in *Explorations in Applied Linguistics 2.*

Using poetry in the classroom

Collie, J. and Slater, S. (1987) *Literature in the Language Classroom,* Chapter 10.
Ramsaran, S. (1983) 'Poetry in the language classroom', *ELT Journal,* **37,** 1.
Tomlinson, B. (1986) 'Using poetry with mixed language groups', *ELT Journal,* **40,** 1.

Textbooks using poetry

Collie, J. and Porter-Ladousse, G. (1991) *Paths into poetry.*
Mackay, R. (1987) *Poems.*
Maley, A. and Moulding, S. (1985) *Poem into Poem.*

Useful poetry anthologies

Heaney, S. and Hughes, T. (eds.) (1982) *The Rattle Bag.*
Lewis, N. (ed.) (1985) *Messages.*
Rosen, M. (ed.) (1985) *The Kingfisher Book of Children's Poetry.*
See also the list in J. Collie and S. Slater (1987) *Literature in the Language Classroom,* p. 260.

7 Materials design and lesson planning: Plays

This chapter, which examines the place of plays in the language classroom, begins by discussing the distinctive features of plays and how plays can be exploited in the classroom. Ways of using both play extracts and whole plays are examined. A section on using play extracts with learners at lower levels and a section on preparing students for a theatre visit are included.

7.1 What is distinctive about plays?

Following the pattern of the previous two chapters, we will begin by discussing what is meant by a play and its similarities and differences to other literary genres. First let us examine the two quotations below.

A. . . . drama is not made of words alone, but of sights and sounds, stillness and motion, noise and silence, relationships and responses.

(J. L. Styan, 1975, *Drama, Stage and Audience.*)

B. However familiar or unfamiliar the world of a tragedy, comedy, farce or melodrama may be, everything that we experience has its source, in the long run, in words. (Gareth Lloyd Evans, 1977, *The Language of Modern Drama.*)

Task 1

a) Think about a play that you know well, either in English or another language. If you have seen the play performed, what examples of 'sights and sounds, stillness and motion, noise and silence' do you remember from the play? What examples of 'relationships and responses' can you remember? If you have read it, were you able to recreate these in your imagination?
b) How important were the words in the play? Could you imagine the play rewritten in another style? Would it still have the same effect?
c) What do you think the relationship is between the text of a play and its performance?
d) Think about a group of language learners that you are teaching or have taught in the past. Do the quotations above suggest any possible features of plays which could be exploited with your learners? What kinds of tasks and activities could be devised to make use of these features?

7.2 The language of a play ☆

In Section 7.1 it was suggested that words, or language, are central to the meaning of a play. By examining a few lines from a play, we can pinpoint some of the ways in which this might be true. Here are some lines from a play by Tunde Ikoli called *The Lower Depths*, which is adapted from a play by Maxim Gorky. It is set in a house in a poor neighbourhood of London. Most of the characters living in the house are renting rooms from a landlord called Mr Koli. The dialogue you are going to read takes place between two characters called Teacher and Rutter.

Task 2 🔑

As you read the extract below you will see that some lines of the dialogue have been left out. These can be found underneath the dialogue. Decide where each one of the missing lines belong. When you have done this, look at the key at the back of the book – is your version of the dialogue the same, or different from, the original play?

1 TEACHER: D'you have a spare tea bag?
2 RUTTER: No.
3 TEACHER:
4 RUTTER: No.
5 TEACHER:
6 RUTTER: That's right. No!
7 TEACHER: But why?
8 RUTTER: Buy your own.
9 TEACHER:
10 RUTTER: So, what d'you want me to do about it?
11 TEACHER: A cup of tea, please?
12 RUTTER: No.
13 TEACHER:

Missing lines:
a) I would if I could but I can't.
b) I see . . . What's happened to the fellowship of man, brotherly love?
c) No?
d) Perhaps I could share the one you have?

Task 3 🔑

Look at the dialogue again, and answer these questions:
a) What kinds of connections between the lines in the dialogue helped you to put the missing lines in the appropriate places?

b) In line 3, Teacher makes a request of Rutter. Why does Teacher say 'perhaps' and 'could'? Could this request be made in other ways? How would this change its effect?

c) In line 5, Teacher repeats Rutter's 'No' of the previous line. Why does he do this? Try saying this 'No' aloud – how does your intonation affect the meaning it conveys?

d) In line 13, Teacher says 'What's happened to the fellowship of man, brotherly love?' What does he really mean when he says this? What is he implying about Rutter by saying this? Does his question reveal anything about what kind of person *he* is – his character, education or background?

e) What do you think the relationship between the two characters is? Are they equals? Do they like or dislike each other? For which one do you feel the most sympathy?

Task 4

If you were teaching an extract from a play you could remove certain lines from the dialogue and ask your students to fill the gaps as we have just done. What would be your aims in doing so? Think particularly about your linguistic aims.

7.3 The performance of a play

In the last section, we thought about the language of a play and some of the ways in which it could carry meaning. But in Section 7.1 it was suggested that a play took on many more meanings in performance, by using gestures, movement, costumes, sets, etc. It is important, when considering using plays in the classroom, that the performance aspect is also taken into account.

Task 5

Imagine that you are directing a performance of the extract of the play discussed in Section 7.2. Jot down some ideas about how you picture the following aspects of performance.

A play in performance

Costumes	Sets	Lighting
Music	Props	Gestures

Task 6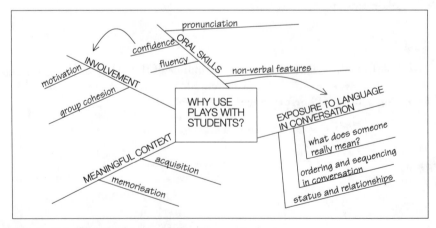

Could you get your own students to imagine they were directing a performance of a play by thinking about costumes, sets, lighting, etc. as you have just done? What would be your aim in doing so?

7.4 Why use plays in the language learning classroom?

Figure 7.1 contains brief notes about some of the reasons for using plays or extracts from plays with the language learner. This figure is a summary of the text which follows.

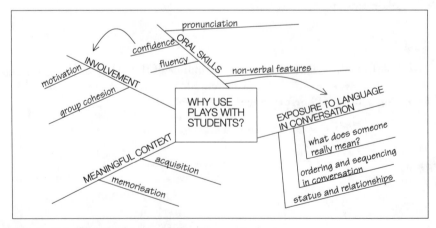

Figure 7.1 Using plays with language students

Task 7

Before you read the text look at the notes and try to predict what will be in the text. Jot down any questions you have about the notes – are they answered in the text? Can you think of other reasons which are not mentioned for using plays or extracts from plays in the language classroom?

In Section 7.1 two distinctive features of plays were mentioned – that a play exists in performance, but that it also exists as words on a page, or a text. Of course, neither of these views are mutually exclusive, since all performances begin from an interpretation of words on a page; and without those words the gestures and movements of the cast, the sets and costumes, the lighting and music would be meaningless. But thinking about performance and text separately can direct our attention to some of the benefits of using plays, or extracts from plays, in the classroom.

Let's begin with the words on the page. Since most plays are rich in dialogue, using a play with students is a useful and exciting way of focussing on conversational language.[1] Dialogue in a play clearly differs from dialogue in everyday conversation in that it is 'tidied up' in some ways. It probably contains few of the hesitations, pauses, incomplete sentences and interruptions of everyday conversation. However, it can be used to highlight certain important features of conversational discourse.[2] In Section 7.2 we examined an extract from a play in which one character, Teacher, says to the other, Rutter, 'What's happened to the fellowship of man, brotherly love?' It is clear that he is not engaging in some casual philosophising, but how, exactly, are we to understand his question? Is it a pointed sarcasm, a sad rhetorical question or a sharp rebuke to the other character for refusing to give him a teabag? On the surface, a question about brotherly love at this point in the conversation may seem irrelevant. We can only see its relevance if we understand it to imply that Rutter is being less than brotherly in refusing to give Teacher a teabag. And we reach this interpretation of his words from our contextual knowledge of what has come before in the conversation, as well as Teacher's probable motives for making this comment. In other words, in order to make sense of the dialogue we need to move beyond the surface meaning of Teacher's words to an interpretation of what is implied by what he says. And by asking our students to try to tease out what lies behind the apparent meanings of dialogues from plays such as this one, we are broadening their understanding of conversational discourse. At the same time, we will be exposing them to other features of conversational language – how conversations are ordered and sequenced in English, what kinds of formulaic expressions it is appropriate to use in different contexts, how what people say in a conversation reflects their relationship and relative status.

Studying the dialogue of a play provides students with a meaningful context for acquiring and memorising new language. Students often pick up new phrases or formulaic expressions by studying how these are used by the characters in a play, particularly if the text is read or performed in class. And there are other advantages in asking students to act out or perform a play, or extracts from a play. Getting students to work together on a mini-production of a play, or simply to read an extract from a play aloud in class, is an excellent way of creating cohesion and cooperation in a group. A strong sense of involvement is fostered which helps to motivate students and encourages them to learn through active participation. The human conflicts, moral dilemmas or political issues communicated in a play engage students intellectually and emotionally, and can provide a valuable source for discussion. Student confidence improves, not least because students have a written text as a basis from which to develop their oral skills. Shyer or more inhibited students often find working from a written text or script a less threatening way of doing a roleplay than having to improvise. Students get a chance to improve their pronunciation by experimenting with different patterns of intonation, and practising different sounds.

Non-verbal features, such as gestures and body language, how far people stand from each other when they talk to each other and for how long they maintain eye contact when speaking, could all be analysed and discussed during the acting out of the play. Students might be asked to what extent these features reflect the relationships of the characters in the play and their attitudes towards each other, as well as the students' own cultural background.[3]

7.5 Using play extracts to think about language in conversation ☆

In Section 7.4 we thought about some of the reasons why extracts from plays can help students gain greater insights into conversational language. In this section, we examine a series of tasks and activities which aim to encourage students to develop these insights. We begin by looking at two extracts from different plays. Both extracts deal with a first meeting between two characters. Read them carefully and then think about the questions which follow the extracts.

TEXT A

> JERRY: I've been to the zoo. (*Peter doesn't notice.*) I said, I've been to the zoo. MISTER, I'VE BEEN TO THE ZOO!
> PETER: Hm? . . . What? . . . I'm sorry, were you talking to me?

JERRY: I went to the zoo, and then I walked until I came here. Have I
5   been walking north?
PETER: *(puzzled)* North? Why . . . I . . . I think so. Let me see.
JERRY: *(pointing past the audience)* Is that Fifth Avenue?
PETER: Why yes; yes it is.
JERRY: And what is that cross street there; that one, to the right?
10 PETER: That? Oh, that's Seventy-fourth Street.
JERRY: And the zoo is around Sixty-fifth Street; so, I've been walking
         north.
PETER: *(anxious to get back to his reading)* Yes: it would seem so.
JERRY: Good old north.
15 PETER: *(lightly, by reflex)* Ha, ha.
JERRY: *(after a slight pause)* But not due north.
PETER: I . . . well, no, not due north; but, we . . . call it north. It's
         northerly.
JERRY: *(watches as Peter, anxious to dismiss him, prepares his pipe)*
20   Well, boy; *you're* not going to get lung cancer, are you?
PETER: *(looks up, a little annoyed, then smiles)* No, sir. Not from this.

(from Edward Albee (1962) 'The Zoo Story' in *The Zoo Story and Other Plays*,
Jonathan Cape, pp. 113–114.)

TEXT B

MERRIMAN: Miss Fairfax. *(Enter Gwendolen. Exit Merriman.)*
CECILY: *(advancing to meet her)* Pray let me introduce myself to
         you. My name is Cecily Cardew.
GWENDOLEN: Cecily Cardew. *(moving to her and shaking hands)* What a
5   very sweet name! Something tells me we are going to be
         great friends. I like you already more than I can say. My
         first impressions of people are never wrong.
CECILY: How nice of you to like me so much after we have known
         each other such a comparatively short time. Pray sit down.
10 GWENDOLEN: *(still standing up)* I may call you Cecily, may I not?
CECILY: With pleasure!
GWENDOLEN: And you will always call me Gwendolen, won't you?
CECILY: If you wish.
GWENDOLEN: Then all is quite settled, is it not?
15 CECILY: I hope so.
         (A pause, they both sit down together.)

(from Oscar Wilde, *The Importance of Being Earnest*
from *Four Plays by Oscar Wilde*, The Unicorn Press, 1944, pp. 330–331.)

Task 8 🗝

After you have read the two extracts, think about the following
questions.

a) What do you think is the setting for each text? What is the relationship between the two characters?
b) With what level of students could you use both these texts?
c) How would you exploit these texts in the classroom?

Task 9

Now read through the following tasks and activities which are designed to exploit the two texts. Are any of them similar to ones that you had anticipated using with your students? Check through the answers that you might need to prepare for students when doing Activities 5, 6 and 7. These answers may be found in the key at the back of the book.

Tasks and activities for use with Texts A and B

ACTIVITY 1

Divide the students into pairs. Each pair should be given one of the rolecards below. Tell the students to 'rehearse' a short roleplay using the rolecards. After a few minutes they will be asked to 'perform' this roleplay for the other students in the class. (A variation on this activity is to get students writing mini-dialogues using the instructions on the rolecards. This works well in groups who are not very confident about their oral skills.)

Roleplay Card 1
You are sitting on a park bench. Somebody who you do not know comes up and tries to start a conversation with you. What do you say to each other?

Roleplay Card 2
You are at a very formal party where you meet somebody who is a friend of one of your friends. What do you say to each other?

ACTIVITY 2

Ask some of the students to 'perform' their roleplay for the other students. While they do so, ask the other students to answer these questions:

a) Where are the two characters?
b) What is the relationship between them?

Ensure that you have at least one 'performance' of Roleplay Card 1 and one of Roleplay Card 2.

Using play extracts to think about language in conversation

ACTIVITY 3

If you wish, you could use this part of the lesson to revise the functional area of what you say in English when you first meet someone or try to initiate a conversation with someone you don't know. You might wish to focus on how this differs depending on the formality of the occasion or the setting. For example, at a party at the home of a friend you might initiate a conversation with a stranger by saying, 'Hi! My name's X' or 'You must be X' or 'So how do you know X (mutual friend)?' In a more formal setting you could make some pleasant comment about the surroundings, for example, 'Isn't this a lovely room!' When initiating a conversation with a stranger in a public place a statement like, 'Nice day today, isn't it?' is quite usual.

If it is appropriate to your group of learners, you could also discuss with them how the topic of a conversation when you first meet someone differs from country to country. In some cultures, for example, conversations with strangers might be initiated by discussing the weather, as above. In some countries it is considered acceptable to continue the conversation by asking 'personal questions' (about family, marital status, children, etc.) while in others this is not the case.

ACTIVITY 4

Ask the students to read Texts A and B. While they do so, they should decide:

a) Where are the two characters?
b) What is the relationship between them?

You might also ask students to point out any phrases or expressions in the texts which they had used in the roleplays in Activities 1 and 2. Do the texts differ in any way from their roleplays? For example, students often notice that the first text is quite odd in that Jerry dispenses with any of the usual conversational preliminaries like comments about the weather. In Text B, on the other hand, the conversation is so formal that at times it becomes comic.

ACTIVITY 5 ☛─⚷

Ask students to study the texts in more detail now, by answering the following questions in pairs or groups:

Text A

a) How does the conversation in this text begin? What does this suggest about Jerry?
b) Peter says to Jerry, 'I'm sorry, were you talking to me?' (line 3). What answer would you expect Jerry to give? What does his reply suggest about his thoughts or his character?

c) Peter says to Jerry, 'It would seem so.' (line 13). What other phrases could he have used in replying to Jerry? What does his response suggest about him and his feelings towards Jerry at that moment?

d) When do we usually use the phrase 'good old . . . '? What is the effect of using it in this context?

e) When do we call someone 'boy'? Why does Jerry call Peter 'boy' in line 20?

f) How do you think Peter feels about Jerry?

g) What do you think is going to happen next? How do you think the relationship between the two characters is going to develop?

Text B

a) In what way does Cecily introduce herself to Gwendolen? Why does she use the word 'pray'?

b) In her reply to Cecily, Gwendolen uses these phrases:

a *very* sweet name
great friends
more than I can say

Are these phrases appropriate on a first meeting? Do they suggest anything about Gwendolen or her attitude to Cecily?

c) What is suggested by Cecily's reply to Gwendolen in lines 8 and 9?

d) Cecily asks Gwendolen to sit down, but Gwendolen doesn't. Why?

e) Why does Cecily say 'If you wish.' in line 13? What is implied by saying this?

f) What does Gwendolen mean in line 14 when she says 'Then all is quite settled, is it not?'

g) What do you think the two women *really* feel about each other?

h) What do you think is going to happen next? How is the relationship between the characters going to develop further?

ACTIVITY 6 🔑

When you have discussed the answers to the questions in Activity 5, ask students to compare the two texts by filling in the chart below. Then ask students to think about how the texts might differ from ordinary, everyday conversation. Could they imagine actually overhearing such conversations?

	Text A	*Text B*
Setting		
Period		
Relationship between the characters		
Type of language used		

After you have discussed the chart with students, and if it is of interest to them, you could tell them something about the plays from which the two extracts are taken and the playwrights who wrote them.

ACTIVITY 7

An optional activity for a class at a higher level is to ask students to look at the texts again, but this time to find ways in which the different characters in the text try to establish their *control* or *conversational superiority*. For example, Cecily asserts her superiority by saying, 'If you wish.' when Gwendolen asks to be called by her first name. She thereby implies that she herself would rather address Gwendolen more formally.

You could then ask students to think about other ways in which people assert themselves or express their status or superiority in conversation. This is obviously something that differs from one country to another and one language to another and is always very hard to pin down, but a few possible areas for encouraging discussion are mentioned in the questionnaire on the next page (Figure 7.2). While it is quite useful to do this activity immediately after studying Texts A and B, it can also be used at the very end of the lesson as a possible alternative to Activity 8.

Questionnaire

Write down short answers to the questions below:

1. You are talking to someone in your own language who keeps interrupting you. Are you:

    a) very good friends?
    b) from the same family?
    c) colleagues at work of the same status?
    d) that person's boss?
    e) that person's student?
    f) that person's junior at work?

    How do you feel about the interruptions?

2. In your language, if you were speaking to one of these people, how would you address them? What would you call them while speaking to them?

    a) your brother?
    b) your boss?
    c) your daughter?
    d) your colleague at work?
    e) your doctor?
    f) an old friend?
    g) a taxi–driver?
    h) your boyfriend/girlfriend?

3. You are in a situation where someone is asking you a lot of questions. You do not ask too many yourself. Are you:

    a) at the doctor's?
    b) at school?
    c) at a job interview?
    d) with a good friend?
    e) with your father?
    f) in a taxi?

    Why do you ask fewer questions than the other person? What would happen if you started to ask more questions yourself in this situation?

    Now discuss your answers to the questions above with your teacher and the other students in the class. Ask your teacher to explain what he or she would do in English. Is it very different from your own language? Can you think of any other ways in which people show their status in a conversation – in your own language and in English?

Figure 7.2 Questionnaire to encourage discussion of status

Using play extracts to think about language in conversation

Either of these two follow-up activities could be used after reading and studying the texts:
a) Students in pairs choose one of the texts and write a continuation of the dialogue, trying to 'resolve' it in some way.
b) Students choose one of the two letters below and complete it:

Letter A

312 Seventy-fourth Street
Manhattan

Dear Mom,
You're never going to believe what happened to me! There I was, sitting in Central Park, just minding my own business when
....
Love
Peter

Letter B

Chesterfield Lodge
Hertfordshire

My dearest Mama,
I hope this letter finds you in good health. I am writing to tell you of the rather annoying meeting I had recently ....
With fond regards
Cecily

Task 10 ⚷

After you have read through the activities, look at this list of possible aims for using them. Decide which aim most applies to each task or activity. You may find some aims overlap with different activities.

a) to encourage students to read for gist
b) to revise and consolidate the functional area of initiating conversations and meeting someone for the first time
c) to practise writing letters which are both formal and informal
d) to use stylistic analysis to analyse the relationship between speakers in a dialogue
e) to provide students with fluency practice
f) to increase student awareness of how speakers demonstrate their status or assert their control in conversation
g) to expand students' awareness of how language use differs according to setting, period and social roles by contrasting two texts
h) to stimulate the students' imagination
i) to encourage students to listen for gist.

Think about your own students. Which of the activities above would you like to use with them, and which ones would you avoid using with them? Which ones could you adapt to suit the needs, interests and level of your students?

Task 11

Figure 7.3 summarises the sequence of activities we have just discussed. After you have looked at it, think about:
— what extract from a play you could use with your own students
— whether you would be able to develop a lesson incorporating the stages and activities in the diagram
— what other tasks and activities you could use at each stage of the lesson (some more ideas for these are given in Section 7.9).

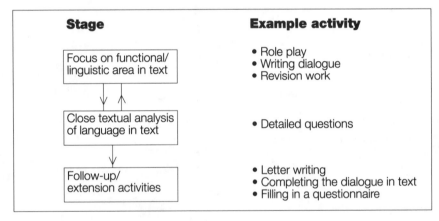

Figure 7.3 Using a play extract to focus on conversational language

7.6 Using play extracts to improve students' oral skills ☆

In the beginning of this chapter we mentioned that much of the meaning of a play was conveyed in performance. We also said that getting students to act out an extract from a play was a useful way of improving their oral skills. In this section, we focus on how the performance aspects of a play can be used as a useful source of classroom activities.

We begin by reading an extract from a play called *Hello and Goodbye* by Athol Fugard.

Imagine you wanted to use it with a group of students to improve their oral skills. For what level and age of students would it be suitable? What kinds of activities or tasks could you use to do this?

TEXT C

JOHNNIE: You used to throw stones at me.

HESTER: Not really.

JOHNNIE: You did, you know.

HESTER: I mean I never really aimed at you.

5 JOHNNIE: (*persistent in his memory*) Once or twice . . .

HESTER: When you wouldn't go back!

JOHNNIE: . . . they came quite close.

HESTER: 'Where you going, Hester?' 'Can I come with Hester?'

JOHNNIE: Because you were supposed to look after me.

10 HESTER: Didn't I?

JOHNNIE: Not always.

HESTER: What you complaining about? You're still alive.

JOHNNIE: That's true.   (Oxford University Press, 1973, p. 30.)

Lesson plan for Text C

Below is the first half of a lesson plan for using the extract from *Hello and Goodbye* with a group of intermediate learners. As you read it, think about the aim of each activity.

PRE-READING ACTIVITY

Divide the students into pairs and groups. Ask them to discuss these two questions:
– What kinds of things can cause conflict between brothers and sisters? What can bring them closer to each other?
– Do you have any brothers or sisters? Do you get on with them? What do you like or dislike about them?

WHILE-READING ACTIVITY

Hand out copies of the text, and ask the students to read silently. Deal with any linguistic problems that students have with the text. Then follow this procedure:
1. Assign roles, so that in each pair there is one student taking the part of Hester, and another the part of Johnnie. Tell the students to read the text aloud according to their roles.
2. When all the pairs have finished reading out their texts once, tell them to do it again – but this time with more feeling. They should think about intonation, facial expressions and even gestures while they do so.
3. Ask the pairs to stand up and read the text aloud once more, but this time they should 'act out' the scene by moving around as they think

F

the characters in the play might do. This activity obviously works best if the desks in your classroom are arranged in a semi-circle with an open space in the centre for students to move about in. If your classroom is not arranged so that there is much room for students to move about, let them stay where they are and encourage them to use a lot of gestures.

4. Get the pairs to change partners, so that students still retain the same roles. Each student playing Johnnie will now be paired with a different Hester. Tell the students to read the text again with their new partner, paying attention to intonation, gestures and facial expressions.

5. Now tell students to put their texts away. Ask them to act out the scene again, this time supplying the words themselves. They do not need to reproduce the text perfectly, and can improvise as they wish, but they should aim to keep broadly to its content.

6. Students improvise an ending to the scene.

7. Ask one or two pairs to perform this scene in front of the class.

Task 12 ☞─◦

Here is a list of statements about using the procedure, described in the lesson plan, with a class. Write A next to the statement if you agree with it, and D if you disagree. Be clear about your reasons for this.

Opinions about the lesson plan

– Asking students to talk about their own experiences before reading the text is threatening and invasive.
– Shy or inhibited students get a lot of non-threatening practice in pairs.
– The teacher should only correct pronunciation while unobtrusively monitoring the pairs.
– The activity can get very noisy.
– Students will find improvising relatively easy after reading aloud a number of times.
– The teacher doesn't need to provide any background to the text before the students read it.
– The teacher shouldn't explain too much vocabulary or grammar before the students read the text.
– Students might get very bored reading the text aloud so many times.
– Changing partners during the activity confuses students.
– The activity can only be used at intermediate level and upwards.
– The activity is difficult to do with large classes.

Now think about any of the more problematic points mentioned above that you think you might experience with your students. Suggest a few ideas for overcoming them.

148

Task 13

In the activity described in the lesson plan for Text C, students were performing the play, rather than simply studying its language. In Section 7.3 some of the elements contributing to a performance were mentioned. These included gestures and movement, but also sets, lighting and costumes. Can you suggest any ways that these elements could be incorporated into a lesson using Text C?

Other activities for use with Text C

Here are some activities which could be used with the students after they have read Text C and acted it out. The overall aim of using these activities is to encourage students to think about the different kinds of meaning that can be communicated by the costumes, sets and acting in a performance of a play. At the same time, the students would be practising their reading and speaking skills.

ACTIVITY 1: THE CHARACTERS

With your partner, discuss these questions. Use your imagination:
a) Who are Hester and Johnnie?
b) What is their relationship?
c) How do they feel about each other?
d) What do you think they look like?
e) How old are they?
f) How do you think they move around the stage?
g) What kind of gestures do you think they might use?
h) What sort of voices do you think they have?
i) For which one do you have the most sympathy? Why?

ACTIVITY 2: THE SET

Look at the description of two possible sets for the play. Discuss which one you think provides the background for the dialogue between Hester and Johnnie.
a. The stage is empty of furniture except for a kitchen table and four chairs. A single electric bulb hangs above the table, on which there is a jug of fruit squash. The rest of the stage is a jumble – three or four old boxes and suitcases have been opened, and their contents are all spilling out onto the stage. Piles of old clothes and newspapers litter the stage. Hester is sitting looking at an old photograph album.
b. On the stage is an elegant dining table with four chairs. To the right stands a tall lamp with a silk shade, to the left a large potted plant. Behind the plant is a window revealing a view onto a well-kept garden. The back wall is covered with watercolours of birds, nicely

framed. Hester is paging through three leather-bound photo albums spread out on the table.

ACTIVITY 3: THE COSTUMES

Look at the sketches for costumes for Hester and Johnnie (Figure 7.4). Discuss which ones you think the actor and actress playing Johnnie and Hester should wear. Why?

Figure 7.4 Costumes for Hester and Johnnie

ACTIVITY 4: SOME BACKGROUND

Look at the extract from the notebook of the playwright, Athol Fugard, who wrote *Hello and Goodbye*. While you read it discuss any words you don't know with another student or look them up in the dictionary.

> 16/9/63
> Last night before sleep, found myself thinking about Johnnie – the local street-corner derelict I made a few notes about some months back. I remembered a thought I had about a sister and suddenly I saw very
> 5 clearly the germinal situation of a play. Thinking about it this morning I am again excited.
>   Johnnie is living with his father in a two-room shack in Valley Road. The father is blind and a cripple . . . victim of a blasting accident when he worked for the South African Railways. Johnnie looks after him –
> 10 feeding, washing, dressing, carrying. They exist on an old man's pension – old age or disability. One night, after ten or fifteen years absence, his sister arrives back unexpectedly at the little house. All she possesses in the world she has with her in an old and battered suitcase. Her purpose is revealed. She believes the old man was paid 'hundreds
> 15 of pounds' compensation by the S.A.R. for the accident. It is in a box under his bed. She wants the money. Is ready to steal. Eventually, even prepared to kill the old man to get it. None of these possibilities happens. She leaves Johnnie and the old man together.
>
>   (from Athol Fugard, *Boesman and Lena and other plays*, Oxford University Press, 1985, p. xiv.)

In the final version of the play, Johnnie's father is already dead when Hester comes looking for the money, but the basic plot is the same as that mentioned in Fugard's notebooks. Now that you are familiar with the story of *Hello and Goodbye*, think again about the characters, the set and the costumes. Do you still imagine the characters, sets and costumes in the same way? Or would you change how you see them? If there is time, try acting out the dialogue again – would you do it any differently this time?

Task 14

In this section, we considered how to use an extract from a play as oral practice for students. We also thought about some ways in which the costumes, sets and gestures and movement of the actors could be incorporated into classroom activities. Can you think of any other ways of exploiting these aspects of a play with your students? A few more will be mentioned in Section 7.9.

7.7   Using play extracts with lower levels

Although plays are used most often with intermediate or advanced level students, extracts can also be used at lower levels as well. Here is an extract from Harold Pinter's *The Dumb Waiter*.

Read Extract D and think about a few ways you might exploit it with students at lower levels.

TEXT D

	BEN:	What's that?
	GUS:	I don't know.
	BEN:	Where did it come from?
	GUS:	Under the door.
5	BEN:	Well, what is it?
	GUS:	I don't know. (*They stare at it.*)
	BEN:	Pick it up.
	GUS:	What do you mean?
	BEN:	Pick it up!
10	GUS:	(*Slowly moves towards it, bends and picks it up.*) What is it?
	GUS:	An envelope.
	BEN:	Is there anything on it?
	GUS:	No.
	BEN:	Is it sealed?
15	GUS:	Yes.
	BEN:	Open it.
	GUS:	What?
	BEN:	Open it! (in *Plays: One*, Methuen Paperbacks, 1960, p. 139.)

Task 15   🗝

Below are six possible activities which could be used to exploit Text D with a class of lower intermediate students. Look at the activities and then answer these questions:
a) Which one(s) of the activities would you use and why?
b) How would you order the activities to make a coherent lesson plan? Which one(s) could you use before students read the text and which one(s) after students have read the text?
c) What other possible activities could you incorporate into your lesson?

Activities to use with 'The Dumb Waiter'

ACTIVITY 1 🗝️

Working in pairs, the students read the possible descriptions of Gus and Ben and decide which one they like best. Then they write the rest of the dialogue between Gus and Ben.

a) Gus and Ben are two brothers, who share the same house. They are getting old now, and cannot always see or hear very well. Ben is older than Gus and likes to tell him what to do.

b) Gus and Ben work in the same office together. Ben is the boss and likes telling Gus what to do.

c) Gus and Ben are two hired killers who work together. They are nervously waiting for their instructions about who they must kill next.

d) Gus and Ben are two students who share the same room. Gus is very quiet and shy, but Ben is very confident.

ACTIVITY 2

The teacher brings three or four packages into the classroom which contain small objects, perhaps objects which are fairly unusual. For variety include an envelope, something wrapped like a gift, something in a carrier bag, etc. The students have to try to guess what is in each package by asking questions about the objects. The teacher is only allowed to provide one-word answers to the questions. Before starting this activity, you may wish to revise any questions that the students might find useful, for example, 'Where does it come from?' and 'What's it made of?'

ACTIVITY 3

When the students have finished writing the dialogue in Activity 1, each pair reads it out aloud to the class who have to guess which one of the descriptions of Gus and Ben the pair chose before completing the dialogue.

ACTIVITY 4

Students in pairs look at the pictures in Figure 7.5 and discuss which picture best fits the dialogue.

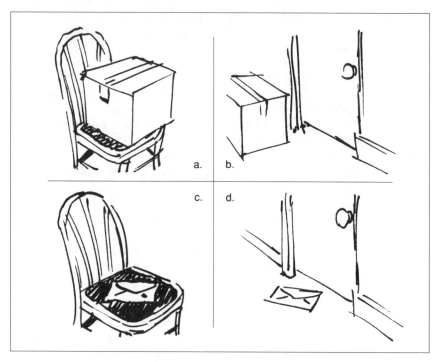

Figure 7.5 Illustrations for 'The Dumb Waiter' – Activity 4

ACTIVITY 5 🔑

Students do the following exercise:
1. Complete the dialogues below by inserting one of these phrases:
   - What do you mean?
   - What?

   a) SUE: Look, Jim, I think you're a lovely person, but I don't think things are going very well between us at the moment.
      JIM: ....
      SUE: Well, I think it's better if we don't see each other any more.

   b) MARIA: Where did you put the butter?
      PETE: ....
      MARIA: If you turn off the television, you'll be able to hear me!

   c) BILLY: We won, we won the match!
      BILLY'S MOTHER: ....
      BILLY: Yes, I know . . . it's a great surprise!

   d) MS KELLY: I don't think I can stay late to work anymore.
      MR YOUNG: ....
      MS KELLY: Well, my boyfriend is starting to get suspicious.

2. We usually say 'What?' if we didn't hear what someone said, or if we are very surprised by what someone says. We usually say 'What do you mean?' if we don't really understand what someone means, and we want them to explain more clearly what they mean. How are these two phrases used in the text from the play? Does this tell you anything about the characters or their relationship?

ACTIVITY 6

Working in pairs, try to complete the following text about Gus and Ben. Use your imagination!

Gus and Ben are ....

They live ....

Gus is ....

Ben is ....

One day ....

....

So ....

....

....

7.8 Anticipating student problems

We have already looked at a number of tasks and activities for exploiting an extract from a play with students. But before deciding what kind of activities and tasks are to be used with students, it is important, when planning your lesson, to try to anticipate some of the difficulties they may have with a particular text. The tasks and activities you use in the lesson can then be adapted to help overcome some of these problems. Below is a checklist of some possible questions which might be useful.

Checklist for anticipating student problems

THE BACKGROUND TO THE TEXT

- Will you need to give students a summary of the plot leading up to the text you are using, or can the context be easily inferred?
- Is there any cultural or historical information students will need to have in order to make sense of the text?
- Is it useful to know anything about the author's life or other works?
- Do students need to know what genre the play is in order to make sense of it?

Materials design and lesson planning: Plays

– Are there any words or phrases in the text which will be unfamiliar to students? Should you preteach these? If so, which ones? Or should you encourage the students to check the meaning in a dictionary or provide exercises to help students deduce the meaning from context?
– Are there any grammatical structures or functional areas which are not familiar to students? Should you preteach these or focus on them after students have read the text?
– Are there any discoursal features of the text that might cause students difficulty; for example, sudden changes of topic, characters meaning something different to what they are saying, etc.? Does the dialogue seem to follow the usual norms of conversation, or does it disrupt these (as in many modern or Absurdist plays where there often seems to be little logic in the way characters respond to each other)?
– Is there anything unusual or non-standard about the language of the text? For example, is it written in rather dated or old-fashioned language? Slang? Does it use any dialect words?
– Are any rhetorical or literary devices used which may be difficult for students to understand (e.g. complicated metaphors, apostrophe, synecdoche, etc.)?
– Are there any particular features of pronunciation which the extract could be used to pinpoint?

MOTIVATING AND INVOLVING STUDENTS

– How can the theme or topic of the extract be made relevant to the students' own experience? By providing questions for discussion? By asking students to complete a questionnaire? By asking students to think of situations they know which are similar to the one in the text?
– In what skill do students need the most practice, and how could the text be used to help them with that skill?
– What activities would most suit the learning style of the students? Working on their own with a dictionary? Working in pairs? Being asked to memorise sections from a dialogue? Being asked to give a personal opinion in English?

What other questions could you add to this list?

Applying the checklist

Figure 7.6 is a text from Shakespeare's *Julius Caesar*. It has been annotated using the checklist above. Some of the possible difficulties for students when studying the text have been underlined or circled. A few notes have been made about the possible problems and ideas for classroom activities (Figure 7.7). After you have read it, try to do the same on an extract of your own choosing.

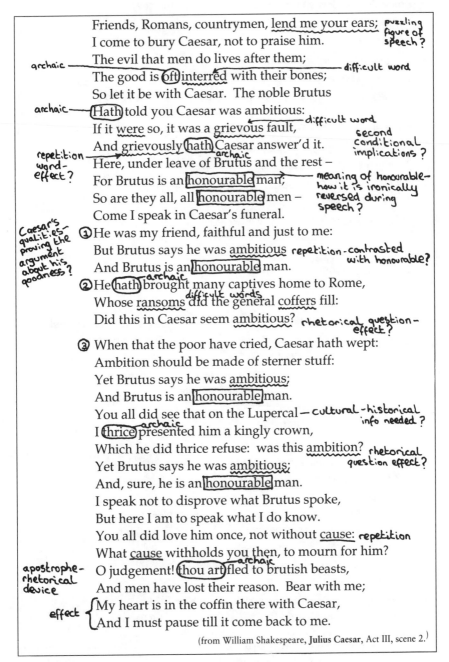

Friends, Romans, countrymen, <u>lend me your ears;</u> *puzzling figure of speech?*
I come to bury Caesar, not to praise him.
The evil that men do lives after them; — *archaic*
The good is (oft) interrèd with their bones; *difficult word*
So let it be with Caesar. The noble Brutus
(Hath) told you Caesar was ambitious: — *archaic*
If it <u>were</u> so, it was a grievous fault, *difficult word*
And grievously (hath) Caesar answer'd it. *second conditional implications?* *archaic*
Here, under leave of Brutus and the rest — *repetition word-effect?*
For Brutus is an |honourable| man; *meaning of honourable — how it is ironically reversed during speech?*
So are they all, all |honourable| men —
Come I speak in Caesar's funeral.
① He was my friend, faithful and just to me: *Caesar's qualities — proving the argument about his goodness?*
But Brutus says he was <u>ambitious</u> *repetition — contrasted with honourable?*
And Brutus is an |honourable| man.
② He (hath) brought many captives home to Rome, *archaic*
Whose <u>ransoms</u> did the general <u>coffers</u> fill: *difficult words*
Did this in Caesar seem <u>ambitious</u>? *rhetorical question — effect?*
③ When that the poor have cried, Caesar hath wept:
Ambition should be made of sterner stuff:
Yet Brutus says he was <u>ambitious</u>;
And Brutus is an |honourable| man.
You all did see that on the Lupercal — *cultural-historical info needed?*
I (thrice) presented him a kingly crown, *archaic*
Which he did thrice refuse: was this <u>ambition</u>? *rhetorical question effect?*
Yet Brutus says he was <u>ambitious</u>;
And, sure, he is an |honourable| man.
I speak not to disprove what Brutus spoke,
But here I am to speak what I do know.
You all did love him once, not without <u>cause</u>: *repetition*
What <u>cause</u> withholds you then, to mourn for him? *archaic*
O judgement! (thou art) fled to brutish beasts, *apostrophe — rhetorical device*
And men have lost their reason. Bear with me;
{ My heart is in the coffin there with Caesar, *effect*
{ And I must pause till it come back to me.

(from William Shakespeare, **Julius Caesar**, Act III, scene 2.)

Figure 7.6 Mark Antony's speech to the Romans – annotated

157

Level of class: LATE–INTERMEDIATE/ADVANCED

Possible problems with the background to the text:

1 _Understanding plot_ up to this point - death of Caesar, role of Brutus, Mark Antony, etc.
2 _Historical background_ - Roman Empire, system of government, role of Caesar, class system, etc.
3 _Setting_ for the speech - What Mark Antony is aiming to do

Possible problems with the language:

1 _Difficult vocabulary_, e.g. grievous, interred, coffers, etc.
2 _Archaic words_ - hath, oft, etc.
3 _Rhetorical/literary features_ - repetition, apostrophe, rhetorical questions, etc.
4 _Irony_ - changing meaning of "honourable"?
5 Following _stages of speech_ - proof of Caesar's goodness, appeal to emotions, etc.
6 Uses of _conditional_ - implication?

Ways of motivating students:

1 _Involving_ students in _human dilemma_ - Mark Antony's plea for a friend?
2 _Modern day politicians_ - tricks and campaigns? Discussion
3 _Importance of reading skills_ - a) for gist
                                         b) understanding meaning from context
                                         c) silent reading using dictionaries.

Ideas for classroom activities

1 Planning Mark Antony's political campaign in groups. What arguments will he use to persuade crowd?
2 Read text - what arguments does he use? (gist)
3 Close study of language:
   a) multiple choice questions for difficult vocabulary?
   b) Discussion: meaning **ambitious**
                              honourable
   c) Modern English equivalents for archaisms?
   d) literary aspects - effect?
4 **Follow-up** - write newspaper article describing speech in style of
   • a tabloid paper
   • a serious paper?

Figure 7.7 Notes on possible problems with Mark Antony's speech

7.9 Further activities for play extracts

In the previous section we considered the kinds of problems it is useful to try to anticipate when preparing a lesson based on an extract from a play. In this chapter, we have already looked at quite a few tasks and activities for exploiting extracts from plays in the classroom. Here are some more tasks and activities you could use after you have predicted some of the difficulties students might have with a text. For convenience, they have been divided into four main categories:

– Pre-reading activities
– Activities for increasing students' language awareness
– Activities for practising oral skills
– Follow-up and extension activities

Obviously, there is some overlap between the different categories. For example, while doing a task which encourages fluency, students may also be expanding their vocabulary. An activity used to stimulate students' interest in a text before they read it might equally be used as a discussion task after they have read the text.

Pre-reading activities

1. Students are given the situation in the extract – the setting, relationships between characters, etc. They develop their own roleplay around it.
2. The teacher outlines the social, political or historical background to the play. The students take notes.
3. The teacher explains what the genre is of the play the extract is taken from (e.g. farce, melodrama, comedy of manners, Absurdist play, etc.). The students make predictions about the play.
4. Students are given four lines from the play. They decide which characters are speaking the lines and in what setting. They then improvise the rest of the dialogue.

Activities for increasing language awareness

1. Students are asked to identify what language function is fulfilled by the different lines in the text – is a particular line an apology, threat, promise, etc.? (This works particularly well with Pinter's plays where the characters' utterances are so often ambiguous.)
2. Students compare two extracts – the original of a non-contemporary play and a version of it written in modern English. They try to pinpoint differences in grammar and vocabulary, and the effects conveyed by these. (This works particularly well with Shakespeare.)

3. Students compare a text in their own language with two different translations into English. They decide which translation they like the most and why.
4. Students are divided into two groups (if you are using an extract which only involves two characters). One group is given all the lines spoken by character A only, and has to write the responses of character B themselves. The other group is given the lines of character B only, and has to write the missing lines for character A. The groups then compare their version with the original lines spoken by both characters. (This can also be done with three groups using an extract involving three characters.)

Activities for practising oral skills

1. Students mark out the text for word stress and sentence stress. They then read it aloud, paying special attention to its emotional meaning.
2. Students annotate the different lines in the text by describing *how* the line should be said, for example, coldly, aggressively, with a sneer, in a loving voice, etc. (If necessary you could supply them with a list to choose from.) They then read the lines out aloud, keeping as closely as possible to these annotations. Other pairs or groups try to guess what the annotations were.
3. Students discuss the characters in the text by answering a short questionnaire about them. The questions might include:
   – Which character do you most admire? Why?
   – Which character do you find the least appealing? Why?
   – For which character do you have the most sympathy? Why?
4. Students are divided into groups, each with a different extract from the same play. The groups write five questions about the text they have been given. They rehearse reading it out aloud, and then either perform it for the class or record it so that the recording can be played to the class. The other students then answer the questions which have been set. When all the questions on all the texts have been answered, the students try to piece together the full story in the play. They can do this by thinking of questions to ask the teacher, who should be able to supply the answers!
5. Students are each asked to bring three accessories to the lesson (these could include different kinds of hats, umbrellas, jewellery, scarves, handbags, walking sticks, belts etc.). In pairs or groups they rehearse a scene from a play, and then choose accessories for each character before performing the scene in front of the class.
6. Students are given a dialogue from a play and asked to rehearse reading or saying it aloud. They should aim to make it sound as close to real everyday conversation as possible. (E.g. they should hesitate,

interrupt each other, stammer, use phrases like 'sort of' or 'you know', repeat themselves and so on.)

7. Students in groups act out an extract from a play, paying special attention to gestures and movement – how far characters stand from each other, how they use their hands, if they touch each other at all, etc. At various points during the performance, the teacher stops the action and asks other students in the class to comment on these metalinguistic features. Would it be more appropriate to their roles, for example, for students to be standing further apart? For one to be standing and the other sitting? For one character to be slouching forward while the other looms over them, etc.? (This activity only works in classes which are very relaxed with each other, or where the students acting out the roles are very confident and don't feel inhibited by being interrupted.)

Follow-up and extension activities

1. Students discuss a series of controversial statements about the theme/topic of the extract.

2. The students discuss the theme or subject of the play in light of their own experience. For example, if a play is about the problems which arise between parents and children, then students could be asked what they think causes conflict between parents and children, and how these conflicts might be resolved.

3. Students in groups or pairs invent mini-biographies for the characters in a play by imagining a past for them. These are then read aloud to the class and compared.

4. The teacher plays students three or four short pieces of music. In groups they decide which one they would choose as their 'theme tune' if they were filming the extract from the play.

5. Students discuss the values and world-view which are either implicitly or explicitly expressed in the text. Do they agree with them?

What other activities or tasks could you add to these lists?

7.10   Using a whole play with students

In this chapter we have concentrated mainly on using selected extracts from plays with students. But you may find that you need, or want, to use a whole play with your students. In this section we look briefly at activities which can help to provide students with a skeleton outline for understanding a whole play.[4] This skeleton can be used in one of two ways:

1. Students could be asked to read the whole play at home over a period of a few weeks. This would solve the problem of insufficient class time to read the play. The activities or tasks from the skeleton outline could be used at various points in class to ensure that students have a basic grasp of the plot, themes and characters in the play. The use of these activities could be interspersed with some of the tasks and activities described in the previous section (7.9) in order to practise students' oral skills and increase their language awareness.

2. The activities in the skeleton outline could be used in one or two preparation sessions before students attend a live performance of a play or see a film of it. Students would not necessarily need to read the play before going to the performance. The aim of the activities used in class would be to prepare students for the basic plot, characters and themes of the play so that they would be free, while watching it, to concentrate on understanding the language of the play and possibly some of its more subtle nuances. The activities themselves would not aim to help the students directly with the language of the play. But a sense of anticipation and interest in the play should be created by these activities.

Task 16

Think about a group of students with whom you are planning to or would like to use a whole play. Then complete the following information:

Level of students: ....

Name of play to be used: ....

Purpose of activities/tasks to be devised: (please tick either A or B)

A. To guide students in their extensive reading of a play by providing classroom activities which check and reinforce their comprehension of the text.

B. To prepare students for a live performance of a play by providing them with a skeleton outline of the plot, themes and characters in the play.

Classroom hours available to work on play: ....

Homework hours available to read play: ....

When you have completed the information above, look at the following chart. Each section lists a typical problem that students might experience when reading or viewing an entire play. Jot down any ideas you may have for a task or activity you could use with the group of students you described to help them overcome this problem.

Problem	Tasks and activities to overcome the problems
Understanding the genre of the play	
Understanding the setting/ social milieu of the play	
Understanding the characters and their relationships	
Understanding the plot	
Understanding the main themes of the play	

When you have jotted down your own ideas read through the following list of tasks and activities. Some of them will be suitable for checking and reinforcing students' overall comprehension while or after reading a play, some will be better used as preparation for a theatre visit. Some could be used for both these purposes. While you go through the list select any activities you feel would be suitable for use with your own students in order to overcome the problems listed in the chart.

Tasks to help students before reading/seeing a whole play

UNDERSTANDING THE GENRE OF THE PLAY

1. Students are told what genre the play is, and are then given a list of characteristics commonly associated with this genre. What expectations do they now have of the play? For example, if the play is described as a 'fable' will they expect some kind of moral lesson? They could also be asked to think of examples of that genre in their own language.
2. Students are given a list of characteristics of different genres all jumbled up. Which ones do they find exemplified in the play?

Materials design and lesson planning: Plays

UNDERSTANDING THE SETTING/SOCIAL MILIEU OF THE PLAY

1. Students are given the playwright's description of the setting of the play and asked to jot down any associations it has for them, or any expectations they may have of what the play could be about.
2. Students are given a short reading/listening comprehension about the social or historical background to the play and asked to discuss it.

UNDERSTANDING THE CHARACTERS AND THEIR RELATIONSHIPS

1. Students are given the list of characters from the play with a very brief description of each one. They are asked to imagine a past life for each character and to guess how they are connected with each other.
2. Students are given a sociogram to fill in which illustrates the main characters and their relationships to each other. Figure 7.8 shows a sociogram based on a play by Arthur Miller called *The Man Who Had All the Luck*.

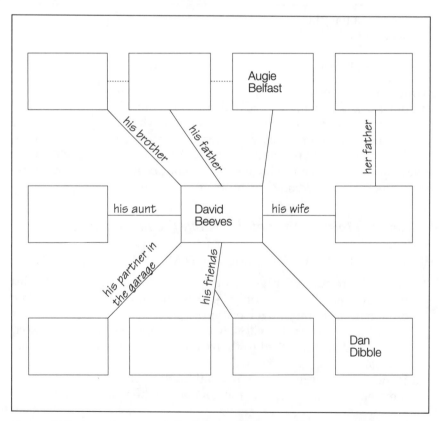

Figure 7.8 A sociogram of the relationships in 'The Man Who Had All the Luck'

3. Students are given a list of descriptive adjectives and asked to describe each character using one of the adjectives.

UNDERSTANDING THE PLOT

1. Students are given a summary of the first few scenes of the play and asked to predict what will follow this. They check their predictions against their reading/viewing of the play.
2. Students are given a list of jumbled sentences which summarise the plot of the play. They have to put the sentences in the correct order.

UNDERSTANDING THE THEMES OF THE PLAY

1. Students are asked to discuss certain quotations by the playwright which point to the main themes of the play.
2. Students are given an extract from the play with phrases or sentences pertaining to the main themes of the play underlined. They are then asked to discuss the issues arising from the underlined sections.

Task 17

Now think of any tasks or activities you could use with students after they have read or seen the play. Write down your ideas, and then compare them with the list below.

Tasks to use after reading the play

1. Students select a few episodes of the play to act out. They write a summary linking these episodes which is delivered by a narrator. This playlet is then performed for other students.
2. Students in groups design a poster or advertisement for the play for other students to read.

Tasks to use after seeing the play

1. Classroom discussion on any aspect of the play that the students found difficult to follow.
2. Students read different authentic reviews of the play and decide with which ones they most agree.
3. Students write their own reviews of the play.

Endnotes

1. In exploring this idea I was helped by reading an unpublished M.A. dissertation by J. R. Smith, *Stylistics and the pedagogic implications for dialogue in drama and text books* (M.A. in Language and Literature in Education (TESOL), September 1985, London University Institute of Education).
2. For a more detailed discussion of some features of conversational language relevant to the dialogue in plays see Chapter 8 'Some Aspects of Dialogue' in Fowler (1986). A thorough discussion of discourse analysis and its application to dramatic texts is contained in Short (1981).
3. A breakdown of some of these non-verbal features of communication is provided in Genelle G. Morain, 'Kinesics and cross-cultural understanding' in Valdes (1986).
4. For a full discussion of the wide range of tasks and activities that can be used to exploit a whole play see Collie, J. and Slater, S. (1987) Chapter 8.

Suggestions for further reading

On the discourse in drama

Fowler, R. (1986) *Linguistic Criticism*, Chapter 8.
Short, M. H. (1981) 'Discourse Analysis and the Analysis of Drama', *Applied Linguistics*, 2, 2.

On practical ideas for using plays in the classroom

Collie, J. and Slater, S. (1987) *Literature in the Language Classroom*, Chapter 8.
Wessels, C. (1987) *Drama*.

Classroom materials

Shackleton, M. (ed.) (1985) *Double Act*.

See also the list of plays in Collie, J. and Slater, S. (1987) *Literature in the Language Classroom*, p. 262.

8 Reflecting on the literature lesson

In this book so far, we have looked at some of the issues underlying the use of literature in the language classroom, possible approaches towards using literature, and a range of tasks and activities. In this chapter we turn our attention to the actual teaching of the lesson and ways of reflecting on this process. This reflection should then help you to change or modify what you do, when necessary. The chapter also discusses the value of classroom observation – whether you are observing an experienced teacher on video, you are being observed yourself, or you are 'sitting in' on the lesson of a colleague or friend.

8.1 Thinking about observation

At some stage in their professional careers, most teachers will have observed or been observed teaching a lesson. The following question-naire helps you to focus on your own experiences.

Personal experience

Please identify the statements which apply to you.

REASONS I HAVE OBSERVED ANOTHER TEACHER IN MY CAREER

To assess the progress of the teacher (in my capacity as director of studies, senior teacher, etc.).
To write a report on which that teacher's promotion will depend.
To watch one particular language student in the class.
To gain new insights which will help me to improve my own teaching skills.
To learn more about classroom interaction.
To learn about a class I was going to take over.
To help the teacher as part of a training course.
To learn a new activity or technique.
To check the physical factors in the room (e.g. acoustics).

REASONS I HAVE BEEN OBSERVED IN MY PROFESSIONAL CAREER

To be assessed on a training course.
To be assessed for promotion.
To help in the training of novice teachers.
To be helped in solving a problem (e.g. with a student, by a colleague or director of studies).

To share a new idea/activity with a colleague.

To let a colleague see a class that she/he is going to take over.

To gain new insights into my teaching by reflecting on it with an observer.

MY FEELINGS ABOUT OBSERVATION

1. How do you feel about observing other teachers?
2. Do your feelings change depending on the reasons for observing them?
3. How do you feel about being observed?
4. Do your feelings change depending on the reasons for being observed?

Observing for professional development

In the questionnaire above we pinpointed some of the reasons why people observe lessons or are observed teaching. However, in this chapter we focus on a single major reason for observation – the continuing professional development of ourselves and our colleagues. This includes all those kinds of observation which are done to observe the behaviour of a class or individual student, to share ideas or activities, to try to improve our own teaching and to develop our teaching skills and abilities.

Observation can have a very important developmental function. It can help us to become more aware of what we do in the classroom, and what our students are doing. It can help us to gain deeper insights into what happens in class and to reflect on our own teaching practice so that we can set our future goals more clearly and realistically (Williams, 1989, p. 85).

Observation can also help us to make the distinction between 'ritual teaching behaviour' and 'principled teaching behaviour' (Maingay, 'Observation for Training, Development or Assessment?', in T. Duff (ed.), 1988, pp. 118–119). 'Ritual teaching behaviour' is based on unthinking and automatic procedures which have become divorced from any principled awareness of why they are being used. 'Principled teaching behaviour', on the other hand, involves a self-reflective awareness of the principles behind the way we do things. By thinking about our own lessons, or observing those of other people, we can ensure that our lessons involve 'principled teaching behaviour'.

How we observe our own lessons and those of our colleagues is of crucial importance in helping us to develop professionally. In order to reflect in a principled way on lessons we have taught, or those we observe, we need to examine the data or evidence that we find in these lessons and draw conclusions from it. This is often difficult to do since our own judgements and prejudices can interfere with the process of recording what has happened in a lesson. Of course no observation can ever be entirely free of the judgements or values of the observer, but it is useful for our professional development if we can at least try to stand back a little from these in order to gain a fresh perspective on our teaching practice.

In this chapter you will find a series of observation tasks which are intended to help you reflect in a principled manner on the way in which you or other teachers have used literature in a language lesson. The aim of many of these tasks is to help both the observer and the person being observed to focus on any recordable data or evidence that they find in the lesson and from this evidence to reach certain conclusions about the effectiveness of different aspects of a lesson. Reflecting on observable evidence in the lesson can help both the observer and the person observed to develop greater insights into their own teaching, and may spark off new and creative ideas about alternative ways of doing things.

The observation tasks in this chapter can be used in a number of different ways. You can use them yourself to think about your own teaching, taking the roles of both 'teacher' and 'observer'. One useful procedure for this is to record all or part of your lesson on audio or video cassette for analysis later. Or you could simply use the observation task to guide you in your reflections on your lesson.

Another way of using the tasks is to discuss them with someone (e.g. a trainer or colleague) who has observed your lesson. This observer could be particularly helpful in gathering data for you so that in the discussion following the lesson you can jointly suggest solutions to any of the problems that came up in the lesson.

Alternatively, you can use the tasks to observe another teacher's lesson – whether this is a colleague 'micro-teaching' or your trainer teaching your own group. Your role here would be to make notes about certain aspects of the lesson so that you and the person being observed can reflect on these and any new insights they provide.[1]

There are two important points to bear in mind while using these observation tasks. Firstly, since the subject of this book is the use of literature in the language classroom, all the tasks are concerned directly with this, rather than with more general teaching techniques or prac-tices.[2] Secondly, you may find it useful to use a particular task after you have read or studied a specific chapter or section of this book, so that you get an opportunity to experiment in the classroom with some of the ideas discussed in that part of the book. For example, Task 3 which focusses on dealing with linguistic problems in the literature lesson could be used after you have read Sections 2.2 and 2.3 which address this topic.

8.2 General observation of the literature lesson

The observation task which follows can be used to focus very generally on a lesson using literature. It should help you to plan your lesson as well as to reflect on the teaching of it. You can either use it by yourself or you can discuss it with an observer who has taken notes during your lesson.

Observation task 1: Getting an overview of the lesson

BEFORE THE LESSON

Ask yourself:
1. What are your aims in this lesson?
2. What text have you chosen and why?
3. What tasks and activities have you devised and why?
4. What opportunities have you provided for students to participate and respond personally to the text?

DURING AND AFTER THE LESSON

Ask yourself:
1. What evidence was there that the students found the text interesting and relevant/boring and irrelevant?
2. What evidence was there that your tasks and activities helped students to understand and enjoy the text?
3. Did you notice any examples of students participating and responding personally to the text? What helped them to do this?
4. Do you think you achieved your aims in this lesson? Why?
5. What did you learn from doing this lesson? How would you like to improve/develop the way in which you use literature in future lessons?

8.3 Micro-tasks for reflecting on specific areas of teaching

The following tasks are intended to help you focus on specific aspects of using literature in the language classroom. You can choose what task you would like to use, or you would like an observer to use, depending on which area you wish to think about. You can use some of the tasks yourself to think about a lesson both while you are planning it and after you have taught it. Other tasks are best used in discussion with an observer. You might also like to use each task during or after reading particular sections of this book.

Observation task 2: Experimenting with different approaches

This task can be used in conjunction with Chapter 2.

BEFORE THE LESSON

Ask yourself:
1. What text(s) have you chosen to use with students and why?
2. What approach have you chosen to exploit this/these text(s)? What are your reasons for doing so?
3. How have you staged your tasks and activities? Why?
4. What do you hope your students will learn from this lesson?
5. How does the lesson fit in with your scheme of work? What lesson preceded it? What lesson will follow it?

DURING AND AFTER THE LESSON

Ask yourself:
1. What evidence was there that the text(s) you have chosen was/were suitable for the students?
2. What evidence was there that the approach you used was appropriate?
3. What evidence was there that your tasks and activities were staged appropriately?
4. What do you think that your students learned from this lesson? Was this what you intended?
5. What do you plan to do in your next lesson? Why?
6. What have you learnt from this lesson? What ideas, activities, techniques, procedures would you like to try out in your next lesson?

Observation task 3: Dealing with linguistic problems

This task could be used in conjunction with Sections 2.2 and 2.3 and is probably best discussed with an observer.

BEFORE THE LESSON

1. Note down any linguistic problems you think that students might have with the text you have chosen.
2. How do you intend to help them with these problems?

Reflecting on the literature lesson

1. Note down any evidence that students were having linguistic problems with the text, for example, difficulties in:
   - understanding the meaning(s) of a word or phrase
   - understanding and appreciating textual ambiguities
   - understanding and appreciating any figurative meanings in the text
   - understanding and appreciating any rhetorical devices
   - coping with unusual language use (e.g. archaisms, dialect, etc.)
2. Note down any strategies that were used to help the students with these difficulties, for example:
   - encouraging students to use dictionaries and glossaries
   - encouraging students to infer meaning from context
   - explanation
   - translation
   - providing exercises and activities which explore the language

AFTER THE LESSON

Look at the notes made about the lesson together. What have you both learned from them? Can you suggest any other ways of helping students with linguistic difficulties when using a literary text?

Observation task 4: Dealing with cultural problems

See Chapter 4.

BEFORE THE LESSON

1. Make a note of any cultural difficulties that you think students may experience when reading or studying the text(s) you have chosen.
2. In what ways will you help them to overcome these difficulties?

WHILE YOU OBSERVE/AFTER YOU HAVE TAUGHT THIS LESSON

1. Note down any evidence that students were having cultural difficulties with the text.
2. What techniques or strategies were used to help the students overcome these problems?
3. Can you think of any other techniques or strategies for helping students cope with cultural aspects in the text?

Observation task 5: Involving students personally in the reading

See Section 2.5. This task needs to be used with an observer.

BEFORE THE LESSON

1. What text have you chosen to use with the students and why?
2. Note down any ways in which you intend to involve the students personally in the lesson so that they can discuss their own opinions and feelings about the literary text.

DURING THE LESSON

Record, under the following two headings, any ways in which the teacher involved the students personally in the lesson and/or gave them opportunities to discuss their own feelings and opinions:

What the teacher did	Students' response

AFTER THE LESSON

Look at the notes taken during the lesson together and then think about these questions:
1. What evidence was there that the text chosen in this lesson was relevant and appropriate to the students?
2. What evidence was there that the tasks and activities devised by the teacher encouraged student participation and involvement in the lesson?
3. Can you think of any other useful ideas or techniques for encouraging student participation and involvement in a lesson using literary texts?

Observation task 6: Guiding students towards an interpretation

See Section 1.3. This task should be discussed with an observer.

BEFORE THE LESSON

1. What text(s) have you chosen to use with your students and why? Note down any problems you think your students might have in making an interpretation of the text.

Reflecting on the literature lesson

2. Note down any ways in which you could help your students to make their own interpretation(s) of the text you are going to use with them.

WHILE YOU OBSERVE THE LESSON

Note down any examples of the following ways in which the teacher helped the students to make their own interpretation(s) of the text:

	Task/Method	Student response
1. The teacher guided the students towards a basic comprehension of the text.		
2. The teacher encouraged the students to draw on their own knowledge and experiences when making sense of the text.		
3. The teacher encouraged the students to infer unstated meanings and 'read between the lines' where necessary.		
4. The teacher encouraged students to reach their own interpretation of the text rather than relying on a 'correct' or standard one.		
5. The teacher encouraged students to provide reasoned arguments for their interpretation.		
6. Any other ways?		

AFTER THE LESSON

Look at the notes made during the lesson together and think about these questions:
1. What evidence was there in the lesson that students were helped and encouraged to reach their own interpretations of the text?
2. What techniques or activities seemed helpful for doing this?

3. Can you think of any other activities, tasks or techniques for fostering student self-confidence in interpreting literary texts?

Observation task 7: Providing useful background information

See Section 2.4. This task is best discussed with an observer.
By background information is meant historical, literary, biographical, social facts, etc. which are relevant for understanding the text.

BEFORE THE LESSON

1. What background information do you plan to present in this lesson?
2. How do you plan to present it?

DURING THE LESSON

Record how the teacher presented the background information in the lesson. Construct a table with the following headings and fill in the columns while you observe:

Background information presented	Technique/Method for presenting it	Students' response

AFTER THE LESSON

Look at the notes taken during the lesson together and think about these questions:
1. Was there any evidence that the background information presented in the lesson was relevant/irrelevant to students and helped to make the text accessible/inaccessible?
2. Was there any evidence that the way in which the background was presented was appropriate to both the text and the students?
3. How did students seem to react to the background information provided in the lesson? Why do you think this was so?
4. How would you use background information next time? In the same way or differently? Write down any other ideas you have for how it could be used in the literature class.

Observation task 8: Matching the aims of observer and teacher

This task is to be done by an observer who can then compare the table that has been filled in with the teacher's lesson plan.[3] The observer's notes can then be discussed with the teacher after the lesson, concentrating on any reasons for the differences between the plan and the lesson.

DURING THE LESSON

Construct a table using the headings below and, while you observe the lesson, fill in the columns. Then compare this record of your observation with the teacher's lesson plan. How are they the same? How are they different? If there are any differences or discrepancies can you suggest a reason?

Activity/Task	Aims	Changes/Differences

8.4 Observing a student

It is sometimes instructive to focus on one particular student when observing a lesson, since this can enable the observer to pay close attention to a single learner – an activity that is usually impossible for the classroom teacher. The following two tasks are intended to be used to focus in detail on the individual learner. You can make use of the student questionnaire in Observation task 9 either before or after observing a lesson and completing Observation task 10.

Observation task 9: Interviewing a student

Record the following information about the student you wish to observe. You can either do this by asking questions directly or by gleaning the information in an informal chat.

Name
Nationality
Mother tongue
Level
Reasons for learning English
Number of years spent studying English
Hobbies/interests

Favourite type of reading matter in mother tongue
Favourite authors in mother tongue (if applicable)
Knowledge of literature in mother tongue
Experience of reading literature in English
Favourite authors in English (if applicable)
Interest in reading/using literature in English
Areas an English student most wants to improve (e.g. grammar, vocabulary, reading, listening, etc.)

Observation task 10: Observing a student in the literature class

Note down the following information as you observe your chosen student during a lesson.

1. Note down any evidence that the text(s) used in the lesson seemed relevant to the student's interests.
2. Note down any evidence that the tasks and activities for exploiting the text(s) seemed relevant and challenging to the student.
3. Note down any evidence that the student was having difficulties with any:
   - linguistic features in the text
   - cultural aspects of the text
   - literary aspects of the text (for example, rhetorical devices, figurative language, etc.)
   - other aspects of the text

   Note down any ways in which the teacher was able to help the student with these problems.
4. To what extent did the student participate in the lesson? Can you suggest any reasons for this?
5. What do you think the student learned in this lesson? How useful do you think this would be for the student.
6. Bearing in mind what you may already know about the student or what you guessed from observing him/her, write down some ideas for ways in which the teacher could make the lessons using literature of the greatest benefit to this student. You might like to think about such things as the type of skills being practised, the texts used, the type of tasks and activities, the overall approach to using literature, the match between the student's learning style and the activities in the lesson, opportunities for the student to study further on their own.

8.5 Other ways of monitoring your teaching

In this chapter we have provided a variety of observation tasks for use during lessons in which literature is being used. These tasks can be used by you or by a colleague to monitor your teaching. Below are a few suggestions of other ways in which you can reflect on your lessons and use these reflections as a spur for future development.

1. Keep a teaching diary or log. After each lesson you have taught, write down your thoughts and feelings about the lesson. You might wish to do this in a fairly unstructured way, allowing your thoughts to come at random. Or you could write notes after each lesson under headings such as: *What went well in the lesson? What would I like to improve? Alternative ways of doing things.*

2. Exchange lesson plans with colleagues. Let them teach your materials while you teach theirs. As well as reducing your work load, the insights and experiences of others can help to improve both your planning and your teaching.

3. Try to get as much feedback as possible from your students about which lessons/texts/approaches they found the most enjoyable and useful. You can either do this by chatting with them informally, or by providing them with questionnaires or evaluation forms to fill in either during or at the end of the course.

Endnotes

1. All the tasks in this chapter borrow much from the observation tasks in Williams (1989).
2. For a book which looks in detail at the process of observation see Wajnryb (1992).
3. I heard about this method in a workshop given by Tessa Woodward at The Teachers' Centre, International House, London and I believe she heard it from Hilary Rees-Parnall.

9 Literature and self-access

In this chapter we think about ways of encouraging our students to enjoy literature by themselves by making use of a self-access literature centre. Setting up a literature self-access centre requires planning and resources, the second of which may be in fairly short supply. But even with fairly limited resources it may be possible, with imagination and initiative, to establish a centre of some kind. We begin this chapter by describing a self-access centre and then listing some of the reasons for establishing one. In the rest of the chapter we consider ways in which a centre can be set up and how we can encourage our students to use it.

You will find that Sections 9.3 and 9.4 are best completed through role-playing with colleagues. However, if you are working through this book on your own, then reading these sections should still help you to think about some of the issues and problems involved in setting up a literature reading centre.

9.1 What is a literature self-access centre?

A literature self-access centre is a library or small collection of texts for students to read on their own with minimal supervision. The reading can be done either in class time or for homework. The self-access centre could consist of:
- literary texts such as novels, plays, short stories, anthologies of poetry and/or graded readers in a school library, from which students are encouraged to borrow on a regular basis
- a box or file of literary extracts, short stories and poems kept in the classroom and from which students select and borrow texts
- a small collection of books (novels, short story collections, poetry anthologies, etc.) which are kept in the classroom and from which students borrow regularly
- a collection of video recordings of plays or films based on novels, and audio recordings of literary texts which students are encouraged to work through on their own – perhaps after reading the original literary text.

9.2 Why have a literature self-access centre?

The following are the main reasons for taking the time and effort to establish a centre.
- To provide students with a choice of literary texts to listen to or to read

- To foster the students' enjoyment of literature
- To promote students' language acquisition
- To develop students' reading and listening skills
- To enable students to become more self-confident and independent as learners

9.3 A simulation: First meeting for planning and setting up a literature self-access centre ☆

Imagine that you are a member of a group of teachers at a school who wish to establish a self-access centre to encourage students to read or listen to literary texts. Before having your planning meeting, decide as a group on the following information about your school:

LITERATURE AND SELF-ACCESS: OUR SCHOOL

Type of school: (e.g. private language school, state secondary school, etc.)

Age of students:

Number of students:

Level of students who would use a self-access literature centre:

Resources available: (e.g. Is there already a library in the school? How much money is available to buy books? etc.)

Reasons for wanting to set up a literature self-access centre:

THE ROLES

A number of different members of staff are involved in the planning and setting up of the literature self-access centre. Each one has a slightly different perspective on how to set up and organise a centre of this kind. During your planning meeting take one of the following roles:

Headteacher

You are very keen on the idea of a literature self-access centre, but you are worried about the resources it will require and from where these will come. In the meeting with your staff get them to brainstorm ideas for getting hold of the texts you require, and if necessary for raising any money you need to do this. With your teachers decide what kind of self-access centre is the most practical and appropriate for your school – for example, a proper library or a file or box of extracts in each classroom? Finally, decide on how you could involve parents (if appropriate) and students in the setting up and use of this centre.

Director of resources

You are the member of staff in charge of all of the equipment in the school from blackboards to textbooks. From past experience, you are concerned that books and materials get easily damaged, and sometimes even disappear. You are concerned that if a literature self-access centre is set up, even on a very modest scale, everything should be done to look after it and maintain it properly. Secondly, you know that teachers and students often remain unaware of what is available for their use in a school. You feel it is important that everybody should know about what the literature self-access centre can offer, and be trained in its use. Finally, you are keen to integrate the use of different media in the self-access centre. For example, it might be possible to make available to students for self-study recordings of radio plays to be used while or after they have read the text of the play. Discuss your concerns with your colleagues and see if you can find any ways of dealing with them successfully.

Classroom teacher 1

You feel very positive about the idea of setting up a literature self-access centre, but are concerned that unless such a centre takes account of the needs and interests of your learners it will not work. With your colleagues, think about ways of selecting texts for the centre which will be relevant and motivating to students. Although the intention is to use authentic literary texts, should you also include non-literary texts? What role is there for graded readers in the project? How can you interest and motivate the students to use the centre?

Director of studies/Senior teacher

You are responsible for ensuring that the syllabus of the school is implemented. Your concern is about how the use of the literature self-access centre can be integrated into the overall timetabling of the school. With your colleagues decide how the self-access centre will be used – during class time, for homework, a combination of both, or some other way? How will the use of the centre link with the overall aims of the syllabus?

Classroom teacher 2

Your primary interest as a teacher is in developing your students' reading skills. You believe that a literature self-access centre would be of great benefit, but you are concerned about how your students will get the most from it. You believe that it is important to develop back-up materials, such as worksheets, to assist students in their reading. With your colleagues, decide what kinds of support materials need to be developed and how they would be used.

By the end of the meeting you should have planned the following:

Type of literature self-access centre to be set up:

Who will use it?

Where will the resources for it come from?

How will it be maintained in good order?

How will teachers and students be trained in its use?

How will the texts for the centre be selected?

How often will students use it? When and where?

What kinds of materials will be provided to support students in their reading?

Will any other resources (e.g. video recordings, cassette recordings, etc.) be available to use in conjunction with the reading texts?

9.4 Second meeting for planning and setting up a literature self-access centre ☆

For your next planning meeting decide which member of staff will be responsible for each task related to the setting up of the literature self-access centre. Draw up a plan of action for this or start designing any of the worksheets, questionnaires or materials you might need for the centre.

9.5 Setting up a literature self-access centre: A case study

What follows is a brief description of a literature self-access centre that was set up at a large language school for adults.[1] As you read through it, it might spark off ideas about how you can set up such a centre at your own school, even if it is a very different school from the one being described.

TYPE OF SCHOOL

A large institution combining a language school for adults and a teacher training centre, situated in central London. Adult language learners usually attend the school for between 15 and 25 hours a week for anything from one month to six months. There are over 200 students in the school at peak times.

Setting up a literature self-access centre: A case study

The school had recently decided to expand its provision for self-access learning, so that students working on their own could make use of videos, computers, language laboratories, etc. As part of this programme, it was decided to spend some of the budget on buying more books for the student library, both fiction and non-fiction. It was felt that the collection of graded readers in the library should be supplemented by a good range of authentic literary texts for students to borrow.

CHOICE OF TEXTS

Since it was envisaged that the literature self-access part of the library would be used mainly by students at upper-intermediate and advanced levels, teachers at these levels were asked to consult their students about the kinds of literary texts in English that they enjoyed or would like to see in the library. Often students said that they would like to read a particular novel if they had seen the film on which it was based, so this sometimes influenced the choice of text. Teachers were free to add their own suggestions. Other suggestions for texts were taken from published materials.[2] It was decided that a number of published materials which involve the use of literature in the language classroom would also be included on the list, particularly since many had accompanying audio material.[3] It was hoped that the list would be fairly eclectic and would cater for a variety of tastes. It was intended that it should offer something for the more academic or literary-minded student, but also include texts with more popular appeal. It was divided into the following categories:

Classics (pre 1900)

For example:

The Portrait of Dorian Gray	Oscar Wilde
Pride and Prejudice	Jane Austen

Contemporary novels

For example:

The Prime of Miss Jean Brodie	Muriel Spark
The Color Purple	Alice Walker
The Pearl	John Steinbeck
Things Fall Apart	Chinua Achebe
The Dark Room	R. K. Narayan

Thrillers and detective novels

For example:

After the Funeral	Agatha Christie
The Spy Who Came In From the Cold	John le Carré

Literature and self-access

Collections of short stories

For example:
Someone Like You	Roald Dahl
Something Out There	Nadine Gordimer
An Anthology of African and Caribbean	
Writing in English	(edited by John Figueroa)

Poetry anthologies

For example:
Old Possum's Book of Practical Cats   T. S. Eliot
(later used as the lyrics for the musical
   'Cats')

Plays

For example:
Amadeus   Peter Shaffer
Various plays by Shakespeare, some in very accessible cartoon form
(with original text).

Comics/Cartoons

For example:
When the Wind Blows   Raymond Briggs

Literary criticism

For example:
Biographies of famous authors
Cambridge Guide to Literature in English   (edited by I. Ousby)

HELPING THE STUDENTS TO CHOOSE TEXTS

It was agreed that students often needed help in selecting books to read. Obviously the advice of a librarian or class teacher is invaluable here, but further assistance for students was provided in the form of two files which students were encouraged to browse through before choosing a book.

a) A file in the library which listed all books in the literature self-access section under the following headings: Title, Author, Type of book/genre, Brief description of the book, Number of pages, Level.[4] The brief description might say something like: 'The exciting story of a young woman who travels across Australia on a camel' – just enough information to help the student decide whether the book would be of interest to them or not.

b) A comments file in which students who had read a particular book were encouraged to write down their opinion of the book in the form of a mini-review.

GUIDING THE STUDENTS' READING

Three very general worksheets were developed to encourage students in their extensive reading skills. Such worksheets could be used by students when reporting back on what books they had read, for example once a month to their class (see Section 9.6).

USING THE SELF-ACCESS LITERATURE CENTRE

Students would be free to use this section of the library at any time. Some teachers might like to build its use into their monthly timetable, for example by asking students to select one book to read over a month and then report on it to their class, using the worksheets if necessary. It was stressed that the reading should never become a chore for students – they should only persevere with texts they were enjoying.

9.6　Worksheets to guide students in their reading

On the next page are two different worksheets which students could be asked to complete depending on what kind of book they have read – either a novel or a collection of short stories, or a play. The students should be encouraged to read for gist and not to labour over every single word or phrase – the worksheets ask very general questions in an attempt to encourage extensive reading.

Task 1

After you have looked through the two worksheets on the following pages, design a similarly general worksheet for use with an anthology of poems. A sample is provided in the key at the back of the book.

SELF ACCESS WORKSHEET

I NOVELS, THRILLERS, SHORT STORIES, ETC

FACTS ABOUT THE BOOK

Title:
Author:
Type of book/genre:
When published:

CONTENT

If you have read an anthology of short stories, then answer the following questions about one story in the book.

1 Setting (where the story takes place):
2 When is it set?
3 The plot: This is a story about ....
4 Characters: Write down the names of the main characters, the role of each one in the story, and 2 or 3 adjectives to describe them.
5 Message: Does the book seem to have a 'message'? If so, what is it?

LANGUAGE

Write down 3 or 4 words, phrases or expressions you have learnt from reading this book.

OPINION

1 Choose from the following adjectives to describe the book:

light hearted gripping moving tedious gloomy amusing thought–provoking compelling well–crafted depressing

What other adjectives could you use to describe it?
2 Would you recommend this book? Why?
3 Does this book remind you of any writers or stories in your own language? If so, what?

SELF ACCESS WORKSHEET

2 PLAYS

FACTS ABOUT THE PLAY

Title:
Author (playwright):
When published:
Type of play/genre:

CONTENT

1 Setting (where the action takes place):
2 When is it set?
3 The plot: The play is about ....
4 Characters: Write down the names of the main characters, the role of each one in the story, and 2 or 3 adjectives to describe them.
5 Message: Has the play got 'a message'? If so what do you think it is?

LANGUAGE

Write down 3 or 4 words, phrases or expressions you have learnt from this play.

OPINION

1 Choose from the following adjectives to describe the play:

hilarious gripping moving powerful tedious tragic amusing

   What other adjectives could you use to describe the play?
2 The play is going to be performed and you are the director. Describe the costumes, scenery, lighting, etc. you want for each act.
3 Would you recommend this play to anyone else? Why?
4 Does this play remind you of any plays in your own language? If so, what?

Endnotes

1. This case history is based on the setting up of a self-access centre at International House, London, in 1988. The project was directed by Jim Rose, and I collaborated with him in the planning and setting up of the literature section of this centre.
2. For a list of literary texts useful for language learners see Collie and Slater (1987) p. 256.
3. Some published materials lend themselves particularly well to use in a self-access centre, for example Rossner (1988). This is a collection of short stories with accompanying glossaries, exercises, key and audio cassettes.
4. The idea for this file came from the 'Books at a glance' section in Collie and Slater (1987) p. 257.

Answer key

Chapter 1

Task 3

A6., B5., C2., D1., E7., F4., G3.

Task 7

Metaphor
the frosted wedding-cake of the ceiling (B.)
to run out of steam/her mind isn't operating (G.)
Simile
curtains . . . *like* pale flags (B.)
making a shadow . . . *as* the wind at sea (B.)
Assonance
thr*ee* gr*ey* g*ee*se (F.)
Alliteration
three *g*rey *g*eese in a *g*reen field *g*razing (F.)
*cr*unchiness redolent of fried *c*orn (E.)
Repetition of a key word or phrase
a breeze *blew* through the room, *blew* curtains . . . (B.)
Unusual syntactic patterns
Grey were the geese, and green was the grazing (F.)
Double/multiple meaning of a word
nothing between our ears (D.)
Poeticisms
girolles, odoriferously, swathed (C.) redolent of . . . (E.)
Mixing of styles/registers
Inserting 'I, formerly known, called, addressed as . . . ' in the rather chatty informality of the passage (E.)

Task 8

Repetition of a key word or phrase
songs, political speeches, slogans, advertisements
Unusual syntactic patterns
songs, political speeches, advertisements
Double/multiple meaning of a word
puns, jokes, everyday speech, adverts
Poeticisms
restaurant reviews, travel writing
Mixing of styles/registers
jokes, comedy routines

Task 9

This exercise is intended largely to provoke thought and discussion, so the answers given here are my own opinions rather than the 'correct' ones.
1. b   2. b   3. a   4. a

Task 10

The University of Wisconsin study suggests that we make sense of a text according to our own cultural background. Therefore, it is natural that when using literary texts students will interpret them in terms of their own cultural background. If we expect them to do otherwise, we will need to supply them with the relevant cultural information.

In Aiken's review, Mrs Ramsay is described as a woman cushioned by her class from the world, while in the view of Barbara Bellow Watson she is seen as embodying certain powerful feminist values. To some extent, the readings of both these critics may have been influenced by their personal experiences, political views and the ideology and culture in which they were writing. This difference in reading suggests that any interpretation of a text is likely to be partial rather than definitive, and we should encourage our students to approach literature in this spirit.

Task 12

Other factors which could be added to the list include:
- the reader's political beliefs or views
- the level of education of the reader
- the reader's previous knowledge of the subject of the text
- the reader's age
- the reader's early childhood experience
- the reader's cultural or ethnic background
- the kind of job the reader does
- whether the reader is male or female
- the political system in the reader's country
- the reader's knowledge of other works by the same writer

Obviously, the main factors influencing the interpretations made by a group of learners will vary from class to class, and indeed, from individual to individual.

Task 13

The idea that there is one interpretation of a text and that the teacher must know what it is, is a particularly thorny problem when using literature in the language classroom. To begin with, there may be a cultural problem in that the students' culture might stress the need for a monolithic understanding of a text which is reinforced by a rather authoritarian notion of the teacher's role. In this situation it is up to the individual teacher to decide what role they want, or are able, to play.

A second problem is that the whole system may be heavily weighted in favour of an exam for which students are expected to come up with particular interpretations of a text. Teachers may feel constrained to make sure their students pass the exam. Once again, individual teachers will have to decide how far their classroom methodology will be influenced by the exam.

A third problem is that students may simply lack the confidence to reach interpretations on their own, possibly because their previous learning experience has relied little on the taking of personal responsibility. In this situation it is important not to throw students in at the deep end by immediately demanding personal interpretations from them. It is advisable over the course of a year to gradually introduce tasks and activities which slowly encourage students to become more self-reliant in producing their own interpretations. For example, early lessons might simply include comprehension exercises asking questions of fact about a text, whereas later ones might ask students to infer more information, to choose between alternate interpretations of a text or even to provide their own interpretation based on a series of fairly open-ended questions.

Provided that the students' interpretation can be backed up by intelligent and logical reasons, and is based on a full linguistic understanding of the text then we should probably accept it. With students who have had more exposure to literature or who belong to the background and culture in which the text was written, we might also expect an interpretation which draws on this knowledge.

Task 14

We should devise tasks and activities that promote discussion and problem-solving, rather than those suggesting there is one 'correct' understanding of a text.

Task 17

By the end of the year students should be able to understand:
the plot
the motivation and traits of the characters
the themes of the play
symbolic/metaphorical meanings in the play
the genre of the play
how the dialogue reveals theme and character
how gesture, stage movements, costumes, lighting, sets, props, etc.
   contribute to the overall meaning of the play

Chapter 2

Task 3

1. A language-based approach: advantage 1. disadvantage 2.
2. Literature as content: advantage 3. disadvantage 3.
3. Literature for personal enrichment: advantage 2. disadvantage 1.

Task 4

Before considering any of the groups mentioned in this activity, it is worth bearing in mind one very important consideration – are the students likely to be interested in and motivated by using literature? This clearly depends on the individual group. Even those students who are probably studying English for very specific purposes (as in groups 1. and 6.) may occasionally enjoy studying a literary text, either for variety or because some of the vocabulary or grammar in the text may be useful to their field.

1. (a) Literature may not really be of use if these students are studying English for business, but occasionally they might enjoy a change of activity. (b) Short stories, poems. (c) A combination of Approach 1 and 2.
2. (a) Literature will aid acquisition; with these students there is probably sufficient time to integrate literature into the syllabus. (b) All genres, but possibly select one novel or play as a set book to be studied over a term or year. (c) Combination of all three approaches.
3. (a) These learners may have a more pressing need to improve their functional competence in English than to study literature. On the other hand, an occasional use of literature may help to provide motivating opportunities for discussion, if the texts are interesting and relevant to the students' interests. (b) Short stories, poems, extracts from plays. (c) Combination of Approaches 1 and 3.
4. (a) Literature would be appropriate if it is used as language practice, but not if studied for its own sake. (b) Poems, extracts from plays, short stories – particularly those written specially for children. (c) Mainly Approach 3, but language work should be incorporated informally.
5. (a) May not be sufficient time to use literature with these students. On the other hand, literary texts may provide a novel way of revising grammar and vocabulary, and promoting skills practice. (b) Short stories, poems, extracts from plays. (c) Combination of all three approaches.
6. As for 1.
7. (a) Literature appropriate if student is interested. (b) All genres; novels and complete plays only if she has time to do lots of homework reading. (c) Combination of approaches.

8. (a) Literature may prove highly motivating for these students since the complex meanings in even very simple literary texts may compensate for the frustrations of having to cope at a very simple level linguistically. (b) Linguistically simple poems and extracts from plays (see Sections 6.6 and 7.7 for examples of how to do this). (c) Combination of Approaches 1 and 3; even 2 could be used if information is given in the mother tongue.

Task 6

1. Revision of reported speech with particular emphasis on different verbs of reporting.
2. Extending students' knowledge of descriptive vocabulary.
3. Helping students to read effectively for gist.
4. Developing gist understanding of a text and promoting oral practice around a given situation.
5. Reading for gist, but in this exercise students will be drawing heavily on their interpretive skills since a title of a poem rarely provides just a simple summary of its content.
6. Revision of different tenses.
7. Reading practice, checking understanding of text being reviewed, exposing students to the typical language of critical reviews as a stage in developing their own skill in forming critical judgements.

Task 7

a) It would probably be possible to achieve the same language aims by using non-literary texts for Activities 2, 3 and 6. However, the advantage of using literary texts in all cases is that they offer a highly motivating context for practising the requisite language area. For example, Activity 1 is probably a more vivid and interesting way of revising reported speech than asking students to transform sentences from direct to reported speech.

b) It is difficult to make a strict demarcation between improving linguistic skills and improving literary skills, since literary skills clearly involve linguistic understanding. However, those activities which would help students towards achieving greater literary competence include Activities 3, 5 and 7.

c) Obviously the answer to this question depends on the type of techniques and activities that you usually use in class. The important point to stress here is that many of these can be applied or adapted to the exploitation of a literary text. The aim would be twofold – to teach or revise a particular area of language and to improve the students' understanding and appreciation of literary texts.

Task 8

(a) Scheme A. (b) Scheme B. (c) Scheme A. (d) Scheme B.
Note: For Figure 2.1 and 2.2, each day's activities represent approximately 2 hours of class time.

Task 11

a) Exact details: ten weeks, Mr Biswas' exact address, more than a year, nine weeks, three months' notice, forty-six, four children, three thousand dollars owing for four years, eight per cent interest, twenty dollars, ten dollars ground rent. Such details are often given on a form or official document of some kind since they convey objective factual information. The cumulative effect of using them here is to provide a very vivid description of Mr Biswas' tragedy while doing so in a tone that appears matter-of-fact, and even distanced. Paradoxically, this creates a strong sense of sympathy on the part of the reader for the plight of Mr Biswas and his family.

b) 'Mr Biswas was sacked' is a phrase that is fairly informal and direct, and since it is used in the passive it suggests that Mr Biswas was the passive recipient of others' actions. 'Mr Biswas was dismissed' is a more formal, official way of saying this, and would seem to be less direct and immediate. 'Mr Biswas lost his job' places the emphasis rather more on Mr Biswas than the people who fired him, and would thus make him seem less of a passive recipient of his fate. The phrase 'Mr Biswas was sacked' is thus a very direct, and almost shocking, way of beginning the novel.

c) This phrase is used quite commonly when somebody can genuinely follow no other course of action. The newspaper could possibly have kept Mr Biswas on, but the effect of using the phrase here is to suggest that the management of the paper were driven to fire Mr Biswas against their own wishes. In other words, this phrase is often used when you wish to minimise your personal responsibility for something unpleasant that you have to do.

d) The phrase which is repeated is, ' . . . had no money'. The effect of repeating it here is to emphasise the difficult circumstances of Mr Biswas and his family.

e) The use of the past perfect continuous tense here (some grammatical purists might argue used incorrectly!) emphasises that Mr Biswas had owed the money on his house in the past, and had continued to owe it right up to the time of his death. The fact of Mr Biswas' debt is thus underlined yet again.

f) Feelings of sympathy, compassion and interest. These are created by a very exact and precise description of Mr Biswas' personal affairs.

Task 12

a) Adult learners – Upper Intermediate onwards

c) This text is probably not a particularly useful one to use on its own as a single lesson, since the language aims it could fulfil in close study are too diffuse. However, it might be interesting to contrast it with other texts, for example official documents giving factual information about a person, such as a passport, application for insurance, etc. Both this text and documents of this nature contain factual information, but have very different purposes. Students could be alerted to the way V. S. Naipaul uses factual information to describe Mr Biswas' fate with great precision and sympathy. It would also be useful to study this text with students before they begin reading the novel or parts of it. It is a text which will certainly arouse the reader's curiosity, while providing a very clear and brief synopsis of the end of a story. Using it would thus guide students towards an understanding of the plot, while at the same time encouraging them to make predictions about the events leading up to Mr Biswas' death.

Task 19

The poems are probably best used with adult learners at Intermediate level, although mature adolescents of the same level might also enjoy them. The intention behind the activities in Task 18 is to get the students personally involved in the themes of the poems before reading them. This is partly to stimulate their interest, and partly to make the poems more immediate and accessible to them. Activities a) and b) in Task 18 are probably the most effective warm-ups since they relate directly to the themes of the poems, and all students would probably have something to say about them. Obviously, it is not necessary to use both activities, so you could select whichever one your students are likely to enjoy doing. Activity c) may not leave students enough room to genuinely talk about their own experiences, and may also be more appropriate for students who are parents. Activity d) is a little vague and does not really cue students in to the themes of the poems.

Task 22

Metaphor J. Simile D. Personification G. Paradox B. Oxymoron E. Metonymy C. the *pen* and the *sword* (where the pen stands as a symbol for writing and the sword as a symbol for war – the pen is associated with writing and the sword is associated with war). Synecdoche I. *a pair of ragged claws* (the claws stand for the whole crab). Apostrophe H. Alliteration F. *His crypt the cloudy canopy.* Assonance A. *smoking blueness of Pluto's gloom.*

Answer key

Task 23

You could use an activity of this kind to familiarise students with literary metalanguage. On the other hand, you might decide that this information might simply confuse and alienate them, and so is best avoided. You could also familiarise them with only the more commonly used terms like metaphor, simile and alliteration.

Task 24

Arguments against the use of literary terminology in the language classroom:
1. Students may be merely encouraged to identify figures of speech mechanically without really understanding how they affect the meaning of the text.
2. Complex terminology is alienating and boring for students.
3. There is insufficient time in the classroom to concentrate on this metalanguage – emphasising it may promote unnecessary rote learning and leave little time for more student-centred activities.

Task 25

Adult learners from Upper Intermediate onwards, possibly with a specialist interest in reading or studying literature. Best used with adults, although some adolescent learners who are fairly academic might find it useful.

Chapter 4

Task 1

a) The cultural references which are identified as difficult in these texts will vary from reader to reader, depending on how accessible to, or remote from, the reader's cultural background the text is. Some of the areas which could present a problem are listed in Section 4.2.
b) Different readers report varying responses to the texts, ranging from pleasure at the challenge of reading something new to irritation, and even anxiety, at not understanding the cultural references in the text. Some readers find themselves intrigued by these, others long for an informant who can help to explain what they mean. It is worth bearing in mind that students are likely to have the same range of responses when reading texts from which they are culturally distanced. This may affect their motivation.
c) Text A is an extract from *Arrow of God* by Chinua Achebe (Heinemann 1964, p. 2). A story of village life in Nigeria and the

struggle of the head priest against his rivals and also against Christian missionaries.

Text B is an extract from *Brideshead Revisited* by Evelyn Waugh (Methuen 1985, p. 29). A story of aristocratic British life in the twenties and thirties.

Text C is an extract from *The Dragon's Village* by Yuan-tsung Chen (The Women's Press, 1980, p. 190). An autobiographical account of the Chinese Revolution by a woman cadre helping to carry out land-reform in a remote region.

Chapter 5

Task 2

This activity can be used before students read the story. The main aim is to stimulate student interest in the story, so that they are motivated to read it. When selecting which paragraphs from a story you want students to speculate about, choose those which provide enough information about the basic thread of the narrative to be interesting, but which still leave a lot of unanswered questions. You could either ask students to slowly uncover these paragraphs on a sheet you have given them, or use an overhead projector to reveal the paragraphs one at a time. A lengthier, but useful alternative, especially if you do not have an overhead projector, is to dictate a paragraph to the class and correct it on the board. Students then speculate about it before moving on to the next paragraph.

Task 4

Most people would agree that E. is the most 'storyish' of all the examples, drawing on our unconscious intuition of what a story is. Example B. seems more of a story than A., and C. seems more of a story than B. Many people feel that D. and F. do not seem quite complete enough to be full stories.

Task 5

a) Most traditional short stories (excluding more avant-garde works) have a plot. Plots usually involve chronology (i.e. a sequence of events) and causation (events are in some way connected with each other). For this reason, most people agree that Example E. most fulfils our intuitions of what a story is since it involves a chronological ordering of events (first Miss Muffet sat down, then the spider arrived, then Miss Muffet ran away). There is also a relationship of cause and effect between these events (Why did Miss Muffet run away? Because she was frightened by the spider).

b) It is common in both short stories and novels for the chronological sequence of events to be disrupted, for example through the use of flashback. In addition, relations of cause and effect are often concealed from the reader so that the reader is forced to make their own conjectures about how these are connected, for example by supplying an interpretation of what motivates a character's behaviour. Or the connection between events is only revealed at the end of the narrative, as in the case of the detective novel where the whole motivation for reading the text becomes, 'Who did what and why?' For the language learner it can be difficult to extract a logical chronological sequence of events from the text, and to understand the connections between the events. Students often need help, therefore, with sequencing the events and understanding the connections between them.

Task 6

In actual fact, it would be possible to conceive of a short story in which any of the paragraphs formed the opening lines. But these stories would be radically different in terms of style. Probably Example A. most fulfils our expectations of what we are likely to find in a short story. Its evocation of character and setting is economical, but makes use of telling details. It does not provide factual information (for example about the age and home town of the characters) which is a necessary convention in newspaper reports (see Example D.). Example B. has more of the characteristics of conversational than written language, in its rather colloquial informality, while example C. is a rather bald paraphrase of events. Example C. gives us essentially the same information as Example A., but in an uninteresting way. In other words, it is often the language used in a short story and the effects it creates which make it vivid and absorbing to the reader, rather than the actual situation it is describing.

(Example A. is taken from 'The Rivals' by Martin Armstrong in *Twentieth Century English Short Stories*, edited by Tina Pierce and Edward Cochrane and published by Unwin Hyman.)

Task 7

Students might have problems understanding some of the vocabulary or grammar in the text. They may also have difficulties appreciating the stylistic effects created by the language, and the way these contribute to the meaning of the story or novel.

Task 8

a) Short stories and novels are told by a narrator. This may be an 'omniscient' who has access to the thoughts of all the characters (as in Example B. where the narrator presents both characters Miss Kevin and Mrs Kearney with humorous detachment). Or the story may be told from the point of view of one specific character who participates in it to varying degrees (as in Example A. where the story is told by Roland's father). In this case, events may be filtered through a particular perspective.

b) It is important to students to the extent that the narrative point of view influences the way that events and characters are described; for example a story told by a narrator who participates in the events may give only a partial view of them, so that the reader has to imaginatively infer the rest. Or the position of the narrator in the story may influence which characters the reader feels the most sympathy for. Part of the meaning of the story is thus indirectly communicated in its narration.

Section 5.4

ACTIVITY 8

a) A maze is a system of very complicated passages through which it is difficult to find your way. The phrase 'a maze of distress' suggests that Eveline feels trapped and unable to find a way out of the emotional conflict she is experiencing.

b) i) She asked herself: 'Can I still draw back after all he has done for me?'
   ii) She asked herself whether/if she could still draw back after all he had done for her.

c) Other examples: 'Was that wise?', 'People would treat her with respect then.' In fact, there are many examples throughout the text of *free indirect speech*. The effect of using it is that we are given access to Eveline's thoughts and feelings as if we ourselves were experiencing the events that she is experiencing. This increases our sympathy for, and involvement in, her plight. At the same time, we are aware that this narrative is not a first person narrative (i.e. it is not told by Eveline herself), but that there is a narrator who is describing events. This creates a sense of slight detachment and distance which is finely balanced against our compassion for Eveline. Free indirect speech is very commonly used in literary texts.

d) We usually say 'She didn't answer.' or 'She didn't say anything.' Strictly speaking, 'She answered nothing.' is grammatically incorrect, but the use of the word *nothing* is a way of emphasising Eveline's refusal to answer Frank.

e) The sentences seem to jump about from one topic to another without logical sequence. In this way, they communicate the disorder of Eveline's own thoughts.

Task 11(a): Aims of Activities 1. to 11.

1. To encourage students to guess the meaning of a word from context and to use dictionaries if necessary.
2. To encourage students to write creatively by drawing on features of the style used in the story.
3. To stimulate student interest in the story and provoke discussion relating to one of the themes of the story.
4. To provide students with the historical or cultural background needed to deepen their understanding of the text.
5. To encourage students to read more intensively by taking notes which summarise each paragraph, thereby helping them to understand the plot.
6. To encourage students to read for gist so that they can follow the basic sequence of events and how they are connected.
7. To encourage students to make their own interpretations of the overall meaning of the text.
8. To direct students to certain features of the style and the effect that it conveys. Also, to sensitise students to how the description of events is shaped by a narrator. (In this story, for example, the use of free indirect speech and disconnected sequencing of sentences and paragraphs gives the reader direct and sympathetic access to Eveline's thoughts, while at the same time maintaining a certain objectivity.)
9. To extend students' knowledge of the literary background to the text.
10. To stimulate student interest in the text by relating one of the themes to their own experience.
11. To aid student understanding and interpretation of the text by assessing the characters in the text.

Task 11(b): Possible ordering for the activities

There are a number of ways that these activities could be ordered to make a complete lesson plan. Here is one possibility: Activities 3, 10 and 4 as pre-reading activities; Activities 6, 5, 1, 7, 11 and 8 for use while reading the text; Activities 9 and 2 as post-reading activities or homework. Obviously, there are too many activities to use with one class and you could select only one or two pre-reading activities; only one activity of a more interpretative nature for use while working with the text (either 7, 11 or 8) and only one post-reading activity.

Task 12

a) When selecting vocabulary in a short story it is wise to focus on those words that you believe are crucial for student understanding of the gist of the story, that are impossible to guess very easily from context and that students are unlikely to know. How far you would wish these words to become part of the students' more active vocabulary depends on the nature of the course you are teaching. For example, if you are teaching a course which prepares students for an exam in which they have to write a descriptive essay, then you may encourage students to use the words in the exercise in their own writing.

Other factors to bear in mind when designing vocabulary exercises are how they link up with reading activities. If comprehension questions are designed largely to help students with understanding overall meaning, then the vocabulary exercises should not focus on words that are not relevant to this. If, on the other hand, students are being asked to comment on the style of one paragraph, they would need a more detailed focus on the vocabulary in that paragraph.

b) Activities 2, 4 and 10. Activities designed to elicit a personal response from students are important for involvement and motivation.

c) This particular story has central themes which are likely to have widespread appeal in different cultures. You may feel that it is not absolutely necessary to provide much cultural or historical background information for students, provided students are encouraged to respond personally to the text, and to relate it to their own experience. On the other hand, some information can only serve to deepen student understanding of Eveline's dilemma. A lecture might include information about the economic conditions in Ireland at the turn of the century, the role of women, the role of the church, the reasons for immigration.

d) Activity 6 aims to encourage students to read for gist, Activity 5 for more detail and Activity 7 to read 'between the lines' by drawing out some of the unstated implications or ambiguities of the text. Staged in this order, the activities would guide students from a global understanding to a more detailed comprehension of the text. With students who are competent readers with well developed reading strategies, it may be less necessary to work through all three stages.

e) Activity 9. Students with little interest in literature may feel bored or demotivated by it.

Task 16

S – focusses on a moment of crisis
N – narrative told from different perspectives
S – mood and tone fairly unified throughout the text

Answer key

N – large cast of characters
N – numerous flashbacks to past events
N – highly complicated plot
S – very economic, suggestive use of language

Chapter 6

Task 2

Here is the original version of the poem:

'maggie and milly and molly and may'

maggie and milly and molly and may
went down to the beach(to play one day)

and maggie discovered a shell that sang
so sweetly she couldn't remember her troubles,and

5   milly befriended a stranded star
whose rays five languid fingers were;

and molly was chased by a horrible thing
which raced sideways while blowing bubbles:and

may came home with a smooth round stone
10 as small as a world and as large as alone.

For whatever we lose(like a you or a me)
it's always ourselves we find in the sea
e. e. cummings

Your version of the poem may be different from this, but you may have interesting reasons for ordering it the way you did.

Some of the devices which may have helped you to reorder the poem include:

(i)   The ordering of the verses according to the names in the title (i.e. the first verse is about maggie, the second milly, etc.).

(ii)   Semantic links – lines 3 and 4 are connected because of the collocation 'to sing sweetly', lines 5 and 6 because a star has five 'rays'. The words 'whose' (line 6) and 'which' (line 8) are also important connecting words.

(iii) The fifth verse makes use of assonance (i.e. repetition of similar vowel sounds to create poetic effects).

(iv) There is a rhyme-scheme of sorts in the poem – the lines of the first, fifth and last verse are linked by rhyme.

(v)   The last verse is a kind of conclusion or moral, so that the word 'For' is used to introduce the verse. The use of the capital letter may have suggested that this verse comes at the beginning of the poem.

Task 3

Ordering based on a title, assonance, rhyme.

Task 5

Your aim would be to sensitive students to what devices and means can be used to create cohesion in poetry. The hope would be that this would increase their sensitivity to the concept of cohesion in all forms of discourse. Students would learn some new vocabulary on the way, and would be actively involved in interpreting and understanding the poem. You might need to preteach some of the vocabulary before the students do the exercise, since the meaning of the words is quite difficult to guess from context.

Task 6

Examples A and B: The words underlined here are neologisms, all invented by the poet. Those in *Kangaroo* are easily understood since they are combinations of existing words. Those in *Jabberwocky*, however, are extreme examples of made-up words which may appear resonant with meaning to an English speaker, but are still virtually impossible to define.

Example C: Word order/syntax – usual word order is reversed here. A more standard form would be *the house is silent.*

Example D: This extract mixes up register – the lyrical poetic register of 'Japonica glistens . . . ' is inserted with ironic effect after the four lines which could be quoted from the dry monologue of a rifle-instructor (for a fuller discussion of this example, please see Geoffrey N. Leech, *A Linguistic Guide to English Poetry*, p. 50).

Example E: Archaisms – in this instance the archaisms were probably contemporaneous uses when the poem was written, since Donne is noted for his vigorous colloquial style. But some more modern poetry does self-consciously make use of archaic language.

Example F: Metaphorical uses of language, the sky is described as a cathedral, and the sun as a steeple.

Example G: The poem is written in West Indian/Caribbean dialect.

Example H: Self-conscious use of punctuation and spacing on the page.

Example I: Repetition of certain key phrases, and rhyming of words at the end of certain lines. This example perhaps differs from the previous ones in that rather than 'breaking' certain rules of language, it patterns and orders language more elaborately and tightly than is usual through rhyming and repetition.

Task 10

The poem could be used with students from intermediate level upwards. It is linguistically unusual in its punctuation, which strings names and words together without spacing or commas, and in its use of newly invented compound words like *colourpiano*, *frozenmagazines*, *high-fidog*, *worksofart*, *human money*, *instant children* and *exploding clocks*.

Task 11

Activity 1 is designed to focus on how the punctuation in the poem deviates from ordinary usage and what message this conveys. Activity 2 asks students to come up with some compound words which they can then compare with the unusual compounds given in the poem.

Task 13(a)

(i) comparison   (ii) unlike/different

Task 14

a) A. Evening and the sunset are compared to a housewife sweeping the sky.
   B. Meg is compared to a new broom from the idiomatic expression 'new brooms sweep clean'.
   C. The sun is compared to the day's fire; the gulls are compared to shiftworkers.
   D. The speaker's situation is compared to being in a fire after jumping out of a frying pan.
   E. The woods may be being compared to something, the journey to something else – but it is not clear as to what! Hence, the mysterious and elusive quality of these lines.
   F. The bad financial situation of the firm is compared to being lost in the woods.
b) Examples B, D and F because these are set, or idiomatic, uses – the metaphors have become 'dead' and so have a fixed meaning. The other examples use freshly minted comparisons – the metaphors are newly invented by the poet. The meaning of these metaphors may be less transparent or fixed than those which have frozen into idiom. Students will be unable to find their meaning in the dictionary, and will need help in unravelling the comparison and analysing its effect.

Task 15

Activity 1: (c) then (a)
Activity 2: (b) then (d)

Section 6.6   Example A

2.   Children sleep at night.
      Children never wake up
      When morning comes.
      Only the old ones wake up.
   5 Old Trouble is always awake.

      Children can't see over their eyes.
      Children can't hear beyond their ears.
      Children can't know outside of their heads.

      The old ones see.
  10 The old ones hear
      The old ones know.
      The old ones are old.

4. **Wake–sleep**   **Eyes–see**
   heavy – light   nose – smell
   short – tall   arms – carry
   arrive – leave   hands – write
   thin – fat   mouth – eat
   day – night   legs – walk
   sad – happy   brain – think

Task 17

sentence completion   A(1.), B(3.)
matching words to definitions   B(2.)
predictive writing   (C)
ordering sentences in the correct sequence   D(3.)
writing your own poem   A(5.), D(5.)
gap-fill/cloze   A(2.)
matching words to pictures   B(1.)
checking word meaning in a dictionary   C(5.)
organising words according to lexical relationships   A(4.)

Task 18

(a) B   (b) C   (c) A   (d) D

Answer key

Task 20

- to understand the overall gist of the poem (3.)
- to understand some of the figurative or metaphorical meanings in the poem (4.)
- to stimulate student interest and to encourage personal involvement in the poem's underlying themes (1. and 2.)
- to analyse how the stylistic device of repetition contributes to the overall effect (5.)
- to understand the tone of the poem (6.)

Section 6.8

ACTIVITY 2

Some of the reasons that people might leave their villages to go and live in a big city: to find a job; to escape the boredom of village life; to get a better education; because of drought or bad harvest; to get money to buy luxury goods like radios, etc.; to join members of their family in the city; because of laws which force people off the land; to escape the social constrictions of living in a very close community; to get better accommodation, services and amenities. Obviously these reasons will vary from country to country.

ACTIVITY 7

This is quite a difficult exercise to do for two reasons. Firstly, some of the words may have changed their original meaning since the poem was written. Secondly, such is the complexity of Blake's discourse that certain words could have more than one meaning in the context of the poem. The line between figurative and literal meanings becomes a fine one. In deciding on which definition best fits the word, the reader is therefore engaging in an interpretation of the text, rather than simply matching straight dictionary definitions to words. Here is my own interpretation:

charter'd: (1) seems the obvious literal interpretation here, although (2) links with a recurrent theme in the poem – the power of the state in the person of the king.

marks: (3).

ban: either (1) or (2) where (1) echoes the idea of restrictive laws (in *charter'd*) and (2) anticipates the Harlot's curse in line 14.

appal: either (1) or (2) where (1) picks up on the contrast between 'blackening' and becoming pale, and (2) emphasises the strong emotional effect of the Chimney-sweeper's cry

blast: (1)

blight: the more literal meaning (1) collocates with the word 'plagues', while (2) links strongly with the figurative meaning of destroying the Marriage hearse (the destruction of the institution of marriage).

Task 25

a) – understanding individual words (7.)
   – understanding the metaphorical/symbolic meaning (8., 9., 10., 11.)
   – understanding the historical context (1., 2., 4.)
   – understanding the poet's attitude to what he sees around him (5., 8.)
   – responding personally to the themes (3., 13.)
   Any of the activities which help the students cope with the difficult vocabulary in the poem and respond personally to the poem should help them to feel less intimidated or threatened by the poem.

b) It might not be necessary to use all the pre-reading or while-reading activities, since using all of them could be quite time-consuming. How much background you wished to provide students with would vary according to the time available, and whether students were motivated and could benefit from it. You might, for example, decide to provide activities designed to involve students personally (such as 1., 2. and 3.) while leaving out 4. and 5. Similarly, if students' critical and interpretative skills are fairly well-developed, you could leave out 13. and simply ask students to produce their own interpretations or critical commentaries on the poem.

c) The need to provide this kind of background varies according to the text and the students. There are certainly some poems which refer very directly to certain events and, although they may also address more generalisable or 'universal' themes, students need to know what these events are to fully appreciate the poem. On the other hand, with other poems background information may serve to enhance student understanding of the poem, without being a necessity, provided the themes of the poem are relevant to the students' experience and culture.

d) Providing students with alternate definitions is a way of helping them to decode the meaning of the more difficult words in the poem. But students should be warned that more than one of the definitions could apply to the meaning of each word. For example, it is most likely that the word *ban* (line 7) means some kind of formal prohibition in the poem, and links with other words connoting restrictions and prohibitions (e.g. charter'd); on the other hand, the word *ban* meaning a curse, prefigures the curse of the harlot in the last verse. Making use of alternate definitions is thus a way of leading students into the multiple ambiguities of the language of the poem.

e) Activity 13. is an attempt to help students form a critical appreciation and/or interpretation of the poem. Exercises of this type are best used as a bridge for students – once they can do this more confidently themselves, such tasks become less necessary.

f) Providing students with other poems by Blake to read and compare, perhaps from *Songs of Experience*, from which 'London' is taken; discussion on urban problems and ways of solving them; reading and comparisons with other texts about the urban experience and what it means; a roleplay/simulation about redeveloping slum areas in a city with students taking the parts of residents, developers, directors of businesses and community centres, etc.

Chapter 7

Task 2

In the original dialogue the sequence of lines is as follows:
line   3. (d)
line   5. (c)
line   9. (a)
line 13. (b)

Task 3

a) Pronominal references, such as 'one' (line 3) which refers to 'tea bag' (line 1). 'That's right' (line 6) which confirms Rutter's negative reply in line 4, but which Teacher questions in line 5. The ellipsis in line 9 in which the sentence really means *I would [buy my own] if I could but I can't* and refers back to line 8.

b) Teacher is trying to wheedle a teabag out of Rutter, and so he is trying to sound tentative and therefore polite. He could have said 'Can I share the one you have?' but this would have been much more direct.

c) Teacher's 'No' is rather challenging and questions Rutter's refusal to give him a teabag. Just how aggressive he is being would depend on intonation.

d) He means that Rutter is not behaving in a very brotherly way towards him, and that Rutter is being unkind, uncaring and even cruel. Teacher here uses quite complicated language linked to complicated concepts, which may suggest that he is reasonably well-educated. But he reverts to this style when he is being sarcastic. He is an extremely persistent person, who can be quite nasty and aggressive.

e) They seem to be equals in that Teacher feels free to carry on pestering Rutter, and Rutter feels free to answer Teacher rudely and abruptly.

Task 4

To sensitise students to the way conversational discourse is linked or connected.

Task 6

To give students practice in speaking, since they would discuss this in pairs or groups. At the same time, you would be developing their interpretative abilities in English, since thinking about the performance of a play necessarily involves them in interpreting the text.

Task 8

a) Text A takes place in a park, Central Park in New York City. Text B takes place in a parlour or reception room. In Text A the characters are complete strangers with no previous acquaintance of each other. In Text B they have not actually met each other before, but they belong to the same upper-class social circle so they have heard about each other.
b) Both texts could be used with students at mid-intermediate level and upwards, although Text B is slightly more difficult.
c) There are many different ways of using these texts with your students, depending on your aims in the lesson. Some possibilities are given in the sequence of activities in Section 7.5.

Section 7.5

ACTIVITY 5

Text A
Why people say what they do in a particular context is often a matter of interpretation. Here are some possible interpretations for Texts A and B.
a) Jerry begins the conversation with none of the usual conversational preliminaries you might have with a stranger. His conversational opening is in the form of a statement, which seems to demand Peter's involvement in the conversation. This suggests that Jerry doesn't care very much about the usual social niceties and is rather aggressive.
b) We might expect an answer that is relevant to Peter's question, such as 'Yes, I was.' But Jerry's reply suggests either that he chooses to ignore Peter's question, or is completely preoccupied with thinking

about the zoo. Either way, the effect is to grab Peter's attention and to draw him, rather unwillingly, into the conversation.

c) Peter could have said 'Yes, you have.' or 'Yes, I suppose you have.' or 'Yes, it looks like it.' The use of 'would' in his reply is rather formal, so that it suggests Peter wishes to distance himself from what Jerry is saying. He doesn't really want to participate in the conversation any further. The rather formal ring to this phrase could also imply that Peter is better educated or of a higher social class than Jerry.

d) We use this phrase when we are referring affectionately or humorously to a person we know well, especially after they have done something which we regard as typical of their behaviour or personality. The expression can also be used to talk about a familiar place that we are fond of. We don't usually use it for points on the compass – does this suggest that 'north' has taken on a kind of human quality for Jerry? At any rate, it is a rather odd use of the expression which suggests that Jerry himself is a little strange.

e) 'Boy' in line 20 is intended as a term of abuse. It is sometimes used very offensively, for example, by whites to adult black men. Jerry is presumably using it here to establish his control or superiority over Peter, or to be very aggressive.

f) Initially Peter seems to want to avoid having a conversation with Jerry, and to regard him with annoyance and suspicion. By the end of this extract, he is becoming interested in the conversation.

g) This dialogue forms the opening lines of the play *The Zoo Story* by Edward Albee. Students should feel free to come up with their own predictions about what happens next. In the actual play, Jerry and Peter continue their conversation, revealing much about their own personalities and backgrounds. Jerry describes himself as a 'permanent transient' who lives alone in poverty, while Peter lives a reasonably comfortable middle-class lifestyle with his wife, two children and two parakeets. At one point, they begin to argue very angrily about who has the right to sit on the park bench. Jerry pulls a knife on Peter, but then drops it onto the ground. Peter picks it up and holds it out in front of himself so as to defend himself. Jerry rushes at him, deliberately impaling himself on the knife and causing his own death. Peter runs away in terror and shock.

Text B

a) Cecily's first sentence is very formal, as befits the role of a hostess welcoming a guest. 'Pray' is an old-fashioned way of adding politeness (or sometimes sarcasm!) to a statement or question. In the broader context of the play from which this is taken, Oscar Wilde's *The Importance of Being Earnest*, she is also probably trying to cover up her surprise that Gwendolen is a sophisticated young woman, rather than the elderly lady she has been expecting.

b) All three phrases show rather excessive politeness, and are probably too gushing to be considered sincere at a very first meeting. They suggest that Gwendolen is being rather false.

c) Cecily gives a rather sarcastic reply, although it is said in an apparently polite and approving way. It suggests that she thinks Gwendolen is being rather insincere.

d) She wishes to show that she will do what she wants; and that she can assert herself with regard to Cecily.

e) Cecily's reply in line 13 could suggest that she is not very happy about calling Gwendolen by her first name, because it implies a friendliness and intimacy in their relationship that she would rather not have. She herself does not want to call Gwendolen by her first name, but will do as Gwendolen wants.

f) This phrase suggests that the two women have had some time to assess each other, decide what kind of relationship they want to have, and are now ready to get onto other topics. It might also suggest that they have resolved the competitiveness and cattiness between themselves, even though it has been masked by apparent politeness. Finally, it underlines that the introductions made in this dialogue were of such an elaborate and artificial formality that it is only now that the two characters can move on to other subjects.

g) Suspicious, competitive.

h) Students should feel free to speculate here. In the play *The Importance of Being Earnest* by Oscar Wilde, Gwendolen and Cecily continue this conversation in the same formal, polite vein only to discover that they are engaged to the same man! They become increasingly furious with each other, but since they are well-bred young ladies they are obliged to conceal this.

ACTIVITY 6

	Text A	Text B
Setting	a city park	a drawing room
Period	modern American (early 1960s)	Edwardian England – early part of 20th Century
Relationship between the characters	strangers in an anonymous environment	know each other through mutual acquaintances – part of restricted social circle
Type of language used	informal, colloquial, direct	formal, polite, indirect

These days students would be unlikely to overhear a conversation like Text B, since it is rather old-fashioned in its formality.

ACTIVITY 7

Jerry calls Peter 'boy' (line 20) and persists in asking Peter questions so he is forced to participate in the conversation, initially against his will. Gwendolen carries on standing although Cecily has asked her to sit down.

When discussing the questionnaire with students, bear in mind that there are no set answers to the questions, since the aim is simply to get students thinking about this very interesting, but fuzzy, area of language use. There will certainly be differences in the way users of different languages respond to the questionnaire, as well as the way users of different varieties of English (British, American, Nigerian, etc.) respond to it.

In very broad terms, it might be possible to come up with a few generalisations about Standard British English, for example that interrupting is generally regarded as rude, although the more informal the setting the less this is so. Since interrupting is regarded in this way, it tends to remain the prerogative of the person with the higher status. Similarly, there is some evidence to suggest that in situations of unequal status, such as teacher-student or doctor-patient, the person of higher status controls the discourse by asking questions which demand a restricted, rather than open-ended response. Finally, terms of address are an interesting way of expressing relationships of status. English has lost a formal/informal distinction in the use of the pronoun *you* (as in the

French *vous/tu*), but names can be a way of registering this difference, for example, *sir* as used by a waiter, or an affectionate nickname as used by a friend.

Task 10

(a) Activity 4 (b) Activity 3 (c) Activity 8 (b) (d) Activity 5 (e) Activity 1 (f) Activity 7 (g) Activity 6 (h) Activities 8 (a) and (b) (i) Activity 2

Task 12

Teachers may find they disagree with each other in their reactions to the statements, but here are a few general pointers relating to them. These activities usually work well with students at all levels, even elementary, as students seem to enjoy reading aloud. How much teachers ask students to respond personally to the theme of the text before they read it depends on the kind of students and the degree of informality in the classroom. The staging of the activity encourages students to develop their oral confidence, and can be adapted to the needs of the group. For example, a stronger group might not need to use the script as many times as is suggested in the lesson plan. Similarly, the teacher can decide if students should change partners during this activity or if this will be too confusing. On the whole, teachers should probably avoid correcting pronunciation mistakes during the activity, as this can be inhibiting for students, although this may be done afterwards. Teachers will need to decide how much preteaching of vocabulary to do before the students read the text. Students may be able to guess the meanings of some of the words from context, or explain them to each other. Some teachers may feel it is confusing to provide students with a dialogue which is out of context, and so could explain the setting or even use the background notes later in this section (Activity 4, under 'Other activities for use with Text C') before students start reading the text. The activity can get noisy, and demands clear instructions and good classroom management, particularly if it is to be used with large classes.

Task 15

A few possible ways of ordering the activities to form a lesson plan:
Activity 2 as a warmer, then students read the text, Activity 4 to check their understanding of gist, Activities 1 and 3 as follow-up practice
or
Activity 2 as a warmer, then students read the text, Activity 5 as language and comprehension practice, Activity 6 as creative writing practice.

Answer key

Activities to use with 'The Dumb Waiter'

ACTIVITY 1

In the actual play the two men are hired killers waiting for orders from a mysterious boss.

ACTIVITY 5

By using the phrases 'What?' and 'What do you mean?' in the dialogue, Pinter seems to imply that Gus has not understood Ben (line 8); or is surprised by what Ben says or hasn't heard what he says (line 17). But this would strike an audience as odd, and even comic, as Ben's orders seem completely clear and unsurprising. Pinter is therefore using perfectly natural language in an unusual way, perhaps to suggest a rather sinister breakdown of communication. It is obviously quite difficult to point this out to lower level students – this might be a time when it would be appropriate to discuss this in the students' own language. And for students of a more literary bent, even if their knowledge of English is limited, you could mention that this kind of language use is typical of Pinter's plays, and indeed, the Theatre of the Absurd. Students may be able to come up with some examples of similar plays in their own language.

Chapter 9

9.6 SELF ACCESS WORKSHEET: POETRY

FACTS ABOUT THE BOOK

Title:
Author/Editor:
When published:

CONTENT AND STYLE

Choose one poem in the book and think about it using these
headings:

1 Subject: This is a poem about ....
2 Poetic techniques:
    a) Does the poet use any unusual comparisons or metaphors?
       Are these effective?
    b) Does the poem rhyme? What effect does this have?
    c) Do you notice any unusual uses of language in the poem
       which create particular effects?
3 Does this poem seem to have a 'message'? What is it?
4 Are there any other poems in the book which have the same
   theme as this one? What are the other poems in the book about?

LANGUAGE

Write down any new words, phrases or expressions you have
learnt from reading this poem.

OPINION

1 Choose from the following adjectives to describe the poems in
   this book:

   | moving   tedious   complex   gloomy   amusing |
   | disturbing   tragic |

   What other adjectives could you use to describe them?
2 Would you recommend this book? Why?
3 Do the poems in this book remind you of any in your own
   language?

Trainer's Notes

Introduction

For whom are these notes intended?

These notes are intended to be used by anyone running a training or development session or course which draws on any of the tasks or activities in this book. You might be:
- a trainer working in a teacher training institution where teachers come for initial or refresher training courses
- the facilitator of a teacher development group
- the director of studies at a language school responsible for staff development seminars.

The notes are intended to provide very general guidelines for using the tasks and activities in this book, and should obviously be adapted to the needs of the trainees with whom you are working.

Methodological principles underlying this book

The basic premise underlying the design of the tasks and activities used in this book is that teachers learn best by being actively involved in the training session. This active involvement might entail participating in a discussion, brainstorming ideas in a group or simply setting aside time to read and reflect on a new idea.

A second principle underlying the tasks is that, wherever possible, teachers are encouraged to relate the content of the course to their own experience. Novice teachers on an initial training course may have fairly limited teaching experience and, in that case, you could ask teachers to draw on their own past experiences of being language students themselves – this sometimes yields useful insights.

You will notice that many of the tasks and activities in the book are designed for groupwork and pairwork. I believe that working in this way can be of benefit to most trainees, but it is also true that teachers may be resistant to this way of working, for reasons ranging from personal to cultural. If this is the case in your situation, then you could adapt many of the activities so that teachers work on them first on their own before participating in a plenary discussion which you direct. Or you could structure your course so that you move gradually from a trainer-controlled approach (using more traditional teaching modes, like lecturing, with which most trainees might feel comfortable) to one in

216

which trainees are given greater autonomy and responsibility (for example, using groupwork and pairwork, participating in a workshop or simulation, etc.).

Planning your session or course

There are two main factors which should determine your planning for a session or course on using literature in the language classroom. The first is how much time you have available. At the beginning of the trainer's notes for each chapter you will find a list of core activities in that chapter to help you select the most important areas which need to be covered on a training course.

The second factor determining the planning of a course is the needs of the teachers/trainees on that course. Any course planning should be preceded by a thorough analysis of what it is that your teachers will need or want to find out on a training course. For example, teachers might be working in a very academic school where students are obliged to cover English literature from Beowulf to contemporary writers for an exam and the teachers themselves might have a strong literary background. Or you might be working with a group of novice teachers who want to know how to use literature on an occasional basis with adult learners. Obviously, both of these groups of teachers have different training needs, and these needs may be assessed either by talking informally to the teachers or by making use of some kind of questionnaire (see the sample provided at the end of this introduction).

During the course it is important that the teachers' own experience and opinions are validated. Wherever possible, the tasks and activities in this book are designed to encourage teachers to apply whatever they have learned to their own setting. It should be stressed throughout that, although teachers may find they cannot use the specific activities included in the book with their own students, the underlying principle, procedure or technique behind the activity can often be generalised, and then applied to a different text or group of students. Otherwise, there is the danger that teachers experience training or development in terms of: 'Very interesting, but what we learned is not something I can do with my own students.'

It is also important to ensure that teachers have some kind of say in the structuring of their own training or development programme. This can be done on a purely informal basis by chatting to teachers, or by asking for written feedback such as filling in a questionnaire or keeping a diary during the course which trainers read from time to time.

Integrating methodology and language development

One of the common threads running through the tasks and activities in this book is the link between language development and teaching methodology. With many activities (for example Sections 6.8 and 7.5) the activity can be used, in the first place, to improve the language skills of the teachers with whom you are working. After the teachers have done the task, as if they were students, they could then be asked to put on their 'teaching' hats and to analyse the task in terms of its methodological implications for them as teachers. All the texts marked with ☆ can be used in this way.

If you are working with a group of teachers who are very keen to improve their proficiency in English you could extend this principle even further. For example, during the course you could ask teachers to read a novel which is then discussed in class as a literary work. The second stage is to then make the activities which were used to exploit the novel the object of the teachers' scrutiny. What was the aim behind the tasks? Would they be able to use similar tasks with their own students? and so on.

The link between language development and methodology could also be taken into account when you set any pre-course reading. For example, teachers could be asked to read a play before coming on the course. The play could then be used for language development activities and as a focus when discussing the methodological principles of using plays with students. A visit to the theatre, or the viewing of a film which is based on the play, could then form an integral part of the course. Another project which is often very successful for practising oral skills is to ask teachers to each present a short talk to the group on the important literature of their own country, or their own favourite writer.

Example of a pre-course questionnaire

This very general questionnaire was used to gather information about the needs and interests of a group of teachers from all over the world who attended a thirty-hour course in the United Kingdom on using literature in the language classroom.

1. Name:
2. Nationality:
3. Where do you teach? (For example, state secondary school, private language school, further education college, private lessons, etc.?)

4. *Your students*

    Age:
    Mother tongue:
    Level of English:
    Reasons for studying English:
    Number of hours per week students study English:

5. Have you ever used literature with your students in a lesson? If so, what did you use? (Please be specific about names of books or authors used.)

6. Is any literature included in the syllabus for your students? If so, what? (Please be as specific as you can here by giving any names of textbooks or literary works used.)

7. When using literature with your students what did/do you find were/are the main problems?

    Problems that you experienced:
    Problems that your students experienced:

    If you have not used literature before with your students what kinds of problems do you think you or they might have?

8. Do your students have to do exams? How often? Are they tested on literature in the exam?

9. Have you attended any other training or development course which focussed on using literature in the language classroom? If so, where?

10. What are your reasons for wanting to do this particular course? Please be as detailed as possible here.

11. Are there any areas that you would most like to discuss on the course, for example, using poetry with the language learner?

12. Do you have any favourite writers in English to whom you would like us to refer on the course? If so, please list them.

13. Please write any additional comments on the back of this form.

Chapter 1   Using literature in the language classroom: The issues

As this chapter is intended largely to provoke thought and discussion about some of the issues underlying the use of literature in the language classroom rather than to be of immediate classroom application, it is intended that trainers choose those activities which are relevant and of interest to the group they are training. On very short courses there may not be time to work through any of the activities in the chapter, as the course emphasis might be on activities with immediate classroom application. For longer courses, the core activities are Sections 1.1 and 1.5.

The section on literary competence (1.4) may be of most relevance to those teachers who are teaching literature as a subject, rather than using it as a resource to promote language teaching.

1.1 What is literature?

Aim

To direct teachers' attention to some of the issues underlying the use of literature in the language classroom by considering some definitions of literature and their implications.

Activity type

Writing and comparing of definitions; discussion of definitions; matching definitions to their implications; discussion/drawing of a diagram.

Suggested procedure

This is quite a long and complicated activity, and you may need to adapt or shorten it. If it is the first day of a training course, you may wish to begin the day with something slightly easier and more lighthearted. In that case, you could begin with Section 6.1 *Putting a poem back together again* in Chapter 6. Point out to teachers that they will be able to use many of the activities you do with them on the course with their own students by adapting the underlying procedure or technique behind the activity to texts they wish to use with their students.

When using **Task 1,** teachers could be asked to write their own definitions of literature on slips of paper which are then read aloud to the whole group. The whole group could then be asked to come up with a composite definition which incorporates the most salient features of all the definitions written.

Tasks 2 and 3 can be discussed in pairs or groups. If you think the tasks will be too long and complicated for the group with whom you are working, you may wish to give the group only two or three of the definitions in Task 2 and their matching paragraphs in Task 3 to discuss. Alternatively, the group could be given the task to prepare at home before the session, particularly if a lot of the vocabulary in the two tasks is difficult or unfamiliar to them. A third approach is to give each group only one or two quotations from Task 2 to analyse and discuss before explaining what they think the quotation means to the group as a whole. The whole group could then read and discuss Task 3.

Task 4 is intended to be very open-ended, and you may find that teachers use it as an opportunity to raise problems and concerns dealt with elsewhere in the book.

Task 5 can either be presented on the board or on an overhead projector transparency for teachers to discuss. Alternatively, teachers could be asked to draw up their own mind-map or diagram summarising those points which emerged during this chapter and which they regard as important. A third alternative is to ask teachers to write down all their queries and questions arising from this section, or even this chapter, which are then collated onto a large poster which is displayed throughout the course. As teachers find 'answers' to their questions, the questions can be crossed out. Teachers could be encouraged to use unanswered questions as the basis for a research project of their own.

1.2 What is distinctive about the language of literature?

Aim

To explore whether literary language is distinctive in any way, and to discuss the pedagogic implications arising from this.

Activity type

Analysis and discussion of texts; filling in chart; discussion of statements in pairs and groups.

Suggested procedure

Task 6 can be discussed in pairs and groups, with the text following the task elicited from teachers in a subsequent class discussion. For teachers wishing to improve their proficiency in English the reading of the texts in Task 6 can first be done as a language and comprehension exercise. Encourage teachers to explain any unfamiliar vocabulary to each other or to look up words in the dictionary.

Task 7 can also be discussed in pairs and groups, but ensure that teachers have understood what each linguistic category is before they do the exercise.

Task 8 could possibly be extended to become an ongoing language development project, particularly for teachers wishing to improve their proficiency in English. Teachers could be asked to bring to class for discussion any examples of discourse which are rich in the kinds of features which do seem pervasive in literature – such as proverbs, advertisements, newspaper articles, etc.

Task 9 is intended to generate some open-ended discussion, with the answers in the key representing my opinions rather than any 'correct' views.

1.3   The reader and the text

Aim

To explore the idea that the meaning of a literary text can never be fixed authoritatively, and the implications of this for the classroom.

Activity type

Jigsaw reading; discussion in pairs or groups.

Suggested procedure

Tasks 10 and 11 can be done as a jigsaw reading with teachers divided into two groups, one of which reads and discusses Example 1 and the other Example 2. Each member of the first group is then paired with a member of the second group to report on the summary and the original group discussion. The remaining activities in this section are to be done in pairs or groups.

Since **Tasks 13 and 14** raise the core pedagogic issues in this section, they can provide the main focus with Tasks 10, 11 and 12 being left out if necessary.

1.4   Literary competence and the language classroom

Aim

To consider the concept of literary competence and its implications for using literature in the classroom.

Activity type

Mini-lecture/reading text followed by discussion.

Suggested procedure

Teachers could be divided into two groups to discuss Text A. and B. The groups then swap texts and decide in what way their response to the texts are different.

The text in this section can be delivered as a mini-lecture or reading text after teachers have brainstormed their ideas about the focus questions in **Task 16**.

Task 17 could be discussed in pairs and groups. Since this is quite a difficult activity to expect teachers to do so early in the course, you should not expect a list that is very extensive. It might be instructive to come back to this activity after teachers have considered the chapter on drama (Chapter 7 and particularly Section 7.10) and to ask them what other skills they would add to their original list.

1.5 Why use literature in the language classroom?

Aim

To consider the reasons for using literature with the language learner.

Activity type

Ranking activity in groups/pairs followed by mini-lecture/reading text.

Suggested procedure

There are two main ways of doing this section. Either teachers can discuss **Task 18** in groups or pairs, possibly as part of a pyramid discussion. (A pyramid discussion involves dividing teachers into groups who then discuss a task, two groups are then amalgamated into a larger group for a further discussion, and so on.)

The text in the section can be given as a lecture or homework reading text. Alternatively, before doing Task 18 teachers could either singly or in pairs be given, or asked to choose, one of the reasons for using literature which is mentioned in the ranking exercise. They have to write down as many points as they can think of connected with this reason for using literature before reading the appropriate section of the text. After reading, they give a mini-presentation to the class as a whole on their section. Alternatively, the original groups can be redivided so that each new group contains at least one member who has read a different section of the text. They then exchange information about the sections they have read. This kind of jigsaw reading works particularly well with groups of teachers who are also aiming to improve their proficiency in English.

Chapter 2 Approaches to using literature with the language learner

The aim of this chapter is to familiarise teachers with different approaches to using literature in the language classroom. Those trainers who only require a very general overview of this area should concentrate on Task 2, which is the core activity, after perhaps doing Task 1 as a warmer. Sections 2.2, 2.3, 2.4 and 2.5 develop many of the ideas introduced in Task 2 in greater detail. Section 2.2 focusses on a language-based approach in general, Section 2.3 on Stylistics, Section 2.4 on providing the necessary background to literary texts and Section 2.5 on ways of involving students more closely in the text. Those teachers/trainers particularly concerned with the issue of using metalanguage are advised to look at Section 2.6.

2.1 An overview

Aim

To consider three possible approaches to using literature with the language learner and to consider the kinds of students it would be appropriate to use literature with. To examine different approaches and genres to decide which are most suitable for different learners.

Activity type

Pairs/small group/large group discussion; reading, discussion and matching or lecture and note taking.

Task 1 can be used as a warmer before doing Task 2. The quotations from published materials are intended to generate ideas, rather than to provide a clear delineation of approaches.

Suggested procedure

There are two possible ways of doing **Tasks 2 and 3**. The first is to divide teachers into groups and give them the part of the text which sets out the methodological assumptions, selection and organisation of material and to encourage teachers to link these with some of the ideas touched on in Task 1. Then, before handing out the lists of advantages and disadvantages ask the groups to anticipate what these might be, before doing the matching exercise.

The second way of doing this activity is to write the titles of the three approaches in three columns on the board and ask teachers in groups to predict what the methodological assumptions, selection and organisation of material and advantages and disadvantages for each approach might be. You can then give them a mini-lecture on all four of these areas while they take notes. Whichever approach you adopt, at the end of the session you should ask teachers to bring up any other points they would like to add to the lists. This often generates useful discussion about the different approaches to which they may or may not have been exposed, often as language learners themselves.

Teachers could work through the questions for **Task 4** in pairs or groups before feedback involving the whole group. Alternatively, the descriptions of different groups of learners could be written up on separate cards, and different pairs or groups of teachers could select a certain number of cards to discuss. Obviously, the cards could be adapted to describe typical groups of learners that the teachers are likely to encounter. This activity might not be suitable for use with teachers who are likely to remain in one working environment with a particular type of student all their careers.

2.2 A language-based approach to using literature

Aim

To discuss in greater depth the different goals and procedures connected with a language-based approach to using literature.

Activity type

Mini-lecture followed by discussion in pairs or groups.

Suggested procedure

The information in this section is best given as a mini-lecture after giving teachers the initial focus question: 'What is meant by a language-based approach to literature?'

Task 6 should be worked on in pairs or groups. Rather than doing feedback with the whole group, groups or pairs could be re-divided to discuss their conclusions. Group feedback is definitely required for **Task 7** since this task pulls together some of the important issues connected with the approach. **Task 8** could also be discussed in small groups before having a plenary session.

2.3　Stylistics in the classroom

Aim

To introduce teachers to the rationale, method, advantages and dis-advantages of using stylistic analysis with their students.

Activity type

Mini-lecture/reading, followed by discussion in pairs and groups.

Suggested procedure

Teachers consider the focus questions in **Task 9** before reading the text or taking notes from a lecture based on that text.

There are two ways of helping teachers with the procedure for doing stylistic analysis. The first is to write up on the board or on an overhead projector transparency, the procedure outlined under the heading: 'Analysing a text for classroom use'. Groups or pairs can then read and discuss the text and questions connected with *A House for Mr Biswas* (**Tasks 10, 11 and 12**). If you adopt this approach then it is important that teachers get some practice in applying the procedure to their own texts. The day before this session they may need to be told to search out a short text to bring to class for discussion. Or you could get them to apply the procedure to any set texts they will be using with their own students. Alternatively, if you do not wish to use *A House for Mr Biswas* you could simply provide teachers with the two-stage procedure which they then apply directly to a text they would like to use, or are obliged to use, with their own students.

Task 13 is intended to promote discussion and could be done as a pyramid discussion. (In a pyramid discussion, teachers discuss the task in smallish groups with the aim of reaching a consensus opinion; two of these groups are then combined to form a new group which in turn reaches a consensus and so on. Even if consensus is difficult to reach, quite vigorous discussion usually develops.)

2.4   Literature as content: How far to go?

Aim

To evaluate and assess what aspects of the Literature as Content approach are useful in a general English classroom.

Activity type

Reading, summary writing and discussion.

Suggested procedure

Teachers work on **Tasks 14 and 15** alone before discussing the questions in **Task 15** as a group. Responses to Task 15 will vary, as will interpretations of the poem. Teachers should be reassured about this since they illustrate an important principle – some background information is often vital if students are to grasp the meaning of certain texts, although what background is necessary may well vary from reader to reader.

Task 16 is intended as a discussion activity. One way of doing it is to divide teachers into groups according to which response they felt was closest to their own. Each group has to then come up with as many reasons as possible to justify their choice. The reasons are presented to the group as a whole.

Task 17 could simply be given as a list, or the group could be asked to brainstorm a list of this nature themselves which they then compare with the one provided.

2.5 Literature for personal enrichment: Involving students

Aim

To consider some of the difficulties of involving students personally in the text, and ways of overcoming these difficulties.

Activity type

Discussion in pairs and groups; brainstorm followed by mini-lecture/reading.

Suggested procedure

Teachers should work through the exercises in **Task 18 and 19** in pairs and groups.

The questions in **Task 20** can be brainstormed in groups or pairs, and if necessary teachers can read the text that follows, or trainers can give the students a mini-lecture on what is in it.

Task 21 is an important activity for ensuring that teachers apply the content of Section 2.5 to their own materials. If necessary it could be done as a workshop, with teachers finding appropriate materials which can then be discussed with colleagues in a later session. Alternatively, you could supply the materials yourself or ask the teachers to choose one of their set texts to work on.

2.6 The role of metalanguage

Aim

To revise some terms commonly used when discussing literature, and to assess the advantages and drawbacks of using them with students.

Activity type

Matching exercise followed by discussion.

Suggested procedure

Task 22 can be done in two ways. Either all the teachers are given the terms (with their definitions) and examples to match in groups, or, teachers are given a card or a few cards (depending on the numbers in the group) with a term and definition or an example on them. Teachers then mill round the room until they find the example card that matches their term card, or the term card matching the example.

Task 24 involves discussion of disadvantages in groups. Alternatively teachers could be divided into two groups, one to suggest advantages and the other disadvantages. **Task 25** is a group discussion.

Chapter 3 Selecting and evaluating materials

If you are short of time you could go directly to the section in 3.1 titled: 'Other factors to consider when selecting literary texts' (following Task 4). You could then look at the evaluation sheet titled: 'Quickie book evaluation'.

3.1 Selecting texts

Aim

To establish criteria for selecting literary texts to use with students.

Activity type

Filling in a questionnaire; reading texts and assessing their suitability according to a scale; brainstorming ideas to compare against a questionnaire; referring to a checklist.

Suggested procedure

The form in **Task 1** can be filled in by teachers who then discuss their conclusions in pairs or report them to the class.

Task 2 and 3 are also to be done by individual teachers and then discussed in pairs or with the whole group. The texts provided are examples only; depending on what group you have, you might bring in other sample texts to read and analyse. Alternatively, you could ask teachers to bring in their own texts which are then circulated and assessed in terms of the scales. Another way of using these grids is as a kind of troubleshooting exercise after teachers have taught a lesson. If there were any problems during the lesson then perhaps teachers could apply the scales to the materials they used to help clarify why the lesson did not go as planned.

The information about the criteria for selecting texts can either be mentioned by trainers before teachers do Task 3, in order to clarify what is meant by the scales; or teachers could be asked to raise any questions they have about the scales after they have completed the task. Trainers can then elicit the criteria from teachers and clarify or add if necessary.

Task 4 is intended as a brainstorming activity with teachers then comparing their ideas to those in the questionnaire.

The 'Checklist of criteria for choosing literary texts' is intended as a reference. But trainers who prefer not to work through Section 3.1 in detail can simply talk the teachers through this list by writing it on the board or on an overhead projector transparency. Teachers could then be asked to choose which text is most suitable for their students from a range of texts supplied by the trainer or brought into class by the teachers themselves.

3.2 Evaluating learning materials which make use of literary texts

Aim

To help teachers assess and evaluate materials and their suitability for use with the teacher's own students.

Activity type

Writing notes/short paragraph; filling in questionnaires about a particular book/piece of published material and reporting findings to the group; drawing up a list of one's own criteria for choosing published materials.

Procedure

The whole of this section is best done as a workshop in which teachers, either singly or in pairs or groups, assess different books and then, after having decided what their own students need (**Task 5**), report their findings to the group as a whole. The group can then take notes on the books that their colleagues have evaluated. Depending on time available, teachers could use either the 'Quickie' or the 'Detailed' book evaluation form to do this. You could also ask the teachers to do the assessment for homework so that the feedback discussion can be done as a follow-up the next day. If books are not available for assessment, then you could ask teachers to assess a piece of material, either published or 'homemade' using the form for evaluating a piece of material. You could supply different samples of published materials, or ask teachers to bring in their own to evaluate and discuss.

Chapter 4 Reading literature cross-culturally

The activities in this chapter work best if teachers are first asked to put themselves in the position of their students (Section 4.1). But if you are short of time, then teachers could simply be given the checklist of cultural aspects to consider (Section 4.2) with the specific examples from texts deleted, as well as the list of strategies for overcoming cultural problems (Section 4.3).

4.1 Being a student

Aim

To sensitise teachers to the kinds of cultural difficulties which students may experience when reading literature.

Activity type

Reading and discussion of relevant texts in groups and pairs.

Suggested procedure

Depending on the group of teachers with whom you are working, you could select different texts to the ones used here. Obviously, your teachers will experience different levels of difficulty with the texts depending on their own cultural background. If the teachers are having to use texts with their own students, which they themselves are finding culturally difficult, then it might be productive to use precisely these texts for this activity. On the other hand, if the teachers have a good knowledge of the culture which provides the background to the texts their students will be reading, then it is more useful to use texts from outside this culture so as to sensitise them to the cultural problems their students may experience. Since the texts are quite long, it is useful to divide the teachers into groups and to get each group reading a different text and discussing the questions that follow. When the groups have done this, they can then move on to the next text. Before discussing the questions in **Task 1** with the group as a whole, make sure all the teachers have at least had time to read through all the texts. The discussion here is intended to be fairly open-ended, although the responses to Task 1(a) can be collated to make up a checklist similar to the one in Section 4.2.

4.2 A consideration of cultural aspects in texts

Aim

To provide a checklist of cultural aspects in texts which can then be used as a reference by teachers when anticipating student problems.

Activity type

Comparing own ideas with a checklist; discussion of two opposing statements.

Suggested procedure

Both **Task 2** and **Task 3** can be discussed in pairs and groups. If you think that most of the teachers in your group are likely to agree as to which statement in Task 3 is the most convincing you could get them, for the sake of debate, to try to argue the opposite view by brainstorming as many ideas to support it as they can.

4.3 Strategies for overcoming cultural problems

Aim

To suggest various strategies for dealing with students' cultural problems with texts; to apply all the ideas and procedure in this chapter to texts which teachers will be using with their own students.

Activity type

Brainstorming in groups/pairs; comparing own ideas with list provided.

Suggested procedure

Task 4 is best done as a workshop in which teachers generate their own ideas for dealing with cultural problems in literary texts. These ideas can then be compared with the list provided.

Chapter 5 Materials design and lesson planning: Novels and short stories

The ultimate aim of the activities in this chapter is to encourage teachers to develop their own materials for using short stories and novels with students. Although the activities are linked to each other, they are also designed to be used individually. Various approaches to the material in this chapter can be taken:

1. The first is to work through all the sections in order, beginning with the short story (Sections 5.1 to 5.6) and then moving on to the novel (Section 5.7).
2. If you only wish to deal with the short story you could leave out Section 5.7, and if you are rather short of time you might wish to leave out Sections 5.1 and 5.2, which deal with more general background factors, and concentrate on practical classroom activities for using a short story (5.3 to 5.6).
3. If your main aim is to help teachers use a novel in the classroom, then you could begin by focussing on the distinctive features of a novel by using Tasks 4 to 8 for the novel. You could then move on to Section 5.3, although you would need to add the problems discussed in Section 5.7 to the mind-map (Figure 5.1). Teachers could then brainstorm some ideas for tasks and activities to exploit a novel using the headings in Task 13 before comparing them to the list of suggestions in Section 5.5. This list, together with the ideas in Section 5.7, could then be added to Figure 5.1. Finally, teachers could be asked to work on Task 18 and plan their own scheme of work for use with a novel.

5.1 Writing your own story

Aim

To orient teachers towards the content of this chapter.

Activity type

Prediction exercise based on paragraphs from a short story.

Suggested procedure

If you have an overhead projector, then this activity can be done by gradually revealing the paragraphs from the story, while giving teachers sufficient time to build up their own version between paragraphs. Or you could read the paragraphs out aloud, or write them up on the board one at a time. When the pairs or groups have all finished inventing their own stories, ask them to tell their stories to the class as a whole. Alternatively, you could regroup teachers so that each new group has at least one representative of the previous group in it. The different 'mini-narratives' are then discussed and compared.

5.2 Distinctive features of a short story

Aim

To encourage teachers to identify distinctive features of the short story. This may help them to anticipate student difficulties while designing materials.

Suggested procedure

Teachers work in groups followed by feedback and comments by the trainer.

5.3 Anticipating student problems when using a short story

Aim

To encourage teachers to further anticipate typical student problems with reading or using a short story. This should help in designing more effective materials.

Activity type

Teachers brainstorming in groups, followed by feedback.

Suggested procedure

1. Ask the teachers in groups to brainstorm the kinds of problems that students might have with a short story. Encourage them to write down their ideas in the form of a 'mind-map' (i.e. a tree-like diagram in which the main branches represent major points, and smaller branches secondary points – Figure 5.1 is a mind-map). You could provide teachers with some headings to get the discussion going. These could be:
   - Following the plot
   - Lack of motivation
   - Understanding the language

Alternatively, you could provide them with the outline of the mind-map with a few headings supplied, and ask them to fill in the rest themselves.

2. One group can then present their discussion to the class by drawing their mind-map on the board, an overhead projector or poster. It is a good idea to keep the mind-map as a reference until after the activities in Section 5.5, so a poster is often the most effective way to do this. Instead of individual presentation by one group, you could collate the ideas of the whole class on a single poster. At the end of this activity, emphasise that when designing materials trainees should try to bear in mind the potential difficulties for students. For the moment, ways of overcoming these difficulties will not really be discussed, although the mind-map will be re-evaluated after Section 5.5.

5.4 Planning a lesson for use with a short story

Aim

To identify the aims of a range of activities and tasks which can be used to exploit a short story and to order them in a logical sequence.

Activity type

Identifying aims of activities; putting activities in a suitable order.

Suggested procedure.

1. Teachers should read *Eveline*, either at home or in class.
2. In groups, the teachers decide on the aims of the activities and a possible ordering for them (**Task 11**). After the aims of the activities have been discussed with the whole class, each group can then present a possible ordering of the activities to make up a complete lesson plan.
3. When doing the assessment of the lesson plan (**Task 12**) encourage teachers to be as critical of the plan as possible, especially when evaluating to what extent they could apply the activities in the plan to their own classes.
4. If you are working with a group of teachers who are keen to improve their proficiency in English, you could use this firstly as a language development session, before discussing its pedagogic application. In this case, you would do the lesson with teachers as if they were students, after giving them all the activities already appropriately

sequenced. After their answers to the questions have been discussed, teachers could then set about identifying the aims of each activity before moving on to Task 12.

5.5   Further tasks and activities for use with a short story

Aim

To encourage teachers to suggest a range of activities for achieving various aims when using a short story with students.

Activity type

Brainstorming in groups.

Procedure

You can simply ask teachers in groups to brainstorm their ideas under the headings provided. If the list of headings seems overlong, then different groups could be asked to work on different headings. Ideas can be collated, either in group feedback or by reorganising groups so that each new group has at least one member of the previous groups in it. The list of suggested activities is simply intended as a reference for teachers, to which they may refer when designing materials of their own. However, it is important to ensure that teachers make the connection between the activities mentioned here, and the kinds of problems discussed in Section 5.3. If you have kept the poster made in 5.3, then this can be referred to again in the discussion in **Task 14**(b).

5.6   Designing your own materials for use with a short story

Aim

To give teachers practice in designing their own materials for exploiting a short story.

Activity type

Reading of a short story (if this was not done previously as homework), followed by group discussion and a poster presentation.

Suggested procedure

1. Divide teachers into groups and get them to design their own materials for exploiting a short story. Those who prefer to could work alone. You can either provide the story yourself, or ask teachers to select one which they feel is suitable for their own students.
2. Get the teachers to write their ideas on a large poster which can then be put up on the wall and analysed by the other teachers.
3. If possible get teachers to try out their materials on a class of students and report back on how the lesson went.

5.7 Using novels in the language classroom

Aim

To focus on any problems with using novels in the language classroom and suggest ways of overcoming them.

Activity type

Sorting features into two categories; brainstorming solutions to problems; planning a scheme of work.

Suggested procedure

Please see the beginning of the Trainer's Notes for this chapter for ideas on how to use this section if you are concentrating *only* on using the novel with your teachers. If you are working through this section after teachers have done Section 5.1 to 5.6, then **Tasks 16** to **18** can be done by teachers in pairs or groups.

Chapter 6   Materials design and lesson planning: Poetry

This chapter aims to identify the distinctive linguistic features of poetry which may hamper student understanding of a poem, but can also be a valuable source of classroom activities. Sections 6.1 to 6.5 consider these features and their implications in the classroom, while Sections 6.6 to 6.8 provide examples of materials and activities to be used with students at both lower and more advanced levels. Since Sections 6.6 to 6.8 are rather time consuming to do with teachers, it is probably best to do only whichever of these sections is of the most relevance to the group you are training, depending on what level of students they themselves will be teaching. Section 6.9 suggests the kinds of questions teachers need to ask themselves while preparing materials, and Section 6.10 provides a reference list of activities and tasks to use with poems. For those trainers or teachers with limited time, the core sections for this chapter are Section 6.2; Section 6.3; either Section 6.6, 6.7 or 6.8; Sections 6.9 and 6.10.

6.1 Putting a poem back together again

Aim

To orient teachers towards some of the issues of this chapter by using an activity that teachers could use with students.

Activity type

Ordering a jumbled text.

Suggested procedure

In pairs or groups teachers put the text back together again and then discuss the questions which follow.

6.2 What is distinctive about poetry?

Aim

To identify certain unusual linguistic features of poetry in order to ascertain how poetry can best be used in the classroom.

Activity type

Discussion of example texts.

Suggested procedure

Teachers are divided into pairs or groups to analyse what is distinctive about each extract (**Task 6**) – this should be followed by group feedback. With teachers who are also aiming to improve their proficiency in English, care should be taken to explicate the unfamiliar vocabulary in each extract. Teachers should be very clear as to the purpose of this exercise – that by identifying some of the features of poetry, they may then design materials which are relevant and appropriate. **Task 7** is an important follow-up to the analysis of texts – in groups or pairs, teachers should be asked to consider what implications the exercise they have just done has for the classroom. This serves as a lead-in to the discussion and lecture in Section 6.3.

6.3 Why use poetry with the language learner?

Aim

To consider the reasons for using poetry with the language learner despite its unusual linguistic features, and the difficulties students may have interpreting it.

Activity type

Discussion followed by a mini-lecture.

Suggested procedure

For **Task 8** teachers are divided into groups or pairs to discuss the comments – it is best if these are distributed or put up on the board or an overhead projector.

The text for **Task 9** can either be distributed as a reading text or delivered by trainers as a mini-lecture. For teachers wishing to improve their proficiency in English, this could be a useful form of listening practice. Another alternative is for trainers to simply go through each comment suggesting counter-arguments for them or eliciting these from teachers.

6.4 Exploiting unusual language features

Aim

To pinpoint the 'deviant' linguistic features of a poem in order to decide what kinds of activities can be based on them. An important aim following on from this is to evaluate a purely linguistically-based procedure for exploiting poems in the classroom.

Activity type

Discussion of a poem and accompanying materials followed by an evaluation of the procedure used to exploit it.

Suggested procedure

In groups or pairs teachers discuss **Task 10** and **Task 11**. An alternative procedure, useful perhaps for teachers wishing to improve their proficiency in English, is to omit Task 10, and get teachers to do the activities for Task 11 as if they were students. This can then be followed by a discussion about the purpose of these activities.

Task 12 aims to make explicit the procedure behind the activities. Since this procedure is intended to illustrate a generalisable approach for using poetry in the classroom, it is important that teachers understand the steps involved (analysing unusual linguistic features in a poem and then making them the basis for classroom tasks and activities) as well as the limitations of the approach (Paragraph B). Teachers can either be given the two paragraphs to discuss, or they could be asked simply to reflect on the procedure used in the activities and to suggest its limitations.

6.5 Helping students with figurative meanings

Aim

To suggest why figurative meanings in a poem may be difficult for students to grasp and to provide some ideas for helping students with them.

Activity type

Discussion of extracts; mini-lecture; evaluation of materials.

Suggested procedure

Teachers discuss **Task 13** in groups or pairs.

The section titled 'The problem with metaphors' may either be delivered as a mini-lecture by the trainer or the points made could be brought out in discussion with teachers.

Teachers can be asked either in groups or pairs to do the activities in the section, 'Helping students with metaphorical meaning' and then the sorting exercise in **Task 15**. It is very important that teachers understand the generalisable procedure described in Task 15 so that they can apply it to other poems.

6.6   Using poetry with lower levels

Aim

To consider some of the problems teachers may have using poetry at lower levels; to suggest ways of using poetry at lower levels.

Activity type

Discussion of statements; analysis of teaching materials; matching activities to their type; matching materials to their aims.

Suggested procedure

Teachers discuss **Task 16** in pairs or groups providing reasons to justify their choice.

There are two possible approaches to examining the activities for lower levels. Teachers can work through all the activities in groups or pairs; alternatively, teachers can be divided into four groups, each of which is given a different poem and its activities to read and discuss. Each group completes **Tasks 17 and 18** for their poem. Groups are then redivided so that each new group has at least one member from each of the previous groups. Groups then describe the materials they examined to each other and compare the aims of the different activities.

6.7   Using poetry to develop oral skills

Aim

To consolidate some of the ideas and procedures suggested in Sections 6.4, 6.5 and 6.6; to encourage teachers to think about ways of using poetry for choral reading.

Activity type

Discussion of activities/tasks; preparation and performance of choral reading.

Suggested procedure

There are two main ways of approaching these materials. The first is to let teachers work through the activities and to do **Task 20** before devising their own choral reading in small groups to be performed for the whole group. The checklist and the teaching notes which follow can then be used as a reference when teachers use choral reading with their own classes.

The alternative approach, if teachers seem confident in their understanding of the issues and procedures outlined in Sections 6.4, 6.5 and 6.6, is to leave out the activities which accompany 'As It was' and **Task 20** and ask teachers to devise their own materials to use with either this poem or one they have chosen themselves. These materials could then be presented to the class as part of a poster presentation. Then teachers could be asked to devise their own checklist for preparing a poem for choral reading as well as to plan and present a choral reading to the whole group.

6.8 Using a poem with students at higher levels

Aim

To bring together some of the ideas and procedures of the previous sections by devising materials for using a poem at higher levels; to suggest ways of supplying background information which is useful for understanding a poem.

Activity type

Discussion of predicted student problems; analysis of possible tasks and activities to use with students; use of diagram to design own materials.

Suggested procedure

In pairs or groups students work through **Tasks 23 and 24.**

There are two possible ways of treating the activities which go with 'London'. Teachers can work through the activities as if they were students, and then discuss them using the questions in **Task 24.** Alternatively, teachers can analyse what kinds of problems the activities are designed to overcome while they read through them and then go on to do **Task 25.**

N.B. Many of the activities used in the lesson plan are quite difficult (e.g. Activities 5., 6. and 13.) because they are open-ended questions, leading to many acceptable answers rather than a single correct answer. If teachers find this frustrating, you could point out that this is testimony to the multiple levels of meaning in Blake's poem. From a pedagogic point of view, such discourse lends itself to activities that promote discussion rather than 'right answers'.

6.9   Anticipating student problems

Aim

To provide teachers with guidelines to think about when anticipating student problems with a particular poem.

Activity type

Reading a checklist; analysing a poem in terms of the difficulties it may cause students.

Suggested procedure

Teachers read the checklist of questions for predicting students' problems.

Teachers analyse a poem they would like to use with their own students in terms of the checklist, and think of possible tasks and activities to use.

6.10   Further tasks and activities

Aim

To summarise some of the tasks and activities used in this chapter and to suggest others.

Activity type

Examining a reference sheet for teachers to use when designing their own materials.

Chapter 7 Materials design and lesson planning: Plays

This chapter is concerned mainly with using extracts from plays in the classroom. For trainers with limited time, the core sections to use in training sessions are Section 7.4; either Section 7.5, 7.6 or 7.7; Sections 7.8 and 7.9. Section 7.9 is intended largely as a reference for teachers to look at on their own. If you are mainly interested in making use of whole plays in the classroom, then you might want to look at Section 7.10 and also ask teachers to refer to Section 7.9 as a checklist.

7.1 What is distinctive about plays?

Aim

To encourage teachers to start thinking about plays by drawing on their own experience and to draw their attention to the distinction between 'performance' and 'text'. This distinction is a helpful starting point for considering some of the features of plays which differentiate them from novels, poetry or short stories.

Activity type

Discussion in pairs or groups followed by group discussion.

7.2 The language of a play

Aim

To focus on some of the ways that the language of a play is central to its meaning.

Activity type

Completion of gap-fill activity; discussion of questions analysing dialogue.

Suggested procedure

Teachers work in pairs or groups followed by feedback with group as a whole.

7.3 The performance of a play

Aim

To remind teachers of all the aspects of a performance of a play so they can then be incorporated into the activities designed for use with a play.

Activity type

Discussion in pairs or groups, followed by a class discussion.

7.4 Why use plays in the language learning classroom?

Aim

To pinpoint reasons for using plays with the language learner.

Activity type

Prediction activity based on mind-map; mini-lecture.

Suggested procedure

There are a number of ways of doing this section. The first is to give Figure 7.1 to teachers in pairs or groups and ask them to predict what will be in a lecture based on the diagram. You then give them a brief lecture based on the text in Section 7.4.

The second way is to ask teachers to make predictions from the diagram, but to read the text themselves, either in class or at home.

A third possibility is to ask teachers in pairs or groups to prepare their own diagram of reasons for using plays in the classroom and to then add to and modify their diagrams as they listen to your lecture. Points included on their diagrams, but not mentioned in the lecture, can be discussed afterwards.

7.5   Using play extracts to think about language in conversation

Aim

To explore the different tasks and activities which will increase student awareness of language in conversation.

Activity type

Reading and discussion of texts; matching activities to aims; using a diagram as a model for designing own materials.

Suggested procedure

There are two main ways of approaching this session. The first is to follow the progression in the book with teachers reading the two texts and then answering the questions in **Tasks 8 and 9**. Teachers then read through the sequence of activities and discuss the answers for Activities 5, 6 and 7. This can then be followed by discussing **Tasks 10 and 11** in groups or pairs.

The alternative way is to ask the teachers to pretend to be students and to do the lesson to go with the two texts as if they were students. The second approach is often more successful if teachers are keen on improving their own language proficiency, since the session then has the dual function of expanding the teachers' language awareness as well as suggesting how they can design materials for their own students. It is also a helpful way of putting teachers in the position of their students, so that they experience the lesson rather than simply analyse it. After you have taught the lesson with the full participation of the teachers, you can ask them to examine the activities more closely by completing **Task 10**.

Task 11 is an important activity for getting teachers to generalise the tasks and procedures used in the activities. Ideally, teachers should be given plenty of time to design *and* teach their own lessons. Figure 7.2 can be used as an example or model for a lesson plan, although obviously teachers should be encouraged to adapt it to their own purposes.

7.6 Using play extracts to improve students' oral skills

Aim

To suggest ways of using an extract from a play to improve students' oral abilities.

Activity type

Reading and analysis of a text and the lesson plan based on it; evaluation of a lesson plan; reading and discussion of further activities.

Suggested procedure

As in Section 7.5, teachers could be asked to become students. You would then teach the lesson to them, following the lesson plan for Extract C and asking them to remember and note down all the stages of the lesson when you have finished. **Task 12** could then be used as the basis for evaluating the procedure in the lesson plan. At the end of this session it is important to ensure that teachers are able to transfer some of the ideas in this session to their own teaching, preferably by planning and teaching a lesson.

7.7 Using play extracts with lower levels

Aim

To suggest tasks and activities which can be used to exploit texts from plays with students at lower levels.

Activity type

Reading and discussion of texts; choosing and ordering possible activities.

Suggested procedure

Discussion in pairs and groups followed by class discussion.

This section is obviously only relevant for certain teachers with lower level classes. The overall point to be drawn from it is that extracts from plays can successfully be used at lower levels, provided they are carefully chosen. The tasks and activities designed to exploit them need not differ substantially from those used in ordinary EFL or ESL lessons. Provided the language is fairly simple, even plays dealing with fairly difficult subjects can be chosen. They can then be used as a springboard for interesting language and skills practice.

7.8 Anticipating student problems

Aim

To provide a checklist of the type of problems students might experience when using an extract from a play.

Activity type

Pairwork or groupwork followed by individual lesson planning.

Suggested procedure

Teachers brainstorm some questions for predicting student difficulties before looking at the checklist.

Texts of immediate relevance to teachers' own classes can be substituted for Mark Antony's speech for discussion and annotation in groups. It is important for teachers to get an opportunity to try out their own ideas by using texts relevant to their own students.

7.9 Further activities for play extracts

Aim

To provide a bank of tasks and activities to use with plays.

Activity type

Brainstorming; reading reference list.

Suggested procedure

This section is simply intended to provide teachers with a list to refer to when planning their lessons. They should be encouraged to add their own ideas to it. You might get teachers to brainstorm the kind of activities they could use for each of the different categories before looking at the lists. They should also identify which activities are likely to be appropriate with their own students.

7.10   Using a whole play with students

Aim

To suggest ways in which teachers could use a whole play with their students.

Suggested procedure

This section is intended to be used with teachers largely as a workshop, and can be used in one of the following ways:

a) Teachers work through **Task 16**, either individually or in groups, with the purpose of planning how to use a whole play with their students. If the teachers have the opportunity to try out these materials on a class of students, then a later training session could be allocated to discuss how successfully the materials were used.

b) Teachers choose a play in English they would like to see themselves. (For teachers doing a training course in an English-speaking country a visit to a live performance of a play is often the high point of the course.) You prepare a skeleton outline of tasks and activities to guide them in their viewing of the play. You may find that the original text of the play, critical writings on it and a programme (if available in advance) will all be of help here. After the teachers have seen the play, they are asked to discuss the aims behind the activities you devised in your skeleton outline as well as to evaluate how effectively these aims were achieved. If there is time, a later training session could be used to devise a scheme of work for teachers to use with their own students.

c) Teachers are asked to read a whole play, possibly before coming on the course. Some course time is set aside to work through tasks and activities relating to the play, possibly using some of the ideas in Sections 7.9 and 7.10. This may be helpful for teachers who wish to improve their proficiency in English. The second stage is to get teachers analysing why you used the tasks you did so that they can then think of using similar tasks when designing materials to use with their own students.

Chapter 8　Reflecting on the literature lesson

All the tasks in this chapter are intended to be used to assist teachers in their ongoing professional development. They are not intended to be used as the basis for evaluation of teachers on a training course nor as assessment of teachers for promotional or related reasons. Obviously, for these two purposes, assessment methods would need to be developed which reflect the aims of your training course or organisation. The tasks provided in this chapter are designed to let teachers set the pace for their own learning and development. The role of the trainer in this situation is to be positive and supportive, to act as a sounding board and source of ideas and to suggest alternative ways in which teachers can plan and implement their lessons. It is also important for trainers to foster the development of a culture in which teachers come to think of observing others and being observed by others as a useful tool in their own self-development.

Ideally, the observation tasks provided in this chapter should be used by teachers and observers when viewing lessons that teachers are teaching to their own students. This might work well if a training course in using literature is part of the in-service training of teachers, if teachers are doing a training course part-time while continuing to work in their own organisations or if teachers have organised themselves into teacher development groups which meet to discuss techniques and ideas that they can use with their classes. Many training programmes are also able to offer teachers some kind of teaching practice. If this is not possible, then trainees should be encouraged to try out the observation tasks when they return to their usual place of work. During the course, they could try out the tasks while watching a fellow-teacher micro-teaching using colleagues as students, while observing a video of a lesson using literature or while watching the trainer teach a lesson to the group of trainees.

Aims and procedures

Aim

To suggest different ways in which teachers can become more self-aware about the way they use literature in the language classroom and to provide observation tasks which enable teachers to reflect on their own teaching and that of their colleagues.

Activity type

Filling in a questionnaire; filling in observation tasks; making a list suggesting other ways of facilitating teacher development.

Suggested procedure

As Section 8.1 is rather general, it is only necessary to ask teachers to do it if you wish to clarify the purposes of the observation tasks to be used in this chapter. If you do use it, then teachers could complete the questionnaire individually before discussing it in groups or pairs.

The task in Section 8.2 can be used to facilitate general reflections on the literature lesson. You may wish to discuss the first part of the task with teachers while they are planning their lessons. While observing the lesson, jot down a few notes, but try to let teachers lead the way in the discussion following the lesson. (For an interesting and relevant discussion of techniques for facilitating discussion in a post-observation meeting see Sheal, 1989.)

The micro-tasks in Section 8.3 can be used by teachers after various sections or chapters of the book have been discussed in order to make the link between 'theory' and 'practice'. You could use whatever comes out of the observation as the starting point for the next training session.

Section 8.4 could be extended to become a mini-project or assignment in which teachers follow the progress of a single student through a course using literature, and then write a report. The initial interview could be made much longer, and the student's progress could be monitored over a series of lessons in order to see how his/her strategies for coping with literary texts develop.

The suggestions in Section 8.5 could be built into a training course from the beginning of the programme. For example, teachers could be asked to keep diaries or logs of their experiences on the course, which trainers could read from time to time. (See Thornbury, 1991.) Teachers could be encouraged to exchange lesson plans and pool ideas – a display board on which lesson plans are regularly displayed with space for comments and suggestions from colleagues is one way of doing this.

Chapter 9   Literature and self-access

The bulk of this chapter is intended to be used as a simulation in which groups of teachers plan the setting up of a literature self-access centre. If you have limited time, then the core activities for this chapter are in Sections 9.1 and 9.2 and the simulation itself (Sections 9.3 and 9.4).

Sections 9.1 and 9.2

Aim

To list the different types of literature self-access centres and the reasons for establishing a centre.

Activity type

Lists of types and reasons.

Suggested procedure

Either elicit the lists from teachers, or ask them to brainstorm their ideas in pairs or groups.

Sections 9.3 and 9.4   A simulation: First and second meetings

Aim

To make teachers aware of some of the issues involved in setting up a literature self-access centre, and to encourage them to develop a plan of action and materials.

Activity type

Form filling, roleplay, completing meeting report, designing materials/ worksheets.

Suggested procedure

Divide teachers into groups and let them fill in the form 'Literature and self-access: Our school' together. If you are training teachers from different contexts, they will need to decide on what school they will be discussing during the simulation. If the teachers are from the same school, then they might prefer to discuss their own school. In both cases, the role cards could be adapted to be made more directly relevant to teachers. For example, there are no role cards for parents and students, yet in some schools these might have a crucial role to play in setting up the centre. A student role card might look something like this:

> You are keen to improve your English because you only hear or read English when you attend English classes. You don't mind reading some books in English at home, but you would like to read books that really interest you. Tell your teachers about the types of books that you would like to read.

A parent role card might look like this:

> You are keen to extend your son or daughter's knowledge of English by getting them to read more books in English at home, or even listen to cassettes. You are enthusiastic about the setting up of a self-access centre for students, and would like to help raise money for it and to help organise it. Share your ideas about how to do this with the staff at your son or daughter's school.

If the issue of resources is of major importance for some of the teachers all the role cards could be made to refer to this more directly.

Set a time limit for the roleplay itself (usually a maximum of thirty minutes) and ensure that the groups complete the planning meeting report. This could be used to report back to all the other groups in a plenary session. If you are working with a group of teachers who are keen to improve their proficiency in English, you could circulate unobtrusively during the roleplay and note down any errors in the teachers' speech for later discussion.

Section 9.4 could form the basis for a workshop in which teachers design materials for the self-access centre. Some ideas for worksheets can be found in Section 9.6.

Sections 9.5 and 9.6   Notes on a case study and planning worksheets

Aim

To provide models for the setting up of a literature self-access centre and for worksheets which encourage extensive reading of the books in the centre.

Trainer's Notes

Activity type

Reading of case study and worksheets; designing of a worksheet.

Suggested procedure

Teachers read the case study and worksheets for homework, after doing the simulation in class. Occasionally you may find that the group with whom you are working would benefit from reading Sections 9.5 and 9.6 before doing the simulation.

Bibliography

Texts used in tasks and activities

Achebe, C. (1964) *Arrow of God*, Heinemann.

Albee, E. (1961) *The Zoo Story and other plays*, Jonathan Cape.

Berry, J. (ed.) (1984) *News for Babylon – The Chatto book of West Indian–British Poetry*, Chatto and Windus.

Brewster, Y. (ed.) (1987) *Black Plays*, Methuen.

Browning, R. *The Poems, Volume I* (edited by John Pettigrew and supplemented by Thomas J. Collins) Penguin 1981.

Dalby, R. (ed.) (1988) *The Virago Book of Victorian Ghost Stories*, Virago Press.

Dickinson, P. and Shannon, S. (eds.) (1967) *Poet's Choice*, Evans Brothers.

Evans, G. L. (1977) *The Language of Modern Drama*, Dent and Sons.

Evans, M. (ed.) (1982) *The Woman Question*, Fontana Paperbacks.

Figueroa, J. J. (ed.) (1982) *An Anthology of African and Caribbean Writing in English*, Heinemann in association with the Open University.

Freer, A. and Andrew, J. (eds.) (1970) *The Cambridge Book of English Verse 1900–1939*, Cambridge University Press.

Fugard, A. (1973) *Hello and Goodbye*, Oxford University Press.

Fugard, A. (1985) *Boesman and Lena and other plays*, Oxford University Press.

Green, J. (ed.) (1982) *A Dictionary of Contemporary Quotations*, David and Charles.

Greene, G. (1972) *Collected Stories*, The Bodley Head and Heinemann.

Harrison, M. and Stuart-Clark, C. (eds.) (1977) *The New Dragon Book of Verse*, Oxford University Press.

Heaney, S. and Hughes, T. (eds.) (1982) *The Rattle Bag*, Faber and Faber.

Holström, L. (ed.) (1990) *The Inner Courtyard*, Virago Press.

Joyce, J. *Dubliners*, Triad/Panther Books, 1977.

Lewis, N. (ed.) (1985) *Messages: A book of poems*, Faber and Faber.

Longman Active Study Dictionary, New Edition, Longman 1991.

Madden-Simpson, J. (ed.) (1984) *Unwelcome Idea*, Arlen House.

Majumdar, R. and McLaurin, A. (eds.) (1975) *Virginia Woolf: The Critical Heritage*, Routledge and Kegan Paul.

McGough, R. and Rosen, M. (1979) *You tell me – poems by Roger McGough and Michael Rosen*, Kestrel Books, Penguin.

Murray, L. A. (ed.) (1986) *The New Oxford Book of Australian Verse*, Oxford University Press.

Naipaul, V. S. (1969) *A House for Mr Biswas*, Penguin.

Pinter, H. (1960) *Plays: One*, Methuen.

Ricks, C. (ed.) *The New Oxford Book of Victorian Verse*, Oxford University Press.

Rosen, M. (ed.) (1985) *The Kingfisher Book of Children's Poetry*, Kingfisher Books.

Bibliography

Rowe, J. (ed.) (1971) *Modern Poetry: A Selection*, Oxford University Press.

Rumens, C. (ed.) (1985) *Making for the Open*, Chatto and Windus.

Scott Fitzgerald, F. *The Great Gatsby*, Penguin, 1983.

Shange, N. (1987) *Nappy Edges*, Methuen.

Smith, A. J. (ed.) (1971) *John Donne: The Complete English Poems*, Allen Lane.

Styan, J. L. (1975) *Drama, Stage and Audience*, Cambridge University Press.

Thomas, D. (1978) *Collected Poems 1934–1952*, J. M. Dent and Sons.

Townsend, J. (ed.) (1971) *Modern poetry: A selection by John Rowe Townsend*, Oxford University Press.

Wain, J. (ed.) (1981) *Everyman's Book of English Verse*, Dent and Sons.

Waugh, E. (1985) *Brideshead Revisited*, Methuen.

Wilde, O. *The Importance of Being Earnest*, Methuen, 1966.

Yuan-tsung Chen (1980) *The Dragon's Village*, The Women's Press.

Zundel, V. (ed.) (1991) *Faith in her words*, Lion Publishing.

Texts for further reference

Alderson, J. C. and Urquhart, A. H. (1984) *Reading in a foreign language*, Longman.

Brumfit, C. J. (ed.) (1983) 'Teaching literature overseas: language-based approaches', *ELT Documents 115*, British Council, Pergamon Press.

Brumfit, C. J. and Carter, R. (eds.) (1986) *Literature and Language Teaching*, Oxford University Press.

Brumfit, C., Carter, R., and Walker, R. (eds.) (1989) 'Literature and the Learner: Methodological Approaches', *ELT Documents 130*, Modern English Publications in association with the British Council.

Carter, R. (ed.) (1982) *Language and Literature; An Introductory Reader in Stylistics*, Allen and Unwin.

Carter, R. and Burton, D. (eds.) (1982) *Literary Text and Language Study*, Edward Arnold.

Corder, S. P. and Allen, J. P. B. (eds.) (1974) *The Edinburgh Course in Applied Linguistics 3*, Oxford University Press.

Crystal, D. (1988) *The English Language*, Penguin.

Culler, J. (1975) *Structuralist Poetics*, Routledge and Kegan Paul.

Duff, T. (ed.) (1988) *Explorations in Teacher Training – problems and issues*, Longman.

Eagleton, T. (1983) *Literary Theory*, Basil Blackwell.

Fowler, R. (1977) *Linguistics and the Novel*, Methuen.

Fowler, R. (1986) *Linguistic Criticism*, Oxford University Press.

Gillie, C. (1972) *Longman Companion to English Literature*, Longman.

Gower, R. (1986) 'Can stylistic analysis help the EFL learner to read literature?', *ELT Journal* **40**, 2.

Gower, R. (1990) 'Anyone for Beowulf: Literature as a subject in ELT', *Sigma* **3**.

Harrison, B. (ed.) (1990) 'Culture and the language classroom', *ELT Documents 132*, Modern English Publications in association with the British Council.

Holden, S. (ed.) (1988) 'Literature and Language' *1987 Sorrento Conference organised by the British Council*, Modern English Publications.

Jefferson, A. and Robey, D. (eds.) (1984) *Modern Literary Theory: A comparative introduction*, Basil Blackwell.

Lazar, G. (1989) 'Using poetry with the EFL/ESL learner', *Modern English Teacher* 6, 3 and 4.

Lazar, G. (1989) 'Metaphorically Speaking', *Sigma* 1.

Lazar, G. (1990) 'Using novels in the language-learning classroom', *ELT Journal* 44, 3.

Leech, G. (1988) *A Linguistic Guide to English Poetry*, Longman.

Leech, G. N. and Short, M. H. (1981) *Style in Fiction*, Longman.

Lodge, D. (ed.) (1990) *Twentieth Century Literary Criticism*, Longman.

Ousby, I. (ed.) (1988) *Cambridge Guide to Literature in English*, Cambridge University Press.

Ramsaran, S. (1983) 'Poetry in the language classroom', *ELT Journal* 37, 1.

Rimmon-Kenan, S. (1983) *Narrative Fiction: Contemporary Poetics*, Methuen.

Rossner, R. (1983) 'Talking Shop: H. G. Widdowson on Literature and ELT', in *ELT Journal* 37, 1.

Searle, C. (1984) *Words unchained: Language and Revolution in Grenada*, Zed Books.

Selden, R. (1989) *A Reader's Guide to Contemporary Literary Theory*, Harvester Wheatsheaf.

Sheal, P. (1989) 'Classroom Observation: Training the Observers', *ELT Journal* 43, 2.

Short, M. H. (1981) 'Discourse Analysis and the Analysis of Drama', *Applied Linguistics* 2, 2.

Smith, J. 'Stylistics and the pedagogic implications of dialogue in drama and text books', Unpublished dissertation, M.A. in Language and Literature in Education (TESOL), London University Institute of Education, 1985.

Suleiman, S. R. and Crossman, I. (eds.) (1980) *The Reader in the Text: Essays on Audience and Interpretation*, Princeton University Press.

Swartridge, C. (1978) *British Fiction: A Student's A–Z*, Macmillan.

Thornbury, S. (1991) 'Watching the whites of their eyes: the use of teaching-practice logs', *ELT Journal* 45, 2.

Tomlinson, B. (1986) 'Using poetry with mixed ability language groups', *ELT Journal* 40, 1.

Tribble, C. and Jones, G. (1990) *Concordances in the classroom*, Longman.

Valdes, J. M. (ed.) (1986) *Culture Bound*, Cambridge University Press.

Wajnryb, R. (1992) *Classroom Observation Tasks*, Cambridge University Press.

Bibliography

Widdowson, H. G. (1975) *Stylistics and the Teaching of Literature*, Longman.

Widdowson, H. G. (1984) *Explorations in Applied Linguistics 2*, Oxford University Press.

Williams, M. (1989) 'A developmental view of classroom observation', *ELT Journal* 43, 2.

Wynne-Davies, M. (1989) *Bloomsbury Guide to English Literature*, Bloomsbury.

Books to use with students in the classroom

Adkins, A. and Shackleton, M. (eds.) (1980) *Recollections*, Edward Arnold.

Carter, R. and Long, M. (1987) *The Web of Words*, Cambridge University Press.

Collie, J. and Porter-Ladousse, G. (1991) *Paths into Poetry*, Oxford University Press.

Gower, R. (1990) *Past into Present*, Longman.

Gower R. and Pearson, M. (1986) *Reading Literature*, Longman.

Lott, B. (1986) *A Course in English Language and Literature*, Edward Arnold.

Mackay, R. (1987) *Poems*, Modern English Publications.

Maley, D. and Moulding, S. (1985) *Poem into Poem*, Cambridge University Press.

McRae, J. and Boardman, R. (1984) *Reading between the lines*, Cambridge University Press.

McRae, J. and Pantaleoni, L. (1990) *Chapter and Verse*, Oxford University Press.

Pervan-Plavec, M. (1990) *Reading for Study and Pleasure*, Školska Knjiga, Zagreb.

Pierce, T. and Cochrane, E. (eds.) (1979) *Twentieth Century English Short Stories*, Unwin Hyman.

Rossner, R. (1988) *The Whole Story*, Longman.

Shackleton, M. (ed.) (1985) *Double Act*, Edward Arnold.

Tomlinson, B. (1986) *Openings*, Filmscan/Lingual House.

Walker, R. (1983) *Language for Literature*, Collins.

Resource books for teachers

Carter, R. and Long, M. (1991) *Teaching Literature*, Longman.

Collie, J. and Slater, S. (1987) *Literature in the Language Classroom*, Cambridge University Press.

Duff, A. and Maley, A. (1990) *Literature*, Oxford University Press.

Greenwood, J. (1988) *Class Readers*, Oxford University Press.

Hill, J. (1986) *Using Literature in Language Teaching*, Macmillan.

Wessels, C. (1987) *Drama*, Oxford University Press.

Appendix

Eveline

She sat at the window watching the evening invade the avenue. Her head was leaned against the window curtains, and in her nostrils was the odour of dusty cretonne. She was tired.

Few people passed. The man out of the last house passed on his
5   way home; she heard his footsteps clacking along the concrete pavement and afterwards crunching on the cinder path before the new red houses. One time there used to be a field there in which they used to play every evening with other people's children. Then a man from Belfast bought the field and built houses in it – not like their little
10   brown houses, but bright brick houses with shining roofs. The children of the avenue used to play together in that field – the Devines, the Waters, the Dunns, little Keogh the cripple, she and her brothers and sisters. Ernest, however, never played: he was too grown up. Her father used often to hunt them in out of the field with his blackthorn
15   stick; but usually little Keogh used to keep *nix* and call out when he saw her father coming. Still they seemed to have been rather happy then. Her father was not so bad then; and besides, her mother was alive. That was a long time ago; she and her brothers and sisters were all grown up; her mother was dead. Tizzie Dunn was dead, too, and
20   the Waters had gone back to England. Everything changes. Now she was going to go away like the others, to leave her home.

Home! She looked round the room, reviewing all its familiar objects which she had dusted once a week for so many years, wondering where on earth all the dust came from. Perhaps she would never see
25   again those familiar objects from which she had never dreamed of being divided. And yet during all those years she had never found out the name of the priest whose yellowing photograph hung on the wall above the broken harmonium beside the coloured print of the promises made to Blessed Margaret Mary Alacoque. He had been a
30   school friend of her father. Whenever he showed the photograph to a visitor her father used to pass it round with a casual word:

'He is in Melbourne now.'

She had consented to go away, to leave her home. Was that wise? She tried to weigh each side of the question. In her home anyway she
35   had shelter and food; she had those whom she had known all her life about her. Of course she had to work hard, both in the house and at business. What would they say of her in the Stores when they found out that she had run away with a fellow? Say she was a fool, perhaps; and her place would be filled up by advertisement. Miss Gavan would

40   be glad. She had always had an edge on her, especially whenever there were people listening.

     'Miss Hill, don't you see these ladies are waiting?'

     'Look lively, Miss Hill, please.'

     She would not cry many tears at leaving the Stores.

45   But in her new home, in a distant unknown country, it would not be like that. Then she would be married – she, Eveline. People would treat her with respect then. She would not be treated as her mother had been. Even now, though she was over nineteen, she sometimes felt herself in danger of her father's violence. She knew it was that

50   that had given her the palpitations. When they were growing up he had never gone for her, like he used to go for Harry and Ernest, because she was a girl; but latterly he had begun to threaten her and say what he would do to her only for her dead mother's sake. And now she had nobody to protect her. Ernest was dead and Harry, who

55   was in the church decorating business, was nearly always down some-where in the country. Besides, the invariable squabble for money on Saturday nights had begun to weary her unspeakably. She always gave her entire wages – seven shillings – and Harry always sent up what he could, but the trouble was to get any money from her father. He said

60   she used to squander the money, that she had no head, that he wasn't going to give her his hard-earned money to throw about the streets, and much more, for he was usually fairly bad of a Saturday night. In the end he would give her the money and ask her had she any intention of buying Sunday's dinner. Then she had to rush out as quickly as she

65   could and do her marketing, holding her black leather purse tightly in her hand as she elbowed her way through the crowds and returning home late under her load of provisions. She had hard work to keep the house together and to see that the two young children who had been left to her charge went to school regularly and got their meals regularly. It was hard

70   work – a hard life – but now that she was about to leave it she did not find it a wholly undesirable life.

     She was about to explore another life with Frank. Frank was very kind, manly, open-hearted. She was to go away with him by the night-boat to be his wife and to live with him in Buenos Ayres where he had

75   a home waiting for her. How well she remembered the first time she had seen him; he was lodging in a house on the main road where she used to visit. It seemed a few weeks ago. He was standing at the gate, his peaked cap pushed back on his head and his hair tumbled forward over a face of bronze. Then they had come to know each

80   other. He used to meet her outside the Stores every evening and see her home. He took her to see *The Bohemian Girl* and she felt elated as she sat in an unaccustomed part of the theatre with him. He was awfully fond of music and sang a little. People knew that they were courting, and, when he sang about the lass that loves a sailor, she

85 always felt pleasantly confused. He used to call her Poppens out of
    fun. First of all it had been an excitement for her to have a fellow and
    then she had begun to like him. He had tales of distant countries. He
    had started as a deck boy at a pound a month on a ship of the Allan
    Line going out to Canada. He told her the names of the ships he had
90 been on and the names of the different services. He had sailed
    through the Straits of Magellan and he told her stories of the terrible
    Patagonians. He had fallen on his feet in Buenos Ayres, he said, and
    had come over to the old country just for a holiday. Of course, her
    father had found out the affair and had forbidden her to have anything
95 to say to him.
      'I know these sailor chaps,' he said.
      One day he had quarrelled with Frank, and after that she had to
    meet her lover secretly.
      The evening deepened in the avenue. The white of two letters in her
100 lap grew indistinct. One was to Harry; the other was to her father.
    Ernest had been her favourite but she liked Harry too. Her father was
    becoming old lately, she noticed; he would miss her. Sometimes he
    could be very nice. Not long before, when she had been laid up for a
    day, he had read her out a ghost story and made toast for her at the
105 fire. Another day, when their mother was alive, they had all gone for a
    picnic to the Hill of Howth. She remembered her father putting on her
    mother's bonnet to make the children laugh.
      Her time was running out but she continued to sit by the window,
    leaning her head against the window curtain, inhaling the odour of
110 dusty cretonne. Down far in the avenue she could hear a street organ
    playing. She knew the air. Strange that it should come that very night
    to remind her of the promise to her mother, her promise to keep the
    home together as long as she could. She remembered the last night of
    her mother's illness; she was again in the close dark room at the other
115 side of the hall and outside she heard a melancholy air of Italy. The
    organ-player had been ordered to go away and given sixpence. She
    remembered her father strutting back into the sick-room saying:
      'Damned Italians! coming over here!'
      As she mused the pitiful vision of her mother's life laid its spell on
120 the very quick of her being – that life of commonplace sacrifices
    closing in final craziness. She trembled as she heard again her
    mother's voice saying constantly with foolish insistence:
      'Derevaun Seraun! Derevaun Seraun!'
      She stood up in a sudden impulse of terror. Escape! She must
125 escape! Frank would save her. He would give her life, perhaps love,
    too. But she wanted to live. Why should she be unhappy? She had a
    right to happiness. Frank would take her in his arms, fold her in his
    arms. He would save her.

                                    *

Appendix

She stood among the swaying crowd in the station at the North Wall.
130 He held her hand and she knew that he was speaking to her, saying
something about the passage over and over again. The station was full
of soldiers with brown baggages. Through the wide doors of the sheds
she caught a glimpse of the black mass of the boat, lying in beside the
quay wall, with illumined portholes. She answered nothing. She felt
135 her cheek pale and cold and, out of a maze of distress, she prayed to
God to direct her, to show her what was her duty. The boat blew a
long mournful whistle into the mist. If she went, tomorrow she would
be on the sea with Frank, steaming towards Buenos Ayres. Their
passage had been booked. Could she still draw back after all he had
140 done for her? Her distress awoke a nausea in her body and she kept
moving her lips in silent fervent prayer.

A bell clanged upon her heart. She felt him seize her hand:
'Come!'
All the seas of the world tumbled about her heart. He was drawing
145 her into them: he would drown her. She gripped with both hands at
the iron railing.
'Come!'
No! No! No! It was impossible. Her hands clutched the iron in
frenzy. Amid the seas she sent a cry of anguish.
150 'Eveline! Evvy!'
He rushed beyond the barrier and called to her to follow. He was
shouted at to go on, but he still called to her. She set her white face to
him, passive, like a helpless animal. Her eyes gave him no sign of love
or farewell or recognition.

(from James Joyce, *Dubliners*, Triad/Panther Books, 1977.)

Index

References in italics indicate figures. References followed by 'n' indicate a note to the main text.

Index